# VICTORIAN
# BABYLON

# VICTORIAN BABYLON

*People, Streets and Images in Nineteenth-Century London*

LYNDA NEAD

*Yale University Press*
*New Haven & London*

Designed by Gillian Malpass

Printed in Singapore

**Library of Congress Cataloging-in-Publication Data**

Nead, Lynda.
Victorian Babylon: people, streets, and images in nineteenth-century London / Lynda Nead.
p.   cm.
Includes bibliographical references (p. ) and index.
ISBN 0-300-08505-2 (cloth)
ISBN 0-300-10770-6 (paper)
1. London (England)–History–1800–1950.
2. City and town life–England–London–History–19th century.
3. Gas-lighting–England–London–History–19th century.
4. Streets–England–London–History–19th century.
5. Women–England–London–History–19th century.
6. Great Britain–History–Victoria, 1837–1901.
7. London (England)–Social conditions.
I. Title. DA683.N425 2000
942.1′2–dc21

A catalogue record for this book is available from
The British Library

00–031037

*Frontispiece*   J.W. Archer, detail of 'Holywell Street, Strand. Drawn March 1862',
in 'Drawings of Buildings in London and the Environs', vol. 10–3.
Watercolour. © Copyright The British Museum

*For Joe Connor*

# Contents

Detail of fig. 29

# *Acknowledgements*

One of the great pleasures of working on the history of London is using the outstanding archives and collections on the subject. I am indebted to the curators and librarians who helped me to explore these collections, shared with me their encylopaedic knowledge of Victorian London and were a mine of information on the objects and texts in their care. In particular I would like to thank Mireille Galinou, Cathy Ross and Alex Werner at the Museum of London and the staff of the Museum of London Archaeological Service. Ralph Hyde and Jeremy Smith offered advice and help throughout my research in the Department of Prints and Maps at the Guildhall Library. Staff at the Department of Prints and Drawings at the British Museum, Chelsea Public Library, City of Westminster Archives Centre, London Metropolitan Archives, London Transport Museum and the University of London Library were also endlessly patient and enthusiastic about my project. Many friends and colleagues shared their ideas and material with me, in particular Deborah Cherry, Steve Connor, Costas Douzinas, Lindsay Farmer, Jane Gough, Frank Mort and Michael Slater. I have learnt much from these people and places.

THE CREMORNE PLATFORM.

# INTRODUCTION

Detail of fig. 47

# Victorian Babylon

In forming our idea of the great capital of the British Empire and of the nineteenth century, we naturally look for models in the great cities of the past, and
the centres of other empires. We compare London with Imperial Rome; and when
we would express in one word the idea of her greatness, we call her 'the Modern
Babylon'. It is natural, then, that in trying to form an idea of London we should
think of that great Assyrian capital, with her lofty walls, her hundred brazen gates,
her magnificent palaces, and wonderful hanging gardens. ('London, As It Strikes a
Stranger', *Temple Bar*, 1862)[1]

London in the nineteenth century was imagined as a Victorian Babylon. Writers and
journalists drew upon the image of the ancient city to invoke the wealth, splendour
and refinement of the modern metropolis.[2] Like Babylon, London was the centre of
a global commerce that was subjugating the rest of the world; it was the seat of an
empire that was defining contemporary history. But Babylon was a paradoxical image
for the nineteenth-century city. It not only represented the most magnificent imperial city of the ancient world, but also conjured up images of the mystical Babylon
of the Apocalypse. It was a place that symbolised material wonder and tumultuous
destruction; a city whose splendour was its downfall. Babylon and imperial Rome
were indices of London's greatness and also warnings of the dangers of hubris.
These great trading centres and capitals of empires were brought down by luxury,
sensuality and an excessive indulgence in and worship of the commodity. Victorian
Babylon could thus look to its ancient predecessors and find signs of its own
magnificence and traces of its inevitable destruction. Babylon was an uneasy image
for London's identity in the modern world.

Nineteenth-century London displayed an acute awareness both of its present
condition and of its historical past. It understood the need to refashion the city and
to create a spectacular capital suited to the imperatives of a modern nation and
empire, but it was constantly drawn to the images and shadows of its past. Attitudes
to the city were always ambivalent: the image of the straight new thoroughfare was
permeated with the presence of the meandering alley; fast public transport was
obstructed by the figure of the wandering, dreaming pedestrian; and the aesthetics
of glass and iron were compromised by lath and plaster and crumbling old houses.
In many respects, therefore, Victorian London was an unworthy successor to the
urban splendour of Babylon. As the anonymous author of the article in *Temple Bar*
admitted: 'Most of the streets are narrow, crooked, and running in every possible
direction. I am not deficient in locality, and can find my way in pathless forests; but
I have tried to walk a mile in one direction through the maze of London, and after
half an hour found myself forty rods on the wrong side of the place of beginning'

(p. 382). This was the nature of London's modernity; it seemed to obey the spatial logic of the maze rather than that of the grid or the *étoile*, and its characteristic experience was of disorientation, as opposed to purposeful movement. The modernisation of London in the nineteenth century was partial and uneven. It was circumscribed by conflicting urban visions and created as much in relation to perceptions of the city's past as it was in terms of the formation of the new and in the interests of the future.

There are many, often conflicting definitions of the concept of modernity.[3] It is a term that has generated a long and complex debate within political philosophy, from the late eighteenth century to recent postmodern reassessments. One of the central ways in which the meaning of modernity has been understood is in terms of a distinct temporality and the formation of a particular historical periodisation, with its associated social experiences. Part, but not all, of the term's complexity, stems from the fact that it has multiple applications. It designates a social and cultural self-consciousness; a time when the present, with its specific forms of economic and historical experience, was perceived to be quantitatively and qualitatively different from previous historical epochs. Modernity is also used, however, as a category of historical and philosophical analysis and as a way of classifying the particular conditions of that epoch. Most of these usages have produced totalising accounts of historical processes. Nineteenth-century commentators swiftly identified their own epoch as a coherent historical moment, characterised by distinct and identifiable qualities and, more recently, this monolithic periodisation has been reiterated by historians and political philosophers, who have endorsed modernity as an historical given even while they have debated its chronological limits and fought over its positive and negative aspects.[4]

The simplest understanding of modernity is in terms of that which is new or contemporary and represents a distinct temporal break with the past. Within this model, modernity takes form in all areas of historical experience: at an economic level; through the organisation of the state; through social and cultural configurations; and at the level of individual perception. Although there is no reason to doubt the emergence of such a consciousness of contemporary life in a particularly intense manner around the middle decades of the nineteenth century, there can be far less certainty about the unity and coherence behind these perceptions. In his influential study *All That Is Solid Melts Into Air*, Marshall Berman divided the experience of modernity into three separate phases: a first moment from 1500 to 1789; a middle period, 1789–1900; and a third phase from 1900 onwards.[5] All three periods are seen as successive stages in the progressive development and realisation of a global modernity. For Berman, modernity is best defined as a distinct mode of experience, brought about by the transformation of capital and society:

> There is a mode of vital experience – experience of space and time, of the self and others, of life's possibilities and perils – that is shared by men and women all over the world today. I will call this body of experience 'modernity'. To be modern is to find ourselves in an environment that promises us adventure, power, joy, growth, transformation of ourselves and the world – and, at the same time, that threatens to destroy everything we have, everything we know, everything we are.[6]

This modernity is exhilarating and full of potential, but threatens also to dislocate and tear society from all its familiar landmarks. It is precisely this ambiguity that constitutes the unified nature of modernity for Berman. In his account, modernity, as an historical process, is total and inexorable; its ontological progress is plotted in conventional terms of early, middle and late and may be tracked in analogous forms in cities throughout the advanced world.[7]

*Victorian Babylon* is a study of a far more focused instance of modernity: London in the middle decades of the nineteenth century, from around 1855 to 1870. During these years London became part of a highly concentrated discourse on the modern. The fashioning of London into a modern metropolis was given validity by the creation in 1855 of the Metropolitan Board of Works, the city's first comprehensive local government. Support for the creation of a London-wide local authority had been growing in the years leading up to 1855, but its establishment clarified, for a period, the view that London could re-create itself; that it was entering a new era of improvement and modernisation. The language of improvement provided the terms for modernity in London during this period. Improvement was a way of differentiating the city's past from its modern present; it was also, paradoxically, a way of ensuring the enduring presence of the historical past within the narratives of modernity. In the mid-nineteenth century London took flight from its past, but was unable to conceptualise its present or future in any other terms. During the late 1850s and 1860s government officials and engineers embarked on particular projects to improve the city. The building of the city's drainage system remained one of the great successes of the Metropolitan Board of Works, but the Board also widened and straightened roads, and imposed a rational order on the city through maps, cross-sections and diagrams. This was a period of expectation and compromise. There was a reasonable degree of consensus regarding the scale of improvement that was required to modernise London and far less confidence that the Board of Works was capable of carrying it out. Modernity for London in this period was a condition of compromise; between local government and private industry, local vested interests and traditional authorities. Modernity was an accumulation of uneven and unresolved processes of urbanisation; it took the form of the improved street within a district of slums. It was summarised in the image of dereliction, as a sign of the past and of preparation for the future.

The version of modernity that emerges from this history of mid-Victorian London is very different from the grand, historical narrative presented by Berman. It suggests that at any given time, modernity was a configuration of extremely diverse and unresolved historical processes. This is not to abandon the concept of modernity altogether, but it is to pay particular attention to the local elements that constitute modernity and to the tensions and irregularities that create modernity's conditions of existence. *Victorian Babylon* traces modernity through representations of the street; the organisation of urban leisure; the poetics of the city at night; and debates on the production and consumption of mass urban culture. These are the varied strands that make up London's modernity in this period, which advance and stall, and are predictable only in their unpredictability. The aim of this study is to reconstitute mid-Victorian perceptions and representations of the modern and to participate in the larger, ongoing debate on the meaning of modernity. Its focus is the visual representation of urban space and the specific cultural forms through which the modern city was given meaning. Modernisation is not simply a question of the shaping and organisation of space, it also concerns the experience of that space, the expectations and fears of those who occupied the spaces of the modern city.[8] This study brings together these different orders of representation, the public and official, and the personal and emotive. It looks at the ideas and images created within the public representations and how these were reformulated or challenged in private forms of representation. It seeks to extend the history of modernity from the official discourses of government to the intimate experiences of individuals.

This image of the multi-layered nature of modernity, its varied and uneven strands and its multiple levels of representation and experience, owes much to the work of Walter Benjamin.[9] For Benjamin, the city was an accumulation of historical traces, experienced through chance associations of the present with dreams and memories of the past. This generates in Benjamin's writing a kind of archaeology of modernity, in which the sites of the modern city stand on layer upon layer of an underground city, which maintains a hellish and ghostlike presence within modernity. It is in these moments, when the spectral past enters the spaces of the present that Benjamin identified the mythological dimension of modernity: 'the new in connection with that which has always already been there.'[10] Benjamin's city was Paris, seen through a filter of Surrealist urban aesthetics, however his poetic evocation of modernity is also highly suggestive in relation to London's encounter with the modern in the middle of the nineteenth century. Paris has dominated recent histories of modernity and urbanisation.[11] The rebuilding of the city under Napoleon III (1852–70) and his Prefect of the Seine, Baron Haussmann, has been taken as the paradigmatic model of nineteenth-century urban history and of modernity more generally. The spectacular city created by Haussmann and subsequently defined by Walter Benjamin as 'the capital of the nineteenth century', has generated a specific version of the spatial conception of modernity which has excluded other models of interpretation and different versions of modernity.[12]

To shift the object of study from Paris to London in the nineteenth century, is to tell a different story of modernity. London's engagement with the new was equivocal and piecemeal. Confronted with the apparent spectacle of the total transformation of central Paris in this period, London offered a different model of urban planning; one that its supporters argued reflected principles of democratic government rather than the autocratic rule that governed Paris. The conventions of the picturesque were reinvented to represent the contingencies of the modern metropolis, and through these cultural forms London produced a pictorial lexicon of modernity based on a conjunction of the old and the new; destruction and construction; antiquarianism and technology. London had its icons of the new: the pumping stations; gasworks; underground tunnels; and smart shopping streets; but even these could be drawn into an alternative world of dreams, memories and fantasies.

The ambiguities of modernity and its paradoxical engagement with the past and the present have been highlighted within some recent theoretical accounts of urban space. Drawing on the work of such French theorists as Michel Foucault, Henri

Lefebvre and Michel de Certeau, the spaces of modernity have been invoked as a troubling mix of the rational and governable and the fearful and disordered.[13] For Foucault, in essays such as 'The Eye of Power' and related studies, the Enlightenment ideal of transparent space was part of a modern technology of power.[14] The panopticon, with its promise of maximum visibility, becomes a symbol of the operation of power and the control of populations. This concept of ordered, legible space is countered, in Foucault's writings, by the evocation of other kinds of phantasmatic spaces; spaces that are both mythic and contested, which he calls 'heterotopias'.[15] These are types of spaces that resist social ordering and that obey their own rules and logics. Foucault's glossary of heterotopic spaces is appropriately wide-ranging and unpredictable, including brothels and boats; in its general terms, however, it begins to suggest a theoretical approach to the unruly spaces of modernity in nineteenth-century London.

The conjunction of ordered and disordered space within modernity has been more fully considered by Michel de Certeau. De Certeau opposes two views of urban space: the panoptic, aerial viewpoint of the mapmakers and city-planners and the perception of the walker at ground level.[16] The aerial viewpoint articulates a totalising mastery of urban space; it renders the city legible and comprehensible. At street level, however, space cannot be controlled in a single gaze, but is apprehended through a rhetoric of walking and its associated symbolic mechanisms of dreams, memories and fables. The poetic space of the pedestrian is, for de Certeau, a space of resistance, which defies the attempts of the planners and improvers to discipline the contingencies of everyday life. De Certeau's geography of resistance can be read alongside his work on the symbolism of history, generating a fascinating interplay of time and space. In the essays collected in *Heterologies*, de Certeau considers the logic of discourses and the play between the rational order of discourse and its non-representable part, which constitutes the discourse's own other.[17] This account moves beyond the more polarised models of order and resistance that have been considered thus far, towards a far more fundamental sense of the deeply embedded ambiguities within discourse. In *Heterologies*, de Certeau sees these structural ambiguities as signs of the torsions of everyday practice and of the discourse's relationship to its own historical moment of production. This begins to suggest a different way of posing the question of modernity. Drawing on de Certeau's work, modernity can be understood as a set of historical discourses and processes that are profoundly and necessarily caught up with the construction of the past. As de Certeau writes:

> any autonomous order is founded upon what it eliminates; it produces a 'residue' condemned to be forgotten. But what was excluded re-infiltrates the place of its origin – now the present's 'clean' [*propre*] place. It resurfaces, it troubles, it turns the present's feeling of being 'at home' into an illusion, it lurks – this 'wild', this 'ob-scene', this filth, this 'resistance' of 'superstition' – within the walls of the residence, and, behind the back of the owner (the *ego*), or over its objections, it inscribes the law of the other.[18]

There can never be a pure, clean modernity, for the discourses that constitute that historical temporality bear the ghosts of the past, of modernity's own other. The past may be rejected or repressed by the language of improvement, but it returns to disturb and unsettle the confidence of the modern. The present remains permanently engaged in a phantasmatic dialogue with the past.

This is the nature of representations of modernity in mid-Victorian London. The spaces of improvement were caught up in a ceaseless exchange with the spaces of the city's historical past. London's past had to be endlessly rewritten and re-imaged; contained through the conventions of text and image and assimilated within a manageable lexicon of the metropolitan picturesque. It was a task that could never be completed and, at times, the present failed to turn the past into a relic, or to control its most fearful connotations. Obscenity was one of the spectres that haunted modern London. Obscenity was improvement's other; but it was also the progeny of the modern city. Produced, consumed and sold in the shops and streets of the metropolis, obscene publications were a bold and dangerous reminder of the erotics of the city; of those desires and places in the midst of modernity that resisted the rational structures of government.

This is the idea of modernity that is developed in the following pages. Modernity is not understood as a rupture with the past, or as a fresh start, but as a set of processes and representations that were engaged in an urgent and inventive dialogue with their own historical conditions of existence. In this sense, it is possible to speak of the multitemporality of history, or of any object or time. This concept has been power-fully and clearly defined by Michel Serres. He describes a late-model car, which he sees as a 'disparate aggregate' of technical and aesthetic solutions, dating from a multiplicity of historical moments. To this extent, the car can be dated from a number of different eras. In the same way, Serres argues, historical eras themselves are always simultaneously an amalgam of the past, the contemporary and the future: 'every historical era is likewise multitemporal, simultaneously drawing from the obsolete and the futuristic. An object, a circumstance, is thus polychronic, multitemporal, and reveals a time that is gathered together, with multiple pleats.'[19] This image of pleated time is literally visualised by Serres in his metaphor of the handkerchief. Spread out and ironed, the handkerchief represents a metrical, geometric concept of time, in which distance and proximity are stable and clearly defined; but crumpled in the pocket, the handkerchief evokes a 'topological' concept of time, in which previously distant points 'become close, or even superimposed'. Moreover, if the fabric is torn, previously adjacent points may be rendered distant and unrelated. Our experience of time resembles the crumpled version of the handkerchief, rather than the flat, ironed one. Modernity, in this context, can be imagined as pleated or crumpled time, drawing together past, present and future into constant and unexpected relations and the product of a multiplicity of historical eras.

Past, present and future were caught up in an ongoing set of processes that were played out through the spaces of the Victorian city. It should be evident that, in this sense, space is understood as an active agent of modernity. Space is never a passive backdrop for the formation of historical identities and experiences, but is an active constituent of historical consciousness, whether experienced on the street, the under-ground, or from above the city in the car of a balloon.

*Victorian Babylon* examines the forms of visual culture generated by the conditions of this modernity. Part 1 takes the themes of mapping and water in order to examine the ideals of movement and circulation in the mid-nineteenth-century city. Improvement sought to create a city of constant, purposeful movement: of water, air, traffic, people and commodities. In the lines of the Ordnance Survey the city was reduced to its functional essentials. Gradients and water levels were plotted on to the sheets of the map and the city's main drainage system constructed by engineers and labourers. Sewerage created a new urban aesthetics, based on the forms of the tunnel and the vault. It also created a new street architecture of decorative drinking fountains, which symbolised the modern city's dedication to hygiene and flow. But stagnation and blockage could not be eliminated from the city. In spite of the modernisers' dreams, the experience of the city streets remained one of physical proximity and of streams of people immobilised within confined spaces. On the streets, men and women could assume identities and explore new possibilities and the Victorian metropolis was a place of pleasure and danger for its diverse population. Unaccompanied women of the respectable middle classes moved around the city, tracing itineraries between home, friends, work and leisure. *Victorian Babylon* takes respectable women out of the home and places them back on the streets of the city. In this respect, the book challenges orthodoxies of modernity and their Baudelairean typologies such as the *flâneur* and the whore and reintegrates women of the middle classes within the history of modernity.

Part 2 is organised around the issues of gas and light and considers the temporality of space in the city and the organisation and representation of the nocturnal city. The Victorian gas industry was a heavy and dirty industrial process taking place in sites throughout the metropolis. Many gasworks were located in the central areas of the city and the spectacle of the cylindrical gas holders symbolised this new industrial cityscape and the technologies that were required to maintain the modern city. Gas had an economics and a poetics. It created large new private monopolies that competed with each other and with central government and consumer groups for control over the supply of gas. It also produced the dream-images of the city at night; of darkness illuminated by the uneven glow of the gaslights and of an uncanny, nocturnal city that obeyed a different spatial logic from that of the city by day. Gas and glass also created the visual conditions for new forms of modern urban leisure. The world of goods was extended to the hours of night and new leisure spaces, such as Cremorne Pleasure Gardens, reconfigured conventional assumptions concerning public behaviour, taste and morality.

The third section of the book returns to the streets and focuses on the question of obscenity. The nineteenth-century city was seen to have created new forms of mass culture that were dangerous and pervasive. Obscenity was the symbol of these new forms of visual culture; it was cheap and widely disseminated and could create a highly sensual and degenerate public. The debate concerning obscene publications was concentrated on one specific street in central London, Holywell Street, and a micro-study of this site draws out the historical and symbolic functions of urban space in this period. The law was invoked to contain the promiscuous irregularities of obscenity, and the pursuit of obscene publications from the legislators at the Palace of Westminster to the judges in the courts at the Old Bailey created an alternative sexual and moral mapping of London's modernity.

London in the 1860s was the centre of a highly focused set of representations concerning modernity and urbanisation, but it was a present haunted by the image of ruin. The past threatened constantly to obstruct the project of improvement. More fearful, however, was the image of the ruins of the future, when Victorian Babylon was itself reduced to archaeological remains and had become a lesson for new imperial nations. But these ambiguities were the condition and form of modernity for Victorian London. There was no uncompromised newness, just a constant struggle with history.

PART I

# MAPPING AND MOVEMENT

# Introduction

Mid-Victorian London was shaped by the forces of two urban principles: mapping and movement. If the processes of modernisation can be said to have had a primary goal, it was movement. The old city was a place of blocked mobility, of congestion and obstacle. The planners and reformers of Victorian London strove to dispel these obstructions and to facilitate the movement of people, goods, money, water and even air.

Mapping was the necessary second condition of the improver's city. The urban ideal was not irrational velocity or indiscriminate mobility, but ordered circulation through networks of streets, pipes and tunnels. If the city was on the move, however, it had also to be mapped; the lines of communication needed to be retraced in the lines of the map. Maps made the modern city legible and comprehensible. They froze the passage of people and things, the loitering, walking and rushing of the streets, and transformed them into the abstract and orderly signs of cartography. On the sheets of the map modernity could be absorbed in a single glance; gradient and flow could be plotted and progress could be planned. It was a reassuring sight, in contrast to the incoherent sensory experience of the street.

Mapping and movement are drawn into an extraordinary proximity in the planning of London's main drainage system, which was probably the most important building and engineering project in the city in the nineteenth century. Not only did it create a vast network of drains and sewers for the capital (on much of which London still relies), but it also brought into being the governmental and conceptual machinery on which the idea of Victorian London was built.

London needed a flow of water: a regular supply of clean water and a reliable system for the removal of waste. It needed drains and sewers and it needed an accurate map to plot the contours of the land through which the liquids and solids would be carried. The Ordnance Survey Map was a civic scheme carried out by the military; it presented a new and unadorned image of London, ready and waiting for engineers and entrepreneurs.

But maps could never capture or contain the growth of and changes in London. Mapmakers struggled to keep up with the pace of modernisation. In the 1860s much of the city appeared to be a gigantic building-site, as the investors in improvement constructed new streets, railways, bridges and buildings. Change affected the city above and below ground. With the opening of the world's first underground railway in 1863, it was no longer sufficient to have a conception or image of the city above ground level, it was necessary also to imagine the city on the move below the ground. It required a vertical perception of the metropolis, which embraced the telegraph poles and wires above the roofs and pierced the surface of the street to the tunnels and pipes below.

It is difficult to over-emphasise the visual impact of these processes. Modernity in the 1860s forced itself on the eye; it had to be grasped visually, and artists and writers struggled to define the aesthetic of this historical moment. In many ways, modernity in the 1860s was visualised through the reinvention of the past, as much as through the representation of the new. In the images and texts of the city produced in this period there is a constant shifting of register between old and new, demolition and construction, and an uneasy tension between the desolation of loss and the triumph of gain.

There are many types of movement and forms of mapping described in this section. Engineers, tourists, writers, artists, as well as ordinary men and women are traced across the varied spaces of Victorian London. Each had their own itinerary as they moved between work and home, station and shop, theatre and restaurant. At street level the conditions of the modernising city demanded, or desired, a code of behaviour, a system that would enable individuals to become rational modern pedestrians. But the city was not predictable and its occupants evaded the social and cultural stereotypes disseminated both in the period and in the twentieth century. The city could be a place of pleasure or threat but, ultimately, it was an untidy experience, which constantly resisted the attempts of improvers and planners.

# 1    *Maps and Sewers*

Statistics poured forth but were hopelessly inadequate to convey the size and growth of Victorian London. The rate of change in the middle decades of the nineteenth century seemed to demand quantification; it called upon and drained all the numerical skills and literary imagination of writers, legislators and social investigators. Most of these strategies failed, however, to evoke the growth of the metropolis. To describe, in words or numbers, a point in the city's growth was momentarily to halt its expansion and it was the unstoppable nature of the development of London that seemed so distinctive to contemporaries.

In bald numerical terms, London's population did grow significantly. The census returns of 1851 gave a population of 2,362,236; by 1861 the census reported an increase to 2,800,000; and by 1871 the population of London had reached 3,254,260.[1] This expansion was the result of constant migrations. Never simply a product of steady growth, London was the centre for enormous and persistent movements of population. Books about London produced in this period are marked by their dependence on and transgression of the logic of statistical evidence. Pages, chapters and entire books were devoted to numerical information about the metropolis, and writers became increasingly inventive concerning what might count as useful quantifiable knowledge about the city; but it was never sufficient. Writing in the opening pages of *The Criminal Prisons of London* (1862), Henry Mayhew informed his readers of the city's square mileage, the number of houses it contained and its population. These statistics are then rounded off with a final exclamation mark to convey the remarkable nature of the figures. But Mayhew was disappointed by the information and admitted:

> Surely the mind is no more enabled to realise the immensity of the largest city in the world by such information as this, than we are helped to comprehend the vastness of the sea by being told that the total area of all the ocean amounts to 145 millions of square miles, and that it contains altogether 6,441 billions of tons of common salt.[2]

Rather than being containable by statistics, Mayhew suggests that London is sublime; that it has no beginning and no end and resists all attempts at demarcation. But Mayhew could not resist the compulsion to render the city statistically, and within a few pages he was presenting tables and increasingly inventive calculations to enumerate the scale of the city: 'If the entire people of the Capital were to be drawn up in marching order, two and two . . . and, supposing them to move at the rate of three miles an hour, it would require more than nine days and nights for the aggregate population to pass by' (p. 16).

For Mayhew and other writers in the 1860s, London was more than a city; it was a 'province covered with houses',[3] a state, 'a *Great* World'.[4] Where geopolitical comparisons stopped, more literary metaphors continued. London was like a colossal body consuming and producing vast quantities of goods and people. In the many editions of Murray's *Handbook of London As It Is*, a guidebook published throughout the nineteenth century, the size of London is conveyed in terms of the city's consumption of wheat, bullocks, sheep, pigs, ale and water. In addition, the guide refers to the city's 'arterial' system – its water supply – and its 'venous' system – its refuse and sewer system.[5] Here, it is uncertain whether statistics are being used to convey the city as within or beyond comprehension. From edition to edition the figures remained the same and were not updated. Rather than offering any numerical truth about the city, therefore, these statistics evoked a poetic image of London as an immense open-mouthed body, consuming everything that comes within its grasp.

If the city was a body, it might also sicken or become aberrant. For one columnist in the *Illustrated London News*, London had gorged itself and become obese:

> The overgrowth of London may be compared with that of the occasional human body. Walk round, and you see how it has spread. The active piece of humanity of some few years since has become puffy, bloated: coated with a light swollen matter which has doubled the size of his waist and cheeks. So London has got puffy with 'new neighbourhoods' all around her . . . Nobody likes to be told of a superabundance of oleaginous matter. It is unpleasant, because nobody knows how far it really has gone or to what it may not lead. For instance, the stout man, who looks the picture of health, may be carried off in a moment of excitement, and the post mortem proves that he suffered from fatty degeneration of the heart. The

fact is, it is not always possible to become fat without, without becoming fat within; and London is a case in point.[6]

The city's growth is not robustly corpulent but unhealthily swollen; its main arteries are coated and becoming choked and it risks an urban cardiac arrest. The rational city of the urban planner is represented as a social body whose organs and functions are productive and efficient. Motion and circulation in the urban body are read as signs of health and morality.

In his book *Flesh and Stone*, Richard Sennett has traced the projection of Harvey's understanding of circulation in the body on to eighteenth-century attempts to circulate people in cities. By the nineteenth century the virtues of respiration and circulation shaped attitudes to urban reform and modernisation. The metaphor of circulation enabled health reformers to conceive of the city's water supply, drains and sewers as its arteries and veins. This constant motion should continue without cessation in the streets of the city as well as in its water supply. Any blockage or accumulated refuse could result in a crisis of circulation in the social body and consequent breakdown – stroke or heart attack. The principle of circulatory movement was central to debates concerning the design of urban space in the mid-nineteenth century.[7]

The streets of the city were the most visible signs of its progress or degeneration. They were sites of passage, communication and transaction of business, and to many of those involved in the debates about the condition of London its streets were its major defect. They were indirect, narrow and obstructed. Rather than facilitating the flow of movement, they constituted an aneurism in the most vital parts of the metropolitan body. In a series of articles on 'Streets of the World', published in *Temple Bar* in the mid-1860s, particular streets are taken as symptomatic of the cities in which they are located. In the article devoted to Paris and the Passage des Panoramas, the journalist and author George Augustus Sala began with an invective of several pages against the rotting buildings, blind alleys and labyrinthine streets of London. For Sala, these were the legacy of self-interested, feudal land rights, which had been defended for centuries through the law courts and parliament. These claims to individual ownership and birthright had lamed the city; they had resulted in 'the perpetuation of hundreds of miserable little skeins of foot-pavement running, or rather limping, between rows of decayed and fever-haunted houses'.[8] Although the houses sheltered disease, the streets: 'these varicose veins in the limbs of a fair city', could prove just as fatal to the future progress of London. Sala acknowledged that Paris was built after much the same fashion as London and used to have as many filthy lanes and houses; but the French Revolution put an end to the property rights of the nobility and now Napoleon III and Baron Haussmann were transforming Paris into the noblest, cleanest and most handsome city in the world. Where *carrefours*, *impasses*, *ruelles* and *culs-de-sac* once stood, there was now one single, spacious and sumptuous boulevard. For Sala, the glazed arcades of Second Empire Paris were the perfect reconciliation of the old thoroughfares of Paris and the functions of the modern city street: passage, communication and exchange. Rather than demolishing the old it had been rebuilt; lined with handsome shops, uniformly paved, covered in with a glazed roof and transformed into a wonder such as the Passage des Panoramas, an emblem of *la vie parisienne*.

Sala blamed London's urban decay on the perpetuation of outmoded private property rights. Clearly, there were radical political implications in this argument, but they were not developed by Sala, who abandoned them early in his article. Nevertheless, the view that London's planning had remained for too long in the hands of independent civic authorities such as the Corporation of the City of London, with its arcane guilds and businesses, gathered increasing support during the early 1850s. A rational, planned city needed a unified, metropolitan government, rather than the motley collection of parishes, vestries and boroughs that was currently responsible for the running and governing of the city.

Throughout the 1850s the editorial pages and columns of the *Illustrated London News* waged a campaign against the Corporation of London and demanded a rational form of metropolitan government, with overall responsibility for all aspects of London's government. On the front page of the issue for 30 September 1854, beneath its familiar masthead illustration of the panorama of the Thames, with St Paul's Cathedral and the surrounding city, it carried the editorial subtitle 'The Wants of London'. The column rehearsed the litany of urban problems facing the metropolis; it was unwholesome, pestiferous and inconvenient. Although wealthy and commercially successful, it was neglected and impaired. The editorial classified the most urgent wants of London: first, the want of municipal unity; secondly, the want of a system of drainage and sewerage; thirdly, the want of bridges across the Thames; and fourthly, the want of a sufficient number of main arterial streets.[9] These four headings provided the focus for the journal's subsequent campaign for a new London government and set the agenda for the paper's monitoring of the city's improvements through the 1860s. London could no longer be treated as a series of disconnected, separate parts; it had to be governed as a whole. The ancient autonomy of the square mile of the City of London had created a wealthy, independent citadel in the heart of the metropolis. With separate provisions for policing, lighting, paving and water, the City symbolised the resistance to unified metropolitan government. For advocates of reform, such as the *Illustrated London News*, these ancient authorities must be done away with, for there could be no independent states within a modern metropolis. Drawing on the city/body metaphor, the editorial imagines the City as the 'belly' of London: 'The "Belly" must be taught that its interests are identical with those of the "Members". The great civic "Body" must be one in Government, as it is in fact.'

The call for a centralised metropolitan government threatened various forms of existing local interests, such as the City of London, the vestries, water companies and paving commissions, which managed the fabric of London in the first half of the nineteenth century. London's administrative government in this period was a confusion of jurisdictions; in one part of central London, within an area of one hundred yards, four separate authorities were responsible for different aspects of the upkeep of the streets. The drainage of the city was the responsibility of seven independent Commissions of Sewers, with the City of London providing its own independent Commission. In the early years of the 1850s reformers demanding a unified metro-

politan government battled with those who defended local rights, or who called for
government through the national parliament. At the heart of this messy political
debate was the question of London's identity. Was it a single entity, or a conglomer-
ation of many? Did it have sufficient common interests for it to be governed as a
whole? What did London *mean* in the middle of the nineteenth century? These issues
were pulled backwards and forwards between advocates of localism and supporters
of centralisation.[10]

The history of London's government in the nineteenth century is one of confusion and compromise. It is not necessary to rehearse all the details of its chequered
creation and subsequent reforms; the important point to emphasise is this: London's
municipal government emerged out of a fog of local hostility and resistance. Driven
by the exigencies of sanitary reform, it was attended by an incomplete conceptual
image of the city. If the formation of a municipal government failed to define
London's identity, then it fell to the city itself, to the visual culture that it produced
and to the images that were made of it, to put together the conceptual distinctive-
ness of Victorian London.

The debates of the 1850s were temporarily resolved by a crisis in health and
sanitation. The division of London into a number of separate Commissions for Sewers
meant that there was no single, overall responsibility for the capital's water supply.
The water companies were also centrally unregulated and, as a result, appalling levels
of pollution were allowed to accumulate within the city and find their way back
into the water supply. Traditionally, London's waste had been disposed of in cesspools,
which had been emptied by nightsoil men; a system that ensured that none of the
waste contaminated the Thames or other sources of drinking water.[11] But by
the 1820s house drains and overflow pipes from cesspools were being connected to
the common sewers, which then discharged directly into the River Thames at
precisely the same spots from which the water companies drew their supplies.
Widespread pollution of London's water supply was the inevitable consequence of
this chaotic, unregulated system. Edwin Chadwick led the call for the single, centralised management for the supply of water and drainage in London. Chadwick is
a central figure in the history of sanitary reform in the nineteenth century.[12] Through
his reports on the health of towns and his roles as Chief Executive Officer of the
Poor Law Commission and Commissioner of the Board of Health, Chadwick tirelessly, obsessively, advocated the causes of social hygiene and sanitary engineering in
England, its capital and its colonies. Chadwick proposed a single Crown-appointed
commission to provide and regulate drainage, street cleaning and water supply in the
metropolis. Hostility to his proposal came from the obvious sources: the vestries,
water companies and paving commissions who wanted to defend their local interests, and, of course, from the Corporation of the City of London. Setting the shape
for things to come, the Metropolitan Commission of Sewers, which was established
in 1847, was an unsuccessful compromise between reform and local interest. The City
of London was excluded from its overall responsibility and kept control of its own
drainage system.

Chadwick is the critical link between maps and sewers. Chadwick envisaged the
building of a new system of main drainage, but insisted that this could not be done

until the city had been exhaustively mapped and every gradient plotted by the Ordnance Survey. While Chadwick seemed to prevaricate, cholera hit London in 1849; some 14,000 died, and Chadwick was removed from the Metropolitan Commission of Sewers and utterly discredited.

In 1854 there was another catastrophic outbreak of cholera, which forced a radical review of the management of London's water supply. The view that a board of works be created for the entire metropolitan area became more generally accepted and in 1855 the Metropolis Local Management Act was passed, establishing London's first municipal government, the Metropolitan Board of Works. Given its pre-history, it is, perhaps, not surprising that the Board of Works began its existence with limited powers. The new system was a form of partnership between the new Board and the older vestries and district boards. Each of these residual groupings could send one or two representative members to the Metropolitan Board of Works, which was not, therefore, a popularly elected body. In spite of the existence of the Board of Works, therefore, many of the traditional powers of local self-government were left intact.

The Metropolitan Board of Works was essentially a committee for the administration of civil engineering projects. It was given responsibility for paving, lighting and constructing and naming streets in the London region, but its main role was to oversee the construction of a metropolitan sewer system. Minutes of meetings of the Board and the pages of London-based papers and journals convey a strong sense of the visions and realities of the Board in its early years.[13] They testify to meetings abandoned, delayed or postponed and decisions deferred and reversed. Having championed its creation, the *Illustrated London News* kept a particularly close watch on the Board, recording and censuring each of its failures, commending any sign of success. Within months of its constitution, the paper nicknamed the Board 'The Senate of Sewers', a parliament created and primarily devoted to the movement of waste.[14]

In its first years, the Board of Works had only partial control over the capital's sewers. The Metropolitan Commission of Sewers shared jurisdiction with the Board until 1858, when the Board took sole responsibility for constructing the London sewer system. Chadwick had been right; a technically measured plan showing land and watershed levels was needed before an underground sewer system could be built. As early as 1848 the Commission of Sewers, under the leadership of Chadwick, had proposed that the Royal Corps of Sappers and Miners should draw up the London plan.[15] Again, modernisers were challenged by older vested interests; private mapmakers proposed putting together a composite of previously existing maps of the area, while military professionals argued for a new survey of the whole region, drawn up with technical accuracy.

The military won and the Board of Ordnance was given the task of making a new, clear and accurate map of the capital. The Honourable Board of Ordnance dates back to the mid-fifteenth century, when its function was to arrange and carry through public orders or 'ordnances'. Its military connections date from the eighteenth century, when it was given responsibility for ordnance supplies to the Army and Navy, and in 1791 it took over the administration of the National Trigonometrical Survey of Britain, later called the Ordnance Survey.

1  *Skeleton Ordnance Survey of London and Its Environs*, 1851, Sheet 20, right half. Approx. 66 × 97.5 cm. (Southampton: Ordnance Map Office, 1851). Maps O.S.T. (78). By Permission of the British Library.

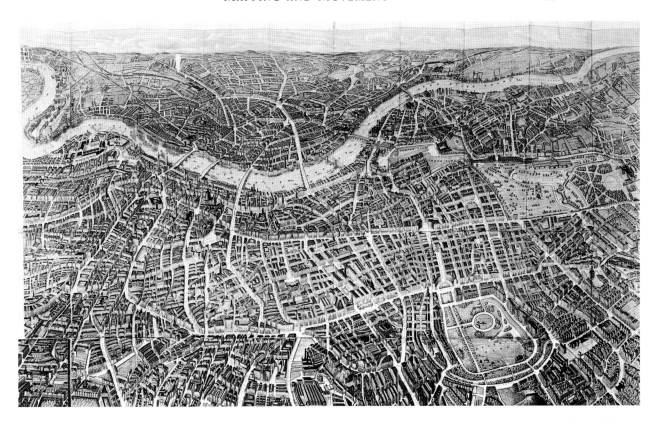

2   John Henry Banks and Co., '*A Baloon View of London*', 1851. Folding map, 60.8 × 102.4 cm. Guildhall Library, Corporation of London.

The Ordnance Survey of London was to cover an area of twelve miles' radius from St Paul's Cathedral, surveyed at a scale of twelve inches to a mile. It was to be a skeletal map, reproducing only main streets and waterways. The Skeleton Ordnance Map for London was completed in three years and was on sale to the public in 1851, the year of the Great Exhibition (fig. 1). The Ordnance Survey was a new way of cartographically imaging London. Abandoning the ornamental and decorative elements that characterised most privately produced, large-scale maps in this period, it was a stylised, abstract tool, which emphasised the connecting structural links of London, rather than its aesthetic or historical landmarks. Chadwick had been quite clear in his instructions to the military professionals; he wanted a block plan with a clear and thorough indication of levels, 'not a minutely detailed plan showing every house and garden and post'.[16] In other words, London was to be represented as potential process, as a geography of flow and movement. For this purpose, individual notation and ornament were in excess. Simplicity, clarity and professionalism were the principles of modern mapping.

Maps can be seen to be embedded in the attempt to modernise London in the mid-nineteenth century. The Skeleton Ordnance Survey marked the transition from an older, static view of the city to its conception as changing and progressive. The surveyor and the capitalist were the two creative forces of the modern map. The accurate, large-scale plan was the means by which tunnels could be excavated and pipes laid. It was the primary tool for entrepreneurial capital expansion; for the destruction and construction associated with the building of London's sewers and railways. The map enabled London to get moving.

In the Ordnance Survey of London, the rules of measurement and the rules of society are mutually reinforcing.[17] Decisions concerning what is shown and what is not shown tell us much about the priorities of official London in the mid-nineteenth century. A comparison with another map of London published in the same year as the Skeleton Ordnance Survey makes this point clearly. John Henry Banks's *A Baloon* [*sic*] *View of London* shows an aerial view, taken from the north towards the south, of the central parts of London (fig. 2). Its contemporaneity is evidenced in the Great Exhibition, which is shown to be taking place in Hyde Park, and yet, in many respects, this panoramic aerial view represents an older and different tradition of cartography. Banks's city prospect offers the viewer the exhilarating experience of viewing the whole of the centre of the city at once, as though from a balloon, above the north of the city. The view is less a functional map than a form of visual entertainment. It gives detailed, individual notation of houses, squares and streets, but it is unscaled. No engineering projects can be planned from this map. Its driving forces are aesthetics and narrative rather than the pragmatism and accuracy of the Ordnance Survey.

In *Utopics*, a fascinating, complex account of spatial power, Louis Marin examines two forms of mapping: the panoramic and the geometric.[18] These two categories help to explain the differences between Banks's map of London and the Ordnance Survey and to understand the significance of the visual codes of the Survey. According to Marin, the panoramic image fixes the viewer in a single spot from which the appearance of the city slowly unfolds in a kind of narrative circuit. Rooftops, steeples, streets and squares have a hidden, potential narrative, waiting to be discovered. But when represented geometrically, the city is given in its entirety, simultaneously. In the geometric map, the city is abstracted into free space and constructed space. The city loses its three-dimensionality and becomes nothing more than surface, marked and unmarked. There is no specific viewpoint; for the view is everywhere and nowhere at the same time. The representation is no longer the mimesis of a particular place, but is an analogic schema created through line and metric rule. Marin concludes: 'There is no staging; simply a map' (p. 208). The Skeleton Ordnance Survey takes the properties of the geometric representation of the city to their extreme forms. Stripped of all outward signs of narration and decorative ornament, it uncompromisingly declares its utilitarian purpose, its cartographic function. And yet, there is still a narrative unfolding on the austere sheets of the Ordnance Survey; a narrative of progress and improvement. The skeletal notations of streets, land and water levels are the resonant signs of modernity. They speak of the city's commitment to professional modernisation and its determination to build a new social order. It is entirely accurate and utterly unrecognisable. It renders the structure of the city on which the culture of modernity can be based.

In the sheets of the Skeleton Ordnance Survey of London, we begin to uncover a new aesthetic, which emerges through the pragmatics of sewerage. The provision

3 'Opening of the First Public Drinking-Fountain for the Metropolis on Thursday Week', *Illustrated London News*, 30 April 1859, p. 432.

of a clean water supply and the safe extraction of the city's waste had a profound effect on the look and experience of London in the period. On the surface of the street, the Board of Works, local authorities and a private, philanthropic association undertook a large-scale project to provide drinking fountains throughout the capital. These were occasionally designed by established academic artists and were unveiled like monuments and with great ceremony (fig. 3).[19] But the construction of a sewerage system also drove home the image of the city below ground and of immense engineering designs creating an uninterrupted flow of water under London. The design for London's drainage system was the work of Joseph Bazalgette, Chief Engineer of the Metropolitan Board of Works.[20] Bazalgette's plan was for a series of intercepting sewers that would remove the sewage before it reached the Thames and take it beyond the currents of London. Three large new sewers were to be built on the north side of the Thames and two on the south side. Crossing London from west to east, they would intercept the old sewers on their way to the Thames. The contents of the new intercepting sewers had to be lifted at intervals by huge pumps, so that gravity could continue the ceaseless movement of muck towards the east. Finally, the waste reached its destination at a huge outfall works below London. The aims of Bazalgette's system were to purify the stinking River Thames and to create an

4    'Main Drainage of the Metropolis: Sectional View of the Tunnels from Wick Lane, near Old Ford, Bow, Looking Westward', *Illustrated London News*, 27 August 1859, p. 203.

uninterrupted flow of matter in the sewers; putrefaction led to infection, movement in the sewers was essential. The *Illustrated London News* reported every stage in the plan's realisation. The construction of the tunnels gave their artists an opportunity to celebrate a new form of heroic, manly labour and a reworking of classical symmetry in the architecture of the vast tunnels (fig. 4). The paper illustrated draughtsmen's diagrams of the pumping machinery,[21] and Abbey Mills Pumping Station, built between 1865 and 1868 in the Venetian Gothic style, was regarded as one of the most splendid examples of industrial architecture in the country. Engines, buildings, diagrams and illustrative compositions were all elements in the visual culture of drains produced in the 1860s.

   Nowhere is the principle of continuous circulation and the aesthetics of sewerage more clearly brought together than in the account by the journalist John Hollingshead of his journey down a sewer in 1862. The account appears in a chapter entitled 'A Day Below', in a collection of essays by Hollingshead on the theme of *Underground London*.[22] Hollingshead was a knowing, prolific, professional writer. His choice of subject shows him to be responsive to the new conditions of the city and also confident of reasonable public interest and sales. In the sewer chapter he explained that he wished to inspect a main sewer from its source to its point of discharge. Jibing at the current tourist literature on London, of which he was himself an author, he comments that he might have called this piece 'A Saunter Through the West End'. But this saunter is below the West End, and Hollingshead guides his readers down into the sewer as he embarks on his subterranean trip. The noise in the tunnel and unfamiliar sources of light disorientate his sense of time and place. Shafts of light through ventilator gratings look like rays of moonlight, and the sound of a boy whistling in the street above makes the journalist feel like an escaped convict. Followers above the ground trace the journey below and shout down their location in the city through manholes. At one point Hollingshead is told he is below Buckingham Palace and he sings the national anthem standing in effluvia.

5   Edward Stanford, *Stanford's Library Map of London and Its Suburbs*, 1862, Sheet 10. 38.6 × 60.8 cm. (London: Edward Stanford, 1862). Maps 11.c.5. By Permission of the British Library.

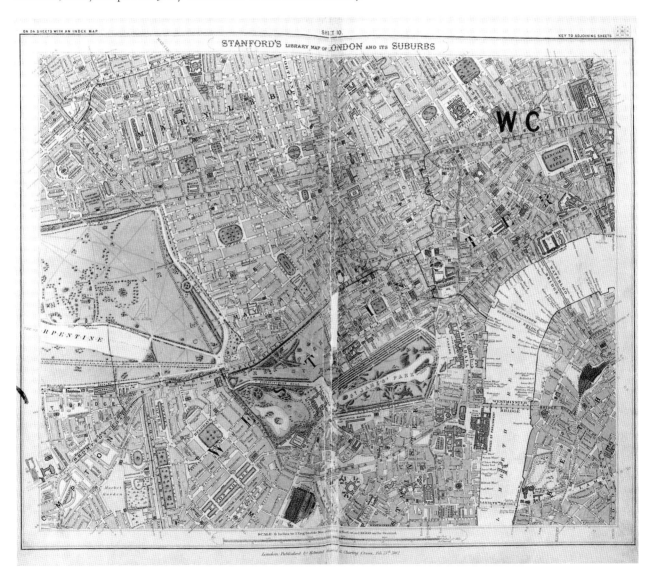

Finally, Hollingshead reaches the River Thames and the end of his journey, having mapped a disturbing, alternative route through the city. Underground space is dislocating; it disorientates the senses and routes can only be plotted and comprehended through the interpolation of place names from the world above. This subterranean city is an impossible place for the moderniser. The rational city is a legible city, in which it is always possible to plot positions and to imagine the relationship of parts to the whole. The modern map performs this function. It compartmentalises, classifies and explains the logics of the metropolis; it lays out its boundaries and priorities.

In 1862, on the occasion of the second International Exhibition to be held in London, Edward Stanford published his *Library Map of London* (fig. 5).[23] Following the passing of the Public Libraries Act in 1850 and its formalisation of the demand for universal knowledge, the *Library Map* was intended for use in libraries, schools and offices. Stanford was an entrepreneurial printer and retailer, who established his own business in London in the early 1850s. He employed engravers but also acquired plates from other firms for the production of atlases and sheet maps. For the 1862 *Library Map* Stanford used a copy of the twelve-inch Ordnance Survey plan, on to which was plotted a huge amount of new detail: public transport routes, postal districts, public buildings and all manner of boundaries – counties, county courts, parliamentary seats, metropolitan local management districts, Poor Law districts, registry districts and sub-districts and so on. The map was then redrawn on a six-inch scale and engraved. Stanford's map is a map of boundaries. It is a cartographic celebration of the modern, public, civic city. Stanford's marketing was impressively flexible; the map could be bought coloured or uncoloured, bound in a volume or in single sheets, varnished or mounted on spring rollers.

By the 1860s London was well and truly mapped. New types of maps were constantly appearing, offering new ways of comprehending the city. There were railway maps, cholera maps, gas supply maps and temperance maps.[24] Visitors and travellers in London could plan their journeys and visualise their location in relation to any other part of the metropolis. In a travelogue-style article, published in *Temple Bar* in 1860, George Augustus Sala parodied the volumes of maps and directories available to the conscientious traveller: '[I] entreated Messrs Kelly . . . to send me their new Suburban Postal Directory, and cutting out the map therefrom, pasted it against the wall and studied it attentively. I consulted the maps and charts of Mr Wyld, of Charing Cross. I read up the literature of Middlesex in Lysons and Faulkner, in Hunt and Mogg, and in many well-thumbed gazetteers and cab-fare statists.'[25] The author is thus prepared to become an informed, rational, modern city traveller, but even in this ordered world of maps, charts and directories, the experience of the street may resist planning and the sensory disturbance of the subterranean city may come to the surface. The logic of the cartographer cannot contain the city of memory and imagination. As a later article in *Temple Bar* enthused: 'The names of the streets are those you have read from boyhood. They are the scenes of a hundred plays and storybooks.'[26] London in the 1860s was not only the city of planning and improvement, it was also the site of fantasy and thrill; it was the location of a constant interplay between rationalism and imagination.

# 2     *Great Victorian Ways*

Some of the most imaginative visions for the improvement of London were never built and remained the personal obsessions of their creators. On 7 June 1855 the Select Committee on Metropolitan Communications heard evidence from an expert witness, Sir Joseph Paxton, architect of the celebrated Crystal Palace. Paxton proposed that a vast arcade should be built which would form a belt around Central London; the projected boulevard and railway girdle was to be called the 'Great Victorian Way'. With the help of a beautiful watercolour of a section of the proposed scheme (fig. 6), Paxton explained his solution to London's traffic problems to the Committee members.[27] The scheme was basically an extension of the principles used in the design of the Crystal Palace. The intention was to form a covered way that would keep out the smoke, dirt and vicissitudes of the London climate. The central nave would incorporate a roadway for the use of heavy goods traffic at night

6    Joseph Paxton, Perspectival drawing of a section of the 'Great Victorian Way', 1855. Pencil, pen, ink and watercolour, 70.6 × 104.7 cm. V&A Picture Library.

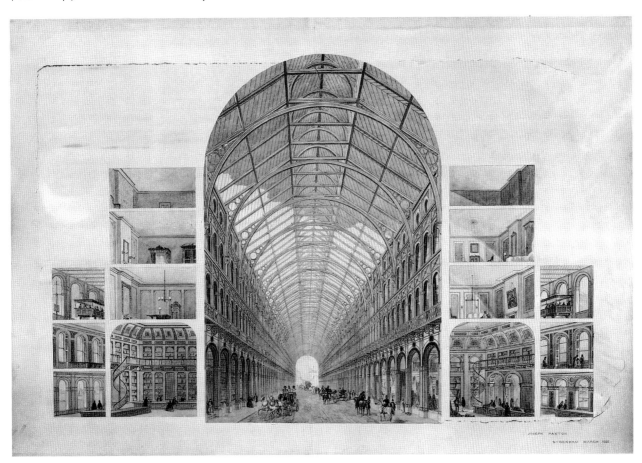

and omnibuses and passenger vehicles during the day. On either side of the roadway would be shops and apartments, and beyond these, within the same structure, would be several of the newly invented, smokeless pneumatic railways and walkways. One of the most radical features of Paxton's scheme was its creation of an artificial environment. Paxton provided details of a grand ventilation system, which would produce an atmosphere as pure as that of the country throughout the arcade. The temperature would also be regulated to ensure constant comfort for the occupants. For the architect, the advantages of the plan were clear: it would be convenient and healthy, and would enhance the value of the property through which it passed. It was a monumental project and would make London the grandest city in the world. Paxton's 'magnificent promenade' would traverse all districts of London and would change its character appropriately. From the City to Regent Street it would be devoted to shops, in the residential west of London it would primarily provide private residences, and in the section passing through Kensington Gardens there would be no buildings and the covered promenade would resemble 'a crystal palace passing through the place'.[28] This is the aestheticisation of movement taken to the point of megalomania. Paxton's perspectival watercolour shows the arcade at a point where it crosses the River Thames. The central section illustrates the immense vaulted cast iron and glass roof, supported by tiers of Italianate arcades. The figures on the road are dwarfed by the scale of the architecture and it is notable that only passenger vehicles are shown within the arcade. The side sections show the interiors of the high-class shops and superior dwellings in this section of the arcade. At the back of the houses, the walkways and pneumatic railways that link the entire scheme are represented.

Paxton's extraordinary proposal creates a micro-city, a mini-metropolis, with its sealed environment and alternating districts. It is not only environmentally regulated, however, it is also socially controlled. Paxton told the Committee: 'It would be possible, and not only possible, but it would be right, to vary the interior of the arcade according to the district, as the circumstances required; it might be in one case desirable to put up a beautiful place for residences, and in another part it might be of a more ordinary description' (p. 82). Paxton's glass boulevard is an exercise in the ultimate control and segregation of urban space. It separates goods and people on the street, it segregates the élite social classes from their inferiors and it even filters the impurities from the air. Whether by means of ventilation or pneumatic railway, the arcade is in a state of constant circulation. Paxton's scheme exemplifies the urban ideal that Richard Sennett has called 'protected openness', that is, an environment that privileges visibility, while ensuring isolation.[29] Perhaps the most extraordinary element of the arcade is its point of transparency; the moment where it ends and the rest of the surrounding city begins. If the strollers on the walkway and passengers on the railway look out of the arcade, what do they see? Perhaps the inhabitants of the outside world looking back at them.

In its report on Paxton's examination before the Select Committee, the architectural journal, the *Builder*, acclaimed his startling scheme, but raised an eyebrow about the projected cost.[30] On balance, however, it supported the project, imagining a new class of Londoner, 'the inhabitants of the Boulevard', who would dwell in the 'noble street'. Paxton's scheme was not built, could not have been built, but the plan remains as a breathtaking example of Victorian futuristic urban planning, suspended half-way between shopping mall and Fritz Lang's *Metropolis*.

The Select Committee on Metropolitan Communications was set up to tackle the problem of traffic in London, in other words, the problem of streets. The newly created Metropolitan Board of Works was given responsibility for street improvement, to include building, widening, straightening, naming and numbering. Among the most substantial of the street improvements undertaken by the Board were the building of Holborn Viaduct and the Thames Embankment. To the disruption incurred by these projects, add the devastating impact of railway construction and station building, and to many it seemed that in the 1860s half of London was being rebuilt or was succumbing to the forces of improvement. The *Illustrated Times* invoked the kaleidoscopic rate of change taking place on the streets of London: 'the whole City and its suburbs are in such a state of transition that a week's absence from town is sufficient to make the oldest inhabitant a stranger in his own parish.'[31] The experience of improvement is described as one of displacement and alienation and the paper accepts that, in this urban context, it is no longer possible 'to know town well'. The political debate provoked by the scale of construction concerned whose interests were being served by 'improvement': those of the city or those of the capital investors. The *Illustrated London News* spent the 1860s shifting between a position as the mouthpiece of reform and alarm at the visual effects of the works. By the middle of the decade it acknowledged: 'for many months London has been in a state of siege and barricade, by reason of the "improvements".'[32] No sooner had the railway builders cleared away their debris than London was taken over by sewer construction. The paper compared the energy of the builders to a military campaign, and tried to evoke the appearance of the streets thus besieged: 'a series of fortifications, mostly surmounted by huge scaffolds that in the twilight resembled the guillotine in the last scene of *The Dead Heart*, and surrounded by stockades that would defy a New Zealand warrior, arose in our chief thoroughfares.'

Change in London was happening so quickly that it seemed by enchantment rather than man-made. London was in the possession of the surveyors and masons, and was undergoing a continuous process of demolition and reconstruction. Familiar landmarks and streets disappeared in clouds of dust, but the new London never seemed finally to emerge. The language of improvement in texts of the 1860s was equally a language of disintegration. The modernising of the city was represented as much in terms of the 'coming down' of old London, as it was through the construction of new projects. In fact, at times it is unclear whether old London was being pulled down or whether it was coming down in a more organic way; in either sense, contemporaries seemed to be witnessing the disintegration of the old fabric of the city. For a period, during the 1850s, the *Illustrated London News* carried a series of reports on 'falling buildings' (fig. 7); cases where old London houses collapsed, either as a result of damage from nearby excavations, or simply through age and decay. The reports give details of damage and injury but, more oddly, convey the idea that the old city, irrespective of improvement, has simply decided to come down.[33] In other images, too, the juxtaposition of old and new suggests a voluntary submission by the old (fig. 8). In its account of recent improvements in the financial

7   'Remains of the Fallen House, no. 184, Strand', *Illustrated London News*, 10 September 1853, p. 705.


districts, the uneven outline of the old buildings is shown in front of a monumental commercial building that seems almost to be growing out of the ruins. It is as though the newness of the modern could not be conveyed in isolation and could be articulated only through its relationship to the old.

   'The nineteenth century sweeps everything old away', 'the "time to pull down" . . . seems to be fast approaching its climacteric in the city of London'.[34] Week after week, the *Illustrated London News* recorded the devastating effects of improvement on

8   'Old and New Buildings in Threadneedle-street', *Illustrated London News*, 10 February 1855, p. 144.

the city. Shortly after the Board of Works started its projects, the paper assumed the role of archivist of the city, and announced its intention to provide its readers with pictorial representations and historical descriptions of ancient buildings removed in the building works. In regular columns with titles such as 'Nooks and Corners of Old England' and 'Archaeology of the Month' it illustrated the disappearing inns and houses of Elizabethan London, creating in its pages a lexicon of the metropolitan picturesque. In nearly every case the text comments on how pictorial the old buildings and streets are, how the artist could not find a better subject for his pencil. Demolition, in the 1860s, gave a new life to the conventional modes of the picturesque.[35]

In their account of the visual representation of early nineteenth-century industrial cities, Caroline Arscott and Griselda Pollock have described the ways in which images manipulate and rework older aesthetic conventions in order to represent an emergent social formation with its new social geographies.[36] Something of this kind happened again in London in the 1860s. The history of the picturesque is now well rehearsed and reasonably familiar:[37] formulated in a number of key texts in the eighteenth century, the picturesque describes a kind of beauty that is capable of being illustrated in a painting. The picturesque is a comfortable aesthetic experience; it does not stimulate dramatic emotions and can be immediately comprehended in a single sweep of the scene. The picturesque is found in contrast rather than in unity, in irregularity rather than in continuity, and in the fragment rather than in the whole. It is an aesthetic of the ruin and of the artistry of age.

By the early nineteenth century the picturesque was a highly conventionalised way of comprehending the social landscape, and guidebooks devoted to tours of picturesque spots proliferated. But the picturesque changed when it crossed from the connoisseurship of landscape to the representation of the city. Although it retained a number of its eighteenth-century features, such as the appreciation of contrast, the admiration of ruins and the pictorial mode of cognition, it came also to represent process and change, the last traces of the past in the present. Even in the eighteenth century the picturesque was a way of aestheticising complex historical and social changes in the landscape, a calming resolution of antagonisms within the frame of a picture. In the mid-nineteenth-century city, however, these changes and conflicts occurred more rapidly and could not be held at a distance, in the sweep of a picturesque eye. In this context, while the picturesque still struggled to contain the full implications of change, it also kept drawing attention to the very processes producing it. The signs of the metropolitan picturesque are thus signs of modernity; they are signs of a changing urban geography and of altered spatial relations.

In illustrations such as the 'Demolition of Hungerford Market', the city ruin is the central motif (fig. 9). The entire foreground is taken up by the representation of absence, of that which is no longer there. Although the teams of workmen may be the Victorian equivalent of Georgian shepherds and gypsies, these picturesque props now signify the forces of change, rather than of rural continuity. Architectural landmarks such as the steeple of St Martin-in-the-Fields punctuate the skyline, but are half hidden by the debris in the foreground. Houses are shown on the brink of destruction, with the spectral lines of demolished ceilings, staircases and floors imprinted on their remaining walls. This is the representation of imminence, of that which is on the verge of becoming; in artistic terms, it is the archaeology of modernity.

Images such as these reveal a constitutive truth in the history of the modern. Modernity leans upon and is haunted by the figure of the past. The discourses of Victorian improvement endlessly declared the finality of the break with the old city. It was the world from which the urban reformers distanced themselves and, as such, belonged to a separate history. But this teleology requires that the past must be constantly rewritten and re-presented. It does not go away, but is a spectral presence in the development of the new. In a fascinating essay on the historical drama of Alexandre Dumas, Michel de Certeau has examined the role of the *ancien régime* in mid-nineteenth-century Republican France.[38] He evokes a disturbing, almost phantasmatic dialogue between the past and the present. Although the present declares its breach with the past: 'the "old" returns. It forbids one to feel at home in the new age. The actual remains engaged in a "fantasy" debate with this phantom, which continues to haunt it' (p. 151). The old disturbs the confidence of the new and unsettles its newly formed values and certainties. But the present can assimilate the past;

9 'Demolition of Hungerford Market: View Looking Towards the Strand', *Illustrated London News*, 27 December 1862, p. 705.

it can subject it to its own interpretations and narratives. This is how the present contains its expelled past: 'little by little, it reconquers it . . . it expresses new fantasies, desires and conflicts . . . That is what re-presenting is. Dis-quieting corpses return to the grave if they become the lexicon of the living. The world of yester-year is summoned to recount *our* history: that is what ensures that it "cannot harm us", that it "presents no danger".'[39] This is surely the key to the meaning of the metropolitan picturesque, that obsessive discourse on the past. In images and texts the picturesque turns the old city into a collection of relics. Demolished areas, old housing, displaced populations are transformed into pleasing images and presented to the public as signs of the emergence of the new. But, as de Certeau reminds us, the success of this operation is never certain and it must be endlessly repeated. This is the cultural process that unfolds on the pages of the Victorian illustrated press.

Photography played an important role in the re-presentation of the past and the transformation of the fabric of the old city into an album of relics. Photographers were routinely sent out to record sites immediately before their demolition for rail-

ways, sewers and roads. This consciousness of the role of photography in document-
ing the city's historical past reached its apogee in the foundation in 1875 of the
Society for Photographing Relics of Old London.[40] The Society was founded by a
number of antiquarians and architects who were anxious to preserve the appearance
of the last remaining old buildings of London. Between 1875 and 1886 twelve series
of photographs were issued, many of them the work of photographers Henry Dixon
and Alfred and John Bool. In these albums, photography not only preserves the image
of the past, it also, in de Certeau's sense, reconquers it.

Perhaps the final move in this particular phase of modernity's engagement with
the past can be traced to the International Health Exhibition, held in South
Kensington in 1884.[41] Here, among examples of the latest in public and domestic
sanitary engineering, the most popular exhibit was the full-scale reconstruction of
an old London street. Visitors were able to walk along the narrow medieval street,
climb in and out of the rickety buildings and marvel, generally, at the filth and lack
of hygiene of the past. When they had had enough of dirt and disease, they could
re-emerge into the rows of gleaming water-closets and spectacular fountains representing the progress of the present. By the end of the century London's past had
been reduced to little more than fairground scenery in the ongoing staging of
metropolitan improvement.

The most significant player in the demolition and transformation of Victorian
London was the railway. In the 1860s the railways ploughed into the heart of London,
causing major displacements of mostly labouring populations through enforced
demolition of housing for new railway construction.[42] In preparing the routes for
their lines, the railway companies usually planned them to pass through working-
class districts, where land and compensation were cheaper. The railways created suburban havens away from the centre of London for the wealthier classes but aggravated
the overcrowding of the poor in the areas where displacements occurred. During
the 1860s rehousing requirements that had been imposed on the railway companies
were not enforced, and the companies continued to evade responsibility until well
into the 1880s. The evicted occupants of demolished buildings were left to their own
devices, which usually meant moving into the already packed houses in adjacent
streets.

Railway building changed the appearance of the city and presented new views of
familiar sights. In its view of the construction of the new railway bridge at Blackfriars, the *Illustrated London News* admired the 'curious juxtaposition' of old and new
in the contrast between the dome of St Paul's and the winches and machinery in
the foreground (fig. 10). Here was a new industrial landscape, located in the heart of
the metropolis.

Charles Dickens had set in place many of the defining features of this wrecked
industrial landscape in his description of the building of the London and Birming-
ham railway at Staggs's Gardens in north London, in *Dombey and Son*, first published
in 1848. It is a memorable piece of writing and worth quoting at length:

> The first shock of a great earthquake had, just at that period, rent the whole neigh-
> bourhood to its centre. Traces of its course were visible on every side. Houses were
> knocked down; streets broken through and stopped; deep pits and trenches dug in

the ground; enormous heaps of earth and clay thrown up; buildings that were undermined and shaking, propped up by great beams of wood . . . Everywhere were bridges that led nowhere; thoroughfares that were wholly impassable; Babel towers of chimneys, wanting half their height; temporary wooden houses and enclosures, in the most unlikely situations; carcasses of ragged tenements, and fragments of unfinished walls and arches, and piles of scaffolding, and wildernesses of bricks, and giant forms of cranes, and tripods straddling above nothing. There were a hundred thousand shapes and substances of incompleteness, wildly mingled out of their places, upside down, burrowing in the earth, mouldering in the water, and unintelligible as any dream.[43]

This is a landscape of chaos and catastrophe in which every physical element has lost its meaning and intelligibility. By the 1860s, however, this scale of demolition had moved from the outskirts of the city into its centre. There are hints of Dickens's insane, illegible space in the illustration of the works at Blackfriars Bridge: ground level is difficult to read and the route of the bridge through the surrounding

10 'The Railway Works at Blackfriars and Opening Towards Ludgate Hill, Viewed from the Temporary Bridge', *Illustrated London News*, 23 April 1864, p. 385.

houses is hard to discern, but otherwise the wilder images of the novelist's prose are curbed by the gentler conventions of curiosity and the engraver's artistic sense of 'juxtaposition'.

Railway construction not only had dramatic effects on the visual appearance of the city, it also brought about a reorganisation of spatial relations. The huge expansion of transport and communication in the 1860s, created by the railways, the electric telegraph and the mass daily press, changed the perceptions of time and space through which daily life was lived. People, goods and information moved more quickly than ever before. The world's first underground railway, which opened in London in 1863, played a significant part in this reconceptualisation of space. Now, instead of traversing space by following the logic of streets and other identifiable external features, people could travel below the ground, on routes that obeyed the logic of their own lines and expediency. They could descend at one point in the city and emerge at another, with little sense of the spaces between, or the meaning of the time taken to make the journey.

The building of the Metropolitan Underground Railway wrecked London. The

11   'Plan of the Metropolitan Railway', *Illustrated London News*, 7 April 1860, p. 338.

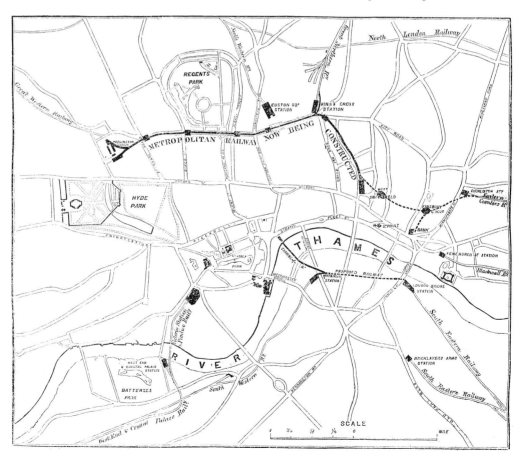

# THE METROPOLITAN RAILWAY.

PROPOSED STATION AT BAKER STREET.

THIS remarkable undertaking—which had been so long in abeyance that the public had well-nigh despaired of its ultimate accomplishment—has now been commenced in earnest, and the contractors are proceeding vigorously with the works at various points. We have, therefore, collected a few details which we think will be of interest to our readers. The need of railways communication between the City and the great series of railway on the north of the Thames, both for passengers and goods, had been long grievously felt, but the difficulties in the way of carrying a railway into the City appeared to be almost insuperable. To have a railway, after the American fashion, passing through a densely-populous district, and crossing on the level our overcrowded streets and thoroughfares, was utterly out of the question; and scarcely less so to carry an unsightly viaduct through the heart of the metropolis. The only alternative was that adopted by the Metropolitan Company—namely, that of an underground communication, by which the most densely-crowded districts could be traversed without the slightest annoyance or obstruction to the existing traffic. A reference to the map will show that the railway starts from opposite the Great Western Railway Hotel at Paddington, with a fork up the South Wharf-road to join the Great Western Railway on the level, near the site of the old passenger station. The line then crosses the Edgware-road, and enters the New-road, which it follows to King's-cross, it being one of the peculiarities of this railway that it occupies, throughout the greater part of its course, the under surface of the existing roadways, thus avoiding the enormous expenditure which would otherwise have been necessary for the purchase of valuable house property.

From King's-cross the line, avoiding the House of Correction at Coldbath-fields, and passing for some distance under the Bagnigge Wells-road, takes an almost straight course to Farringdon-street; and this part of the railway, except when passing under roadways, will be in open cutting.

In addition to the principal terminal stations at Paddington and Holborn-hill, commodious passenger stations will be erected at the Edgware-road, Baker-street, in the triangular plot of ground opposite Trinity Church, Regent's-park, Hampstead-road, Euston-square, and King's-cross. The terminal stations, and the Edgware-road, Regent's-park, and King's-cross stations, will be open, or covered with a glass roof; the others, as that at Baker-street (vide engraving), will be commodious, airy, and well lighted with gas. The ascent and descent to the underground stations, as will be seen by reference to the Great Western station at Paddington and other metropolitan lines.

It is intended to run light trains at short intervals, and calling at perhaps alternate stations, and all risk of collision will be avoided by telegraphing the arrival and departure of each train from station to station, so that there will always be an interval of at least one station between the trains. The traffic is to be worked by locomotive engines of a novel and ingenious construction. In order to obviate the annoyance in a tunnel arising from smoke and the products of combustion, the locomotives will have no firebox, but will be charged with hot water and steam at a certain pressure to be supplied by fixed boilers at the termini, and will be furnished with a large heater to assist in maintaining the temperature. It is estimated that each locomotive will thus carry with it sufficient power to enable it to effect the double journey. In order to test the efficiency of locomotives constructed on this principle the directors have instructed Messrs. Stephenson and Co. to build a broad-gauge engine, which will be employed in the construction of the works.

The general character of the archway may be gathered from the

COMMENCEMENT OF THE TUNNEL AT KING'S-CROSS.

13  'Underground Works at the Junction of Hampstead-Road, Euston-Road, and Tottenham-Court-Road', *Illustrated London News*, 28 May 1864, p. 529.

14   'The Metropolitan (Underground) Railway. – Works in Progress at King's Cross', *Illustrated London News*, 2 February 1861, p. 98.

route passed under central London and excavations were made through built-up residential and commercial areas. Work was begun in the winter of 1860; shafts were sunk at several places along the line of the proposed railway and the huge task of excavation commenced. In the spring of 1860 the *Illustrated London News* provided its readers with images depicting all visual aspects of the project: a map (fig. 11); a cross-section of one of the proposed stations and an illustration of the digging (fig. 12). The construction of the Underground created visual spectacles that were unprecedented in the metropolis. The cross-section became a favourite technique for representing the railway system (fig. 13).[44] In these images the full wonder of the Underground could be displayed; an apparently normal street above the ground and then, below the gas pipes and sewers, another, parallel world of passengers, locomotives and airy tunnels illuminated by gas. The tunnelling itself summoned images of the sublime, with excavations on an apparently limitless scale and tiny figures dwarfed by massive building works. This was a new urban aesthetic built around the forms of the tunnel, the trench, the vault and scaffolding.

In the early 1860s the *Illustrated London News* was kept busy; reporting on the progress of the sewer system and the Underground. Images reveal building works on a massive scale in the middle of London and daily life carrying on in the narrow surrounding margins, apparently inattentive to the devastation at the heart of the city. In one typical image, the vast trench is shown at the centre of the composition, worming its way through the middle of a street in King's Cross (fig. 14). None of the passing crowds pays any attention to the works, apart from a little figure – an echo from the picturesque – peering in through a gate at the tunnelling beyond. The above-ground view of the cutting is accompanied by an underground view of the main tunnel and branch lines. This double vision was essential to convey the uniqueness of the works in progress. The earth beneath this particular part of London was, in fact, already fairly congested, and contractors had to avoid existing sewer, gas and water pipes. They failed: in 1862 a huge sewer containing the River Fleet burst and flooded the excavation, but the *Illustrated London News* advised its readers that the scene was well worth a visit. In spite of setbacks, the system was formally opened at the beginning of 1863 (fig. 15), although construction works to extend the lines continued.

The extension of the system produced even greater disruption of built-up areas in central London. The 'railway people' seemed in control of the city. Parliament assumed a *laissez-faire* approach and made no attempt to intervene in or regulate the works, partly, no doubt, because Parliament itself was invaded by railway interests: some 148 railways directors sat in the House of Commons by 1867.[45] The underground railway works passed through all parts of London, indiscriminately digging up commercial, residential and governmental districts. And the photographers, of course, were there to record it. The visual effects of the railway building are suggested in a staggering series of anonymous photographs, possibly commissioned by the railway contractors. A number show the progress of the works in Westminster and specifically across Parliament Square, the location of the Houses of Parliament (fig. 16). A scene of extraordinary devastation is shown, which surpasses Dickens's description of Staggs's Gardens. The statue of William Canning and the misty shape of the lower part of St Stephen's tower (Big Ben) in the background are the only indicators of the topographical location of the photograph. The entire area is partitioned by wooden fences and piles of bricks, which threaten to obscure the tops of the street lights. The excavations had no respect for status or tradition and, in another image in this series, Westminster Abbey itself seems threatened with destruction (fig. 17).

In residential and commercial areas the excavations tore through shops and houses; railway lines and inhabited buildings were absolutely adjacent (fig. 18). Where once there had been terraces and neighbours, there were now cavernous excavations and teams of workmen. In one photograph a group of three women with children is shown standing on the balcony of a terraced house, amidst a scene of utter destruction. Nothing stands between this house and the immense excavation works next door. The terrace wall literally marks the limits of the demolition. A remaining, tottering chimney in the ruin in front of the figures emphasises the vulnerability of the lone standing house. In these surroundings, the most striking element in the photograph is the calm passivity with which the figures observe the spectacle beside them.

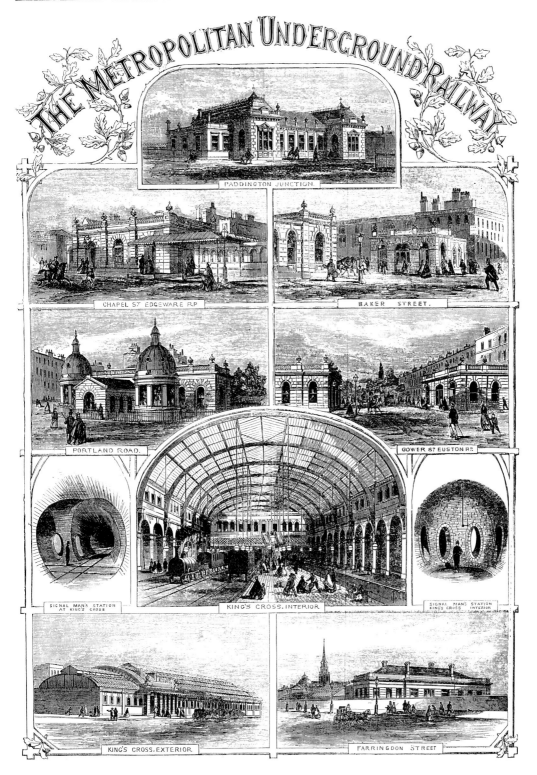

15 'The Metropolitan Underground Railway', *Illustrated London News*, 27 December 1862, p. 692.

16   Excavation for the District Railway across Parliament Square alongside the Canning Statue, *c.*1867. Photograph. London Transport Museum.

Of course the journalist John Hollingshead took on the underground railway, 'a railroad among the sewers', in his study of *Underground London*.[46] But, like other observers, it was the spectacle of the building works that most preoccupied him. Commenting ironically on the proximity of the excavations to domestic residences, Hollingshead noted that Londoners could see how tunnels were made: 'without leaving the warm shelter of their drawing-rooms or bed-rooms' (p. 209). Moreover, the transformation from neighbourhood to building site was fast. One moment the roadway was enclosed and traffic was diverted. Then the steam-engines, horses and 'navvies' arrived. The terrible noise began as scaffolding was erected and shaft-holes sunk. Finally, the household found itself next-door neighbours with the railway works:

17   Clearing the site opposite Broad Sanctuary for the construction of the District Railway, at the eastern end of Tothill Street, *c.*1867. Photograph. London Transport Museum.

18    Completing the tunnel along Praed Street, c.1866. Photograph. London Transport Museum.

huge pieces of timber are planted against some of the houses to prevent their falling into the street. A father of a family looks out of his window one morning after shaving, and finds a large breezy 'clearance' among his neighbours' houses to the right or left, which ventilates the neighbourhood, but fills his mind with doubts about the stability of his dwelling . . . and he strongly objects to a temporary way of wet planks, erected for his use, and the use of passers-by, over a yawning cavern underneath the pavement.[47]

London spent the whole of the 1860s in thrall to railway construction, and excavations were a familiar, if disfiguring, feature of the urban landscape. Its impact on the city was experienced above and below ground and it changed forever perceptions of time and space and metropolitan travel. A carefully executed lithograph of King's Cross, one of the original stations of the underground railway, presents a very different side to underground travel from that given in the photographs of the works

19   Anon., *King's Cross, Metropolitan Line*, 1868. Lithograph. Photo: London Transport Museum.

(fig. 19). Here the architecture and ornament of the station are featured. The locomotive and coaches are given centre place and the Underground is shown to be a
respectable form of travel for the middle classes, and notably, for unaccompanied
women. In the background, the dark tunnels await the trainloads of passengers, and
perhaps it is there that the uncontrollable and chaotic city of the imagination takes
over.

In 1868 the *Illustrated London News* called on Mr Stanford, or some other cartographer, to produce a map of the London railways. Although there were countless
maps of London above ground there was still nothing to guide the traveller in underground London:

We read of outer and inner circles, and of the belts which are nearly complete,
and we get at a sort of astronomical feeling, and are quite sure that from a balloon,
or some commanding position, we should discover symmetry and order, and a

20  'A "Block" in Park-Lane', *Illustrated London News*, 17 December 1864, p. 604.

well-concerted system. But, if anybody understands how the circles and the belt ministers to his convenience, the present writer is not that man.[48]

The experience of the Underground is of disorientation, of revolving 'around London for an indefinite time'; it needed the distant gaze of the cartographer to rationalise and interpret this new space.

While railway building in the 1860s was laying to waste large swathes of London, the Metropolitan Board of Works was undertaking its own projects to relieve traffic congestion and to beautify the streets of the city. The crush and crowding of the main streets were identified as the most pressing problem facing the city. Existing thoroughfares were seen to be narrow and tortuous and the entire metropolis seemed devoid of large open spaces offering direct passage from the east to the west of the city. The old streets did offer opportunities for pictorial comedy and genre painting. Throughout the 1860s the *Illustrated London News* carried full-page engravings depicting incidents and conditions in the streets of the city. A traffic-jam in Mayfair is the excuse for an anecdotal illustration filled with a familiar range of social types and the requisite degree of varied incident (fig. 20), and the paper also carried a series of images depicting the trying conditions of the London streets in different weather and seasons.[49]

Fine artists also took London street life as their subjects. The great majority of these street genre scenes are highly conventionalised and anodyne, but a group of small paintings by Arthur Boyd Houghton is exceptional. The pictures in this group were made between 1859 and 1865, in the years of the first frenzy of improvement, following the creation of the Board of Works. In them, Houghton wove together a number of themes, such as the military, homelessness and street construction, to produce images that are quite unlike conventional Victorian genre scenes. They are strange and slightly disturbing and their composition, style and cast of social types do not offer the comfort of easy legibility.

Houghton was trained as a painter and illustrator.[50] In the 1860s, with little success in finding buyers for his paintings, he concentrated on book and magazine illustration and it was as an illustrator that his work subsequently caught the attention of Vincent Van Gogh. Interestingly, it was Van Gogh, virtually alone among Houghton's critics, who understood the strange quality of the work. He wrote to his brother Theo, '[Houghton] was weird and mysterious like Goya', and he also compared his work to the Parisian Gothic extravagances of Charles Méryon.[51] Although Van Gogh was writing specifically about a series of engravings called *Graphic America*, his description applies just as well to Houghton's London paintings.

One of the earliest of a group taking up the theme of military recruitment in the city, *Recruits* (c.1859) depicts a marching band and soldiers in the streets of London (fig. 21). But this is no orderly panorama of Victorian daily life. The crowds hanging around to see the soldiers look unhealthy and vaguely menacing. Children in the foreground and by the street lamp appear malformed and undernourished, and scrabble around in the dirt of the street. Characters are in close proximity but do not develop the kind of narrative incident favoured by other modern-life painters. For example, the two strange, top-hatted men in the foreground stand close to a young woman with a perambulator, but there is no suggestion of attention or communication between these groups. The whole motley crowd stands in front of a background of tall buildings, smoking chimneys and streets. Houghton ignores contemporary academic conventions of finish and uses a loose painterly brushwork throughout the small canvas.

A number of the characters reappear in Houghton's other London pictures. *Itinerant Singers* (c.1860) shows another crowd, set, this time, against the River Thames in central London (fig. 22). The central family of beggars are starving and dressed in rags, but even the well-dressed figures on the left, who ostentatiously ignore the performance, appear pale and sickly. Houghton brought together his skills as caricaturist and as painter to produce a whimsical but also disquieting image of metropolitan street life. The city itself is represented sketchily in the background. On the right posters plaster a temporary wooden hoarding, beneath a warning 'Bill Stickers Beware'. Across the Thames, the industrial buildings and chimneys of south London are silhouetted against a grey sky; and on the left, just above the shop windows, a single male figure stands looking out of a second storey window.

21   Arthur Boyd Houghton, *Recruits*, c.1859. Oil on canvas, 25.4 × 35.6 cm. The Iveagh Bequest, Kenwood House. © English Heritage Photo Library.

*London in 1865* is undoubtedly the strangest of these unsettling images (fig. 23). In 1865 London meant many things: sewers and railways; congestion and improvement; order and chaos. But what Houghton depicted is a claustrophobic street scene, focused on the central figure of a young woman wheeling a pram. Behind and to the side of this figure is the now familiar crew of military, homeless, bourgeoisie and street children. None disturbs the strangely preoccupied young woman and her stiff, doll-like charges. London in 1865 is crowded, heterogeneous and vaguely menacing. London in 1865 is also a young unaccompanied woman (most probably a nursemaid) walking in the city streets.

Houghton's most crowded street scene is *Holborn in 1861* (fig. 24). The foreground of this painting is the open pit of a road excavation. The scene is located on a street corner, at a print-shop window. Crowds of pedestrians struggle through the congested street, competing with the omnibuses for passage through the city. The crowd is so dense that it seems to have to clamber upwards and children hang on to street

22   Arthur Boyd Houghton, *Itinerant Singers*, c.1860. Oil on canvas, 25.4 × 34.3 cm. The Iveagh Bequest, Kenwood House. © English Heritage Photo Library.

lamp posts on a level with the passengers on top of the omnibuses. Conventional perspective is abandoned and the figures on the small canvas seem to tip forward towards the viewer.

Houghton had an exceptional feel for the changes taking place in London in the 1860s. His choice and treatment of subjects show him to have been highly attentive to the specific debates and particular locations where modern life was concentrated. The district of Holborn, in central London, for example, was about to become the focus of one of the Metropolitan Board of Works' most prestigious building projects, the Holborn Viaduct. The main thoroughfare of Holborn was of particular importance to the commercial and financial life of London, because it linked the commercial West End with the banking district of the City. Passage was hampered, however, by the fact that the road followed the gradient of a steep hill rising from west to east. It was, however, a vibrant commercial district that bombarded the senses; noisy, smelly and packed with advertising, this was 'pre-improvement' Holborn, the

23    Arthur Boyd Houghton, *London in 1865*, n.d. Oil on canvas, 30.5 × 25.4 cm. The Iveagh Bequest, Kenwood House. © English Heritage Photo Library.

24   Arthur Boyd Houghton, *Holborn in 1861*, n.d. Oil on canvas, 30.5 × 40.6 cm. Private Collection.

London of Arthur Boyd Houghton and of the following description from an 1853 tour of the metropolis:

> Holborn is a business street. It has a business character; there is no mistaking it. Shop and plate-glass windows side by side on each hand; costermongers and itinerant vendors all along the pavement; the houses covered with signboards and inscriptions; busy crowds on either side; omnibuses rushing to and fro in the centre of the road, and all around that indescribable bewildering noise of human voices, carriage-wheels, and horses' hoofs, which pervades the leading streets of crowded cities.[52]

The Holborn Viaduct was a raised roadway, with pedestrian routes, subways for sewers, gas-pipes and ventilation and ground-level areas for housing. The roadway was over 1,400 feet in length and formed a wide, level street, which obviated the inconvenience of the steep ascents along Holborn Hill. One of the most striking

25   'Works at the Holborn Valley Viaduct', *Illustrated Times*, 20 June 1868, p. 392.

features of the Viaduct was the ornamental, Gothic-style cast-iron bridge across Farringdon Street; here, engineering and art were seen to be perfectly resolved in the massive arches and piers capable of carrying large volumes of traffic and designed with an eye to metropolitan monumentality.

Like all attempts at 'improvement', work on the Viaduct was preceded by demolition on a massive scale in the surrounding area (fig. 25).[53] Contractors, diggers and builders moved in; wheelbarrows, piles of bricks and timber frames took over, and daily life moved to one side. Work on the project began in the winter of 1866 and took over two years to complete. On 13 November 1869 Queen Victoria made a rare public visit to the City of London to open the new Viaduct, and although scaffolding was still visible, the crowds of people who lined the streets and the press were pleased by the outcome. The *Illustrated London News* finally admitted: 'there is ample reason to be well satisfied with the fruits of local administration in the metropolis . . . London has really been advancing, perhaps more substantially though less rapidly than Paris, in the improvement of its external condition.'[54]

A large watercolour of the Viaduct from the same date expresses a similar optimism and confidence (fig. 26). The image depicts the ornamental bridge across Farringdon Street, with its marble piers, pierced Gothic ironwork, decorative gaslights and statuary. The ground-level accommodation, stairways to the Viaduct and new buildings are also shown. The street is orderly, elegant and modern; it is a great Victorian way.

A number of Board of Works projects came to fruition at the end of the 1860s. The plan and works for the embankment of the Thames occupied the whole decade. The scheme, which was strongly supported by Sir Joseph Paxton, combined the requirements of the new sewerage system with the construction of a new roadway alongside the Thames. The embankment would put an end to rotting waste on the mud banks of the Thames and would unblock the traffic congestion in the nearby main streets. Constructions now spilt over from dry land on to the river bed. A number of different contracts were given to embank sections of the river, and solid ground was gradually reclaimed from the bed of the Thames. Roads, railways, ferries and subterranean tunnels were to be constructed on these new parts of London and the historical relationship between the city and the river was to be permanently changed. The pictorial potential of the project was, of course, seized upon by artists.

26　W. Haywood, *Holborn Viaduct from Farringdon Street*, c.1869. Watercolour and pen, 60.1 × 94.7 cm. Courtesy of the Museum of London.

27    E. Hull, *The Thames Embankment Works Between Charing Cross Bridge and Westminster*, 1865. Wash with bodycolour, 24 × 36 cm. Courtesy of the Museum of London.

The Thames was a traditional subject for London topographical painters and the embankment works offered views of the river that were completely without precedent (fig. 27). But while some artists subjected these novel conditions to traditional modes of representation, others realised that the project's true impact could be visualised only in cross-section, above and below ground and water level (fig. 28). In the execution of the Thames embankments, all the main aspects of improvement that occupied the Metropolitan Board of Works from 1855 were realised: sewers, transport, aesthetics and, above all, movement. In its vision of the Thames Embankment at Waterloo Bridge, the *Penny Illustrated Paper* described a place of perpetual movement: omnibuses crossing Waterloo Bridge; steamers, ferries and barges on the Thames; the underground railway thundering through tunnels; gas and water circulating in pipes buried in the earth; and waste flowing through the low-level sewer, to the outfall beyond London.[55] The modern city was a world devoted to the production of constant motion and was inhabited by a new, ideal citizen: 'locomotive man'.

28  'Section of the Thames Embankment, Showing (1) the Subway, (2) the Low Level Sewer, (3) the Metropolitan Railway and (4) the Pneumatic Railway', *Illustrated London News*, 22 June 1867, p. 632.

In the midst of the building in the 1860s, the *Illustrated London News* took stock of progress in the metropolis:

> The *bouleversement* of London has now become a matter of daily comment . . . We are excavating through strata of civilisation in the execution of these great changes. By scientific appliances of Titanic character, and machinery of automatic power, our engineers and contractors are enabled to effect these changes with such rapidity as to remind us of the Shandean 'Here to-day and gone to-morrow'.[56]

The schemes were bold, the newspaper observed, although not as daring as Paxton's glazed 'Great Victorian Way'. In the last years of the 1860s contemporaries were increasingly willing to compare London to Paris. Although the processes of modernisation and improvement were less rapid in London, they were more solid and lasting; they were the achievements of a democratic government, rather than the vainglorious monuments of a despot.[57] London certainly had a different approach to improvement. Whereas urban space in Paris was treated as a totality, in London

29   John O'Connor, *The Embankment*, 1874. Oil on canvas, 76.5 × 126.5 cm. Courtesy of the Museum of London.

modernity took the form of a collection of partial and unrelated projects for street building and land reclamation. Perhaps the closest Victorian London came to Baron Haussmann's miles of straight, wide boulevards were the eighty or so miles of sewers of Bazalgette's main drainage system.

In 1874, following the completion of the Thames embankment, John O'Connor painted a Canaletto-style view of London, from a terrace overlooking the new roadway (fig. 29). Queen Victoria is Empress of India; the regiment of Grenadier Guards marches east towards St Paul's. The sun shines on a landscape of old and new; on the Gothic hall of Middle Temple and the circular forms of the gasworks, on the dome of St Paul's and the vaulted roof of Cannon Street railway station. This is a new vision of London; drawn from the discourses of the 1860s, but belonging more properly to the later decades of the nineteenth century. It is a vision of London not as metropolis but as capital of an empire.

★ ★ ★

# 3    *Speaking to the Eye*

Metropolitan experience was primarily a visual one. Although the city was noisy and filled with smells, its defining character was seen to lie in its address to the sense of sight. The spectacles of modern life seemed to demand new modes of representation and new skills of description. In 1851, the year of the Great Exhibition, the *Illustrated London News* reprinted an article from the *Economist* called 'Speaking to the Eye'.[58] In fact the item, championing the role of the illustrated press as the medium of modernity, was a shameless piece of promotion for the paper. The article describes the crowds who gather around the offices of the *Illustrated London News* in order to get hold of their weekly copies. The reasons for this new mass popularity are the technical improvements in engraving and printing and the consequent cheapness of the illustrations. Good quality engraved images, the article continues, can thus be distributed in large numbers and at low cost. The chroniclers and archivists of the age are now the artists:

> Our great authors are now artists. They speak to the eye, and their language is fascinating and impressive. The events of the day or week are illustrated or described by the pencil; and so popular is this mode of communication, that illustrated newspapers are becoming common all over Europe . . . The result is a facility of illustrating passing events truly and graphically, which makes the artist, as much or more than the writer, the historian of our times.

Pictures, the article claims, can convey new knowledge in a universal language. All that can be seen can be represented by the artist; it is the age of the image: 'the *pavé* . . . is our main look-out . . . How the parasols gleam, and flash, and glitter in the sunshine! How the eye goes rambling and wandering and is filled with a confused mirage of forms and colours.'[59]

The implications of this euphoric vision of a world of image information went beyond the production of the illustrated press. Although illustrated newspapers clearly came into their own in England in the second half of the nineteenth century, the concept of 'speaking to the eye' also influenced written representations of the city and helped to create a new genre of metropolitan travel writing. These texts often take the form of a vicarious tour of the city streets. There is a peculiar kind of spatialisation in this literature; routes can be mapped and topographical landmarks may be located, but they are never simply tourist itineraries. They construct a fiction of the city that can be consumed from the comfort of an armchair, in the surroundings of a drawing-room or library.[60] The pace of the fictional journey often varies; the reader may be jostled through crowds or may linger in parks, but whatever the mode, the distinctive feature is that the city is written and consumed as visual spectacle.

Cities are saturated by images. They are, as John Tagg put it: 'both a complex of representations and the place of circulation of representations; the effects of the one always articulating into and reworking the other.'[61] The material fabric of parts of the city was recreated in this period and these sights were then represented in the tourist literature of London. In Tagg's terms, London was itself a web of representations and the site for the circulation of representations.

John Timbs's *Walks and Talks About London* (1865) is, as its title suggests, a typical example of the textual perambulation. Written at a time when most of the significant building works in the city were under way, the book focuses on the old parts of the city, which were on the verge of coming down. It is a nostalgic tour through a city in transition and, as such, is indistinguishable from many other texts of its kind. More unusually, however, in the preface Timbs tries to define the nature of the text and its experience for the reader. He refers to it as a 'sort of *mind-walk*' (original emphasis) and later he calls it a '*Book-walk*' (original emphasis) and describes his 'project for a book-walk through the streets of the metropolis'.[62] These attempts to capture the essence of the literary form and the selective emphasis tell us something about the relationship between the spaces of the city and the fictional imagination. The book is a substitution for the city streets and enables the reader to visualise the places in the text as though out walking. It is an intellectual, sedentary form of tourism in which the images of London exist through the text and where walking is achieved by reading.

In Max Schlesinger's *Saunterings In and About London* (1853), the pace is more leisurely and takes the form of a series of strolls by the fictional author and his friend, an Austrian journalist. Less self-consciously instructional than Timbs, Schlesinger's text conforms more to the precedent of the rambling texts of the late eighteenth century and early nineteenth century. The routes that structure this book are through the central business and commercial districts of London; the London of tourists and visitors, rather than of residents. In these places Schlesinger was most struck by the spectacle of street advertising. Advertisements not only covered the walls and temporary hoardings of the city, they also circulated on the roads and pavements. Businesses and shops sent out their sandwich-board men and advertising vans; even advertisements had to be on the move within the metropolitan ethic of unceasing mobility. Schlesinger observed:

> Necessity compels them to strike the gong and blow the trumpet; choice there is none. They must either advertise or perish . . . It seemed as if the world were on sale at a penny a bit. And amidst all this turmoil, the men with advertising boards walked to and fro; and the boys distributed advertising bills by the hundred . . . the Advertisement is omnipresent.[63]

The advertisement is the ultimate synthesis of the central themes of the modern metropolis: movement, exchange and the image. It is part of the visual fabric of the city; it speaks to the eye and sustains the exchange of money and goods. Walked round the streets and pulled on carts, the advertisement creates an alternative mapping of the city, tracing the contours of commodity capitalism.

The streets of London, with their shops, crowds and advertisements, were part of the touristic presentation of the city. In the fictional metropolitan tours and in more practical guidebooks to the city, the streets were part of the tourist itinerary. The development of the railway system in the mid-nineteenth century admitted mass travel for the first time, and in the 1860s London began to emerge as what might be called a modern tourist centre. In his work on leisure and travel in modern societies, John Urry has emphasised the way in which tourist consumption is based on a distinctive gaze.[64] Places are consumed as visual experiences; moreover, this experience is then recreated through the photograph and other souvenirs and memorabilia: 'The viewing of . . . tourist sights often involves . . . a much greater sensitivity to visual elements of townscape than is normally found in everyday life. People linger over such a gaze which is then visually objectified or captured through photographs, postcards, models etc. . . . These enable the gaze to be endlessly reproduced and recaptured.'[65] For Urry tourism constitutes a form of heightened awareness of the visual; it is a new mode of urban perception and experience, which is drawn by and to the visual culture of the city.

Metropolitan improvements gradually made their way on to the tourist itineraries of the 1860s. In the 1863 edition of John Murray's *Handbook of Modern London*, there is a special section devoted to 'Metropolitan Improvements', which includes the north embankment of the Thames, new streets and the underground railways. There is also a separate section on 'Main Drainage', which summarises the scheme and presents an array of related statistics. The streets, though, are the focus of the editions of the *Handbook* throughout the 1860s: 'There is not a more striking sight in London than the bustle of its great streets.'[66] Murray's *Handbook* was the most frequently published and widely used guide to London in the 1850s and 1860s. It takes the form of a discursive introduction to the history and geography of the city, followed by sections on transport, accommodation and a folded map of London, the 'Clue Map', depicting the main thoroughfares, landmarks and railway lines. The guide also included a number of schematic diagrams of the main streets of central London on which were indicated side streets, shops and notable historical associations. The guidebook worked by weaving together the nuanced prose of the introductory sections, with the street diagrams and folding map. The new visitor to London is advised to open the Clue Map at the end of the book while the guide describes to him 'its main divisions and characteristic features' (pp. xi–xii). The stranger is also told how to see London quickly by taking the box-seat of an omnibus or, more slowly, by walking through the city and following the routes set out in the guide which comprise 'the entire *street* architecture of London' (p. xxiii, original emphasis).

Advertisements and tourism offer two extreme instances of the visual presentation and consumption of London in the mid-nineteenth century. Modernity was understood to be a visual phenomenon and its most characteristic forms were those that spoke to the eye. It may seem paradoxical, therefore, that one of the conventional social types who appears routinely in Victorian crowd scenes is the blind man. In the central picture, depicting noon in Regent Street, in William Powell Frith's *The Times of Day* (1862; fig. 30) and in the illustration of the same street during the afternoon in George Augustus Sala's *Twice Round the Clock; Or, the Hours of the Day and Night in London* (1859; fig. 31), the blind man, with and without a guide, is a significant element in the representation of the crowd. In both images, the composition emphasises the diversity and bustle of people and traffic on this fashionable shopping street, evoking an intoxicating mixture of sensory experiences. Within these representations of modern life, the blind man connotes both the pre-eminence of sight for comprehending the city and the significance of the senses *other* than sight – hearing, smell and touch – as he moves or is guided through the throng. As the

30  William Powell Frith, *The Times of Day, 2: Noon – Regent Street*, 1862. Oil on canvas, 38.1 × 68.6 cm. Private Collection.

31  'Two O'Clock P.M.: Regent Street', from George Augustus Sala, *Twice Round the Clock: Or, the Hours of the Day and Night in London* (London: Houlston and Wright, 1859), p. 148.

Detail of fig. 30.

Detail of fig. 31.

character of a blind man in an article in *Temple Bar* explains: 'I love to hear the busy throng of men, the tramping of feet upon the pavement, the rattling of omnibuses and cabs, the crushing sound of cart-wheels grinding the road, the hum of many voices, which go to make up the din of a crowded London street.'[67] Sight governs the modern metropolis, but the other senses that are bombarded on the city streets can only be conveyed in the figure of the blind man.

In his recent essay on vision and consciousness in late nineteenth-century British culture, Daniel Pick has noted that blindness was also a recurrent motif in Victorian fiction.[68] Pick identifies this interest as part of a structural relationship in the period between visibility and invisibility, illumination and obscurity. The late nineteenth century was a world of increasing luminosity; but even as gaslight and electricity were lighting up modern cities at night, the fascination with darkness, invisibility and the unconscious was also developing. Modernity's enhanced visibility was counter-balanced, Pick argues, by an obsession with the forms and truths that were beyond vision.

The image of the blind man as a visionary, devoid of sight, but possessing true knowledge and understanding, has a long tradition. Jacques Derrida examined this trope in his exhibition and accompanying catalogue *Memoirs of the Blind* (1993).[69] For Derrida, the blind man is a representation of the absolute limits of sight and visibility. The eyes of the blind man possess a 'disquieting strangeness' (p. 106). They are stripped of sight and are thus exposed, naked, without the comforting adornment of the animated gaze. As Derrida puts it, the eyes of the blind are:

more naked because one sees the eye *itself*, all of a sudden exhibited in its opaque body, an organ of inert flesh, stripped of the signification of the gaze that once came to both animate and veil it. Inversely, the very body of the eye, *insofar as it sees*, disappears in the gaze of the other. When I look at someone who sees, the living signification of their gaze dissimulates for me, in some way and up to a certain point, this body of the eye, which, on the contrary, I can easily stare at in a blind man, and right up to the point of indecency. (p. 106)

It is possible to historicise Derrida's theoretical account of blindness and to consider its implications for analysing the figure of the blind man in mid-Victorian representations of the city. The blind man interferes with the circulation of the city; he cannot see his way around, but must touch, tap or be guided. He creates an alternative mapping of the city, which is detached from the visual landmarks of improvement, or the imperatives of metropolitan sight. His presence within the crowd creates a momentary hiatus in the unceasing flow of its business and pleasure. The blind man interrupts the exchange of looks and gazes on the streets of the modern city. The eyes of the blind man, devoid of a returning gaze, represent the end of vision and sight and the presence of darkness and invisibility at the heart of the modern metropolis.

There is one further reading of the figure of the blind man. In his analysis of urban space, Michel de Certeau contrasted two viewpoints: the totalising and voyeuristic aerial viewpoint of the city planner or the mapmaker, and the view on the ground, at street level, which is that of the walker, the city's common practitioner.[70] For de Certeau, the aerial, planner's viewpoint is concerned with the imposition of legibility and order on to the city; whereas the walker on the street traces illegible paths: 'The practitioners employ spaces that are not self-aware; their knowledge of them is blind . . . Everything happens as though some blindness were the hallmark of the processes by which the inhabited city is organised' (p. 124). Perhaps, then, sight (or visibility) was the ideal of the mappers and movers of Victorian London; but the condition of the blind man symbolised the experience of the crowds on the city's streets.

# 4    'The Rape of the Glances'

On Tuesday 7 January 1862 *The Times* published an angry letter from 'Paterfamilias from the Provinces'. The correspondent explained that his daughter had been the subject of a cowardly assault while walking in the streets of London. As a stranger to the metropolis, he had been surprised by advice from acquaintances that his daughter should be accompanied by a servant or a relative when out in public. He ignored this advice and was now appalled to inform readers of the paper that his daughter and a female relative had been followed when visiting Oxford Street. It was an outrage, he concluded, that innocent young girls could not walk in London unaccompanied without being bothered by the stares and comments of scoundrels masquerading as gentlemen.[71]

32 [C. J. Culliford], *Scene in Regent Street. Philanthropic Divine:* 'May I beg you to accept this good little book. Take it home and read it attentively. I am sure it will benefit you.' *Lady:* 'Bless me, Sir, you're mistaken. I am not a social evil, I am only waiting for a bus.' Coloured lithograph, *c*.1865. Private Collection.

The publication of this letter from a provincial parent stimulated an intense debate in the letter columns of *The Times* and in the periodical press about men, women, respectability and streets in mid-Victorian London. It is an invaluable source for discovering how women of the middle classes occupied and moved around the streets of London, and for exposing contemporary beliefs concerning the nature of respectable public behaviour. The first to reply to Paterfamilias was 'Puella', who declared that she had walked alone in Oxford Street on many occasions and had never received any incivility. Perhaps the provincial girls had invited attention; if country girls want to go shopping, the letter continued, 'dressed in red cloaks and pork-pie hats with white feathers (a dress most suitable for the country, but hardly consistent with the quiet demeanour necessary for walking in the streets of London), they cannot expect to escape the notice of those despicable idlers . . . who take advantage of the weakness of women.'[72] Really respectable women, who do not wish to attract attention, should assume a quiet dress and manner when unaccompanied in the city.

The argument that began to take form in the correspondence to *The Times* suggests that there were many different ways in which respectable women could inhabit the streets of London, and that respectability itself embraced a range of attitudes to the public domain. The original incident was not a question of the blurring of identities between the respectable woman and the prostitute; the idler does not mistake the country girls for prostitutes, but for naïve young women who may be open to sexual flirtation. This kind of encounter – sought for, or uninvited – was a possibility on the streets of the metropolis. Moreover, the response of Puella confirms that, contrary to some recent claims, women of the middle classes did not need to be chaperoned in the 1860s and that the whole issue of chaperonage was open to debate and interpretation in this period.[73]

There is a fascinating lithograph from this period showing a respectable woman in Piccadilly Circus being accosted by an over-zealous evangelical clergymen. Taking the woman for a prostitute and an appropriate subject for his rescue mission, the cleric offers her a Bible. The woman assures him of her respectability: 'Bless me, sir, you are mistaken . . . I am only waiting for a bus.' And sure enough, it appears just around the corner (fig. 32). At first sight, this interaction might be taken as evidence that fashionably dressed respectable women could occupy the streets of the city only at the risk of being mistaken for prostitutes. It may be more accurate, however, to treat the image as visual confirmation that respectable women did routinely walk around the city on their own, and that social and moral identities were far more diverse than the simple categories of 'pure' and 'fallen' will allow. The joke is on the clergyman, whose enthusiasm and conservatism blind him to the realities of street life and land him in an embarrassing situation.

Paterfamilias sprang to the defence of his daughter and her companion and the doubt cast by Puella on their behaviour. They had not incited any advances, for they had been dressed in 'plain mourning' to respect the recent death of Prince Albert.[74] This detail is offered as incontrovertible evidence of their respectability and of their lack of agency in the man's subsequent insulting behaviour. A few days later 'M', a female teacher, wrote to *The Times* supporting the fears of Paterfamilias about female safety on London streets. M walked between the residences of her pupils and was bothered by 'middle-aged and older men'. She identified herself as one of many women whose circumstances compel them often to walk alone and she recommended any time before 10.30 in the morning as likely to be free from unwanted harrassment.[75]

The last letter in this series of correspondence offers another variation on female behaviour in London streets: girls go out and are deliberately flirtatious and Paterfamilias should come to terms with this. 'Common Sense', the assumed name of the correspondent, claimed that, with its policemen and attentive shopkeepers, there was no safer city than London for unaccompanied women who are not looking for excitement. The letter then imagines the behaviour of Paterfamilias's girls. Fathers cannot believe, it suggests,

that Blanche ever looked kindly at a strange *joli garçon* who appeared struck with her appearance; or that Isabel ever designedly showed rather more than her very neat ankle to a young officer crossing the street. It never occurs to them that bonnets of the 'kiss me quick' build, loud stockings, exaggerated *tournures*, capes and crinolines; vagrant ringlets straying over the shoulder, better known as 'follow me, lads', and suchlike decoys, are all unmistakeably [*sic*] intended to attract the notice and attentions of the male sex . . . Blanche and Isabel take a good deal of notice of the young men in a quiet way when they walk out alone, and are not at all displeased of being taken notice of themselves . . . Many little harmless and interesting adventures may occur to the dear girls during their morning walks of which they say nothing at all when they return home.[76]

Leaving aside the misogynistic hostility of this letter, it takes as a given that girls from respectable families walk unaccompanied in London and that this can provide sought-after opportunities for sexualised encounters with strangers. On the streets, details of dress, gesture and glance are ambiguous and can convey social status or flirtatious availability.

This debate about men, women and streets in Victorian London did not stop at the pages of *The Times*. In February 1862 the *Saturday Review* carried its own response to the correspondence, which it called 'The Rape of the Glances'. The article begins by blaming the problem on the ubiquity of prostitution in the streets of London and, notably, in smart streets such as Regent Street. By the 1860s the association of Regent Street with smart, daytime prostitution had become highly conventional. Nineteenth-century accounts of London's prostitution assigned it a temporal and a spatial geography.[77] Prostitutes, it was claimed, occupied particular places in the city at specific times, and the hours of the day and night in London could be charted according to the shifting locations of prostitution. If the Haymarket was the symbolic locus of London's midnight prostitution, then Regent Street was its midday haunt. The blind men in the Regent Street crowd scenes depicted by W. P. Frith and in the illustration to G. A. Sala, share the street with the figures of well-dressed prostitutes (figs 30 and 31). Indeed, the location is chosen precisely for its mythic and, to a degree, actual associations with prostitution in this period.

Paterfamilias from the Provinces, however, was apparently not aware of Regent Street's reputation when he sent his daughter out shopping in the vicinity:

Unacquainted with the moral geography of the West-End, they innocently trip down the tabooed side of Regent-street. The natural consequence follows. A young gentleman of an amorous disposition, seeing them there, upon the equivocal ground, solitary, sauntering, and attractive, comes to the conclusion that they had rather be looked at than not, and begins to ogle them accordingly.[78]

An important detail is added to the debate; it seems that the ambiguities in the girls' behaviour includes the speed of their movement; their pace is too slow and purposeless, it is out of step with the circulation of the modern metropolis. Moreover, the exchange has now become an exclusively ocular one; it is a matter of how people appear and who has the right to look at whom. To further complicate the analysis, the article then speculates whether the girls encouraged the stranger's gaze, whether 'more than one curious and furtive glance was sent after the bold adventurer'. This has now become a complex and layered set of interactions that converges on the street. A naïve father allows his daughter to walk in a street that is associated with prostitution. This connection sexualises the environment and they are persistently stared at by a male stranger, although they may well have consciously encouraged his attentions. But, after all, the article points out, the offence is only that of stealing a look; there was, it claims, no verbal or physical abuse. The article upbraids Paterfamilias for his naivety. Perhaps he comes from a country 'where nobody looks at anybody' and is shocked, therefore, at 'the ocular freedom of the London streets'. The metropolis is evoked as a world of scopic promiscuity, where the exchange of looks is constant and potent. All pedestrians are caught up in this network of gazes. Perhaps, then, the glance at Paterfamilias's daughter was not purloined, but exchanged freely and knowingly. The conclusion to this inventive piece of writing is a conservative and predictable one. If women want to escape London's web of glances, they must dress unattractively, walk at a steady pace and look straight ahead. To deviate from this set of guidelines is to enter into the space of London's ocular economy.

There is one last element in this discourse on streets and sight. In April 1862 *Temple Bar* published an article called 'Out Walking', by the novelist and journalist, Eliza Lynn Linton.[79] 'Out Walking' is an unequivocal affirmation of the routine presence of unaccompanied respectable women in the streets of mid-Victorian London. For Linton the essential questions raised by the correspondence in the press were:

> Is it a fact that modest women are continually being spoken to if they walk alone? And that even two well-bred, well-dressed, and well-conducted girls together are not safe, however quiet their demeanour and unalluring their attire? . . . What becomes of the modest single women of the middle ranks, who . . . are obliged to walk alone, yet who never dream that they are thereby reduced to the standard of social evils? (p. 132)

Interestingly, the nature of the offence has shifted again, from unwelcome staring to uninvited speech, but Linton's solutions to the problem are socially conservative. No woman need be the object of a strange man's address if she behaves properly, and Linton outlines the codes of female respectability in the modern city:

> If she knows how to walk in the streets, self-possessed and quietly, with not too lagging and not too swift a step; if she avoids lounging about the shop-windows, and resolutely foregoes even the most tempting displays of finery; if she can attain to that enviable street-talent, and pass men without looking at them, yet all the while seeing them; if she knows how to dress as only a lady can, avoiding loud colours and too coquettish a simplicity as equally dangerous, the one for its asser- tion and the other for its seductiveness; if she has anything of purpose or business in her air, and looks as if she understands what she is about, and has really some meaning in her actions; if she has nothing of the gaper in her ways, and does not stand and stare on all sides, like a mark set up for pickpockets to finger – she is for the most part as safe as if planting tulips and crocuses in her own garden. (p. 133)

Any sign that women are enjoying the city, that they are participating in its visual culture and ocular freedom, can be taken as an index of their lack of modesty. Within this conservative discourse, lingering, attracting attention and staring are the charac- teristics of a new, transgressive form of metropolitan femininity. Neither prostitutes, nor conforming to conventional domestic forms of femininity, these are women who inhabit the city for pleasure as well as through necessity. London in the 1860s was governed by the principles of visual exchange; by the display of goods and advertisements, by the fashioning of self and society. The only way for conservative models of femininity to be maintained within this environment was to prove them resistant to the seductions of the city's visual culture. To place them in the city, but not of the city; on the streets, but withdrawn from their specular exchange. This is Linton's conclusion in 'Out Walking'; the truly modest woman is: 'unobtrusive, gentle, womanly, she is just the person to slip through a crowd unobserved, like one of those soft gray moths in the evening, which come and go upon their way, unseen by men and undevoured by birds' (p. 136). Linton's description of diffident women who merge into the background of the city cannot be taken as an accurate account of female respectability in the period. It is further confirmation of the presence of unaccompanied women of the middle classes on the streets of London in the early 1860s, but it is only part of a debate in the period concerning how women should behave in this new public domain. The conditions created by London in this period tested and expanded contemporary definitions of femininity and respectability.

The presence of unaccompanied middle-class women on the city streets has been ignored in recent accounts of modernity and nineteenth-century urbanisation. This is partly the consequence of histories of the middle classes that relate the concept of bourgeois respectability exclusively to the ideology of separate spheres and the location of the respectable woman in the home as wife, mother and daughter. Within these narratives middle-class women are the 'angels in the house', largely confined to the private sphere; whereas men move between the home and the public domain of work and the city.[80] This writing-out of middle-class women from the spaces of the city has been exacerbated by the dominance of Second Empire Paris and its surrounding cultural discourses in histories of modernity and the nineteenth-century city. According to such sociologists of the city as Georg Simmel, Walter Benjamin, Richard Sennett and Marshall Berman, modernity is synonymous with public life and the most powerful experience of modernity is that of the crowd.[81] The crowd produces new types of subjectivity, new ways of behaving and of relating to others. But if middle-class women are believed to be absent from the public sphere, they are effectively absent from the history of modernity. Our descriptions of the development of modern urban life have, it seems, been derived from the male public world, and women, confined by Victorian ideology and twentieth-century historians to the home and occasional shopping trips, are not part of the effective modern world.

The *flâneur* is the paradigmatic figure of this version of modernity. The *flâneur* describes a form of metropolitan existence; a way of consuming the spectacles and experiences of the modern city. The figure of the *flâneur* emerged in the evocations of nineteenth-century Paris in the prose and poetry of Charles Baudelaire. For Baudelaire, the *flâneur* was a man, a poet, who had no place and could find no ease in the private sphere, but was at home in the public spaces of the city. In his essay, 'The Painter of Modern Life', Baudelaire wrote: 'For the perfect *flâneur*, for the passionate spectator, it is an immense joy to set up house in the heart of the multitude, amid the ebb and flow of movement, in the midst of the fugitive.'[82] The *flâneur* is a stroller and a looker whose environment is the city crowd, and who is able to perceive the truth and aesthetic significance in the transient and fleeting experiences of the city: 'The crowd is his element, as the air is that of birds and water of fishes. His passion and his profession are to become one flesh with the crowd.'[83] The *flâneur* is the man of the crowd; he can merge with the crowd, he can be anonymous and unobserved, but he also understands and draws life from it. This unobtrusiveness is clearly of a very different order from the 'gray moths' imagined by Eliza Lynn Linton. The *flâneur* seeks anonymity, but for the sake of his own heightened observation, rather than in the interests of social manners. And above all, he is an observer, at the centre of the city's specular market place and urban flux. Ultimately, for Baudelaire, the *flâneur* was one of the heroic figures of modern life. He was detached and alienated, but also possessed a kind of passion for the empty rituals of modern life. In Walter Benjamin's powerful reading of Baudelaire's work, the *flâneur*'s heroism took on a lyrical nostalgia. For Benjamin, the *flâneur* both reflected and resisted the consumerism of the capitalist city and its circulation of commodities. He was part of the visual spectacle of the city, but resisted its rational planning and mapping. He idled, and watched the constant circulation of goods and people.

The evocation of the *flâneur* and the spaces of modern Paris in the work of Baudelaire and Benjamin is remarkably powerful and moving. Together, they offer a persuasive fiction of the modern city that has exercised a vigorous hold on subsequent histories of Paris and of modernity more generally.[84] Recently, however, feminist cultural critics have begun to question the impact of this narrative of public life on our understanding of the history of women in the modern period. Attempts have been made to assess women's occupation of the city and their particular experiences of modernity. In her influential essay 'The Invisible *Flâneuse*', Janet Wolff has described the failure in the dominant literature of modernity to describe women's experiences. She states unequivocally: 'The central figure of the *flâneur* can only be male.'[85] Wolff also points to the cast of female characters in Baudelaire's account: the prostitute, the widow, the lesbian, the murder victim and the passing unknown woman. All of these women were apparently on the margins of bourgeois definitions of respectable femininity; Baudelaire's city is peopled by men and transgressive women. The prostitute is the female counterpart to the *flâneur*. Although she has none of his analytical agency, she shares his special transgressive relationship with commodity culture. Wolff refers also to Baudelaire's poem *A une Passante*, his fantasy of an exchange of looks between the poet and an unknown passing woman. The key to the poem is the woman's last-moment return of his gaze. Curiously, Wolff questions the respectability of this woman and locates her with the other transgressive types of Baudelaire's female street characters. This is a significant lost critical opportunity. The correspondence in *The Times* and periodical press clearly suggests that there is no reason why Baudelaire's passing woman should not have been a respectable member of the middle classes. The *frisson* of the moment lies precisely in her respectability and in the uncertainty arising from the diverse range of female behaviour on the streets of the nineteenth-century city. The fantasy of erotic encounter was not exclusively male and did not render all women prostitutes. For Wolff, however, Baudelaire's model of modernity is exclusively male because it equates the modern with the public and ignores the private sphere which is the domain of women.

By accepting Baudelaire's roll-call of the population of the modern city, feminist criticism limits the extent of its revision of histories of modernity. Middle-class women can only be reinserted into this narrative, it is claimed, by attending to the private sphere or by examining different spaces of public life, other than the streets, where, it is argued, the presence of middle-class women was allowed. In her essay 'Modernity and the Spaces of Femininity', Griselda Pollock has taken the locations that are referred to in Baudelaire's 'Painter of Modern Life' and are depicted in paintings by male and female artists associated with Impressionism, and plotted them on a grid that differentiates respectable and non-respectable sites.[86] From this, Pollock shows that male artists frequently represented the sexualised places of Baudelaire's Paris, but also moved freely between a masculinised public domain and a feminised domestic sphere. Women's art practice, on the other hand, was strictly confined to subjects within the private sphere or in respectable public sites such as parks and theatres. Pollock traces this gendering of modern space to the pictorial space of the canvas, where she notes a range of formal devices in paintings by women which demarcate the public spaces of femininity from the spaces of the *flâneur*'s city. Furthermore, in paintings of domestic subjects by women, Pollock also identifies an assertion of the private sphere as an alternative and equally viable space for the representation and definition of modernity.

Although this work begins to dismantle the masculinist assumptions of dominant cultural icons of the city, it does not consider the experience of working-class women and goes no way towards challenging the invisibility of middle-class women on the city streets. Historians such as Christine Stansell have persuasively described the central presence of working-class women in public life and in the streets of nineteenth-century New York;[87] but the assumption still remains that the only way to write middle-class women into histories of modernity is by looking at the private sphere, or the history of shopping. Shopping, it seems, was the middle-class woman's entry into the nineteenth-century city. Some of the first department stores opened in London in the 1860s: William Whiteley's in 1863; the Civil Service Stores in 1866; and the Army and Navy Stores in 1871. For some historians, stores such as these presented an escape route for middle-class women from their gilded cages into the excitements of the city. As Jenny Ryan put it: 'The changing culture of consumption provided women with new spaces within which the structuring of "private" concerns of personal appearance, family provisioning, household decoration became increasingly located in "public" and thus their access to the city legitimated.'[88] Shopping imposes a specific chronology on the emergence of women into the public sphere. This begins in the 1870s and grows through the 1880s, so that by the 1890s middle-class women shoppers were familiar figures in the city landscape.[89] This development was augmented, it is argued, by the expansion of philanthropy, which also provided a legitimate purpose for middle-class women to take to the streets.[90]

This all begins to add up to a quite extraordinary picture of the nineteenth-century metropolis, peopled, it seems, by men, working women and middle-class female shoppers. Common sense and the evidence of texts and images from the period should tell us that this cannot be an accurate account of nineteenth-century city space. A different approach is needed. This might start with the formulation of a more complex understanding of the public sphere than has been evident in previous studies of the metropolis. Rather than seeing public life as a monolithic entity, it is possible to conceive a variety of ways of accessing the public world and a number of different public arenas in which women could be involved.[91] In her study of women's politics in nineteenth-century North America, Mary P. Ryan has documented women's routes to public political life through voluntary associations, street protests and parades.[92] Through this presence, Ryan argues, male–female distinctions were severely tested in public space and could be corroded by the everyday practices of real men and women. Life on the streets of the big cities was volatile, diverse and untidy, and the potential for chance, random contact with strangers was a constant feature: 'Along the way to producing, buying and selling, strangers routinely crossed each other's paths, often making brusque physical contact.'[93] Some order could be imposed on the heterogeneous spaces of the city through strategies such as the classification of the city's population into reassuring 'types', through mapping, or through the legal regulation of public space. Still, the female occupants of the city continued to be the focus of concern for the urban planners and improvers of the nineteenth century. The central conflict of the modern city was that which existed between the rational ideals of the cartographers and urban planners, and the new forms of female behaviours and identities fostered by the city's public spaces: 'the city streets offered [women] new attractions, new freedoms, and a veil of anonymity under which to pursue them' (p. 63).

In her work on gender and the city, Elizabeth Wilson has also argued that urban life offered many women new kinds of freedom and the possibility of independent existences.[94] Wilson identifies the city as a place of adventure, pleasure, excitement and risk for women; a place of economic and erotic possibilities. In general terms, however, the liberating potential of the city, in Wilson's account, is available only to working-class women. Bourgeois women, she concedes, were excluded from the spectacular public spaces of the city and were restricted to an expanded private sphere which embraced parks, department stores and so on. Wilson's work does not, therefore, redress the absence of middle-class women from feminist accounts of the modern city streets, but it does introduce the association of female urban experience and pleasure. Although there is risk, this is an inevitable feature of the modern city. Risk and pleasure are both aspects of the unexpected, which is a potential for men and women in the public spaces of the city. As Wilson puts it: 'It is a matter for emphasis whether one insists on the dangers or rather the opportunities for women in the cities.'[95]

Both Mary P. Ryan and Elizabeth Wilson have also challenged the assumption within some feminist criticism that the *flâneur*, the male occupant of the city streets, is 'at home' in public urban space, the omnipotent agent of the male gaze. In a timely corrective, Wilson describes the *flâneur* as a fictional embodiment of a crisis in masculinity; a response to uncertainties regarding public masculinity in the changing social spaces of the city. Wilson argues: '[The *flâneur*] is a figure to be deconstructed, a shifting projection of angst rather than a solid embodiment of male bourgeois power . . . The *flâneur* represents masculinity as unstable, caught up in the violent dislocations that characterised urbanisation.'[96] To dissolve the identity of the *flâneur* is to begin to dismantle one of the central orthodoxies of recent accounts of modernity. It reopens the question of who occupied the streets of the nineteenth-century city and of the experiences of that occupation. This allows a re-examination of the presence of all kinds of women on the city streets; women who were not necessarily prostitutes or other working women, out shopping or on a philanthropic mission, but women of all classes and identities tracing paths and lives in the spaces of the city. Nor were these women necessarily passive victims of a voracious male gaze, but they can be imagined as women who enjoyed and participated in the 'ocular economy' of the city; they were women who looked at and returned the gazes of passers-by.

In the fourth volume of his *London Labour and the London Poor* (1862), devoted to 'Those That Will Not Work', the criminal classes of the metropolis, Henry Mayhew described the common modes of stealing from men and women in the street. After considering the ways in which a gentleman's pockets were picked, Mayhew went on to look at stealing from women:

> A lady's pocket is commonly picked by persons walking by her side, who insert their hand gently into the pocket of her gown. This is often effected by walking alongside of the lady, or by stopping her in the street, asking the way to a particular place, or inquiring if she is acquainted with such and such a person . . . A lady generally carries her gold or silver watch in a small pocket in front of her dress, possibly under one of the large flounces. It is often stolen from her by one or two, or even three persons, one of the thieves accosting her in the street in the manner described.[97]

Mayhew was describing a modern urban experience; a crime made possible because of the heterogeneous population of the city streets and the uncertainties and ambiguities concerning behaviour in public space. Respectable strangers could stand close to each other and engage in conversation. This was a staging of the unexpected, of the pleasures and the risks of the city. Mayhew recalled observing an attempted robbery in the City of London:

> Walking along Cheapside one day, toward the afternoon, we observed a well-dressed, good-looking man of about thirty years of age, having the appearance of a smart man of business, standing by the side of an elderly looking, respectably dressed lady at a jeweller's window . . . Our eye accidentally caught sight of his left hand drooping by his side in the direction of the lady's pocket. We observed it glide softly in the direction of her pocket beneath the edge of her shawl with all the fascination of a serpent's movement. While the hand lay drooping, the fingers sought their way to the pocket. From the movement we observed that the fingers had found the pocket, and were seeking their way farther into the interior.

The robbery is prevented, but the anecdote reads nevertheless as a highly threatening warning to unaccompanied women of the dangers in the city. But, read against the grain, the story reveals other aspects of the city. Identities in the city, based on

33   'The Man in the Club Window', from *The Habits of Good Society: A Handbook of Etiquette for Ladies and Gentlemen. With Thoughts, Hints, and Anecdotes Concerning Social Observances; Nice Points of Taste and Good Manners; and the Art of Making One's-Self Agreeable. The Whole Interspersed with Humorous Illustrations of Social Predicaments; Remarks on the History and Changes of Fashion; and the Differences of English and Continental Etiquette* (London: James Hogg and Sons, 1859), n.p.

appearance rather than personal knowledge, could never be certain. They could be accurate indices of social status, or they could be assumed for deception. The sights of the city invited preoccupation; but the physical proximity of the streets could transform absorption into violation. Mayhew's sections on street theft are woven around the themes of assumed identities and social deception. They describe crimes made possible because of the new social configurations of the city streets and subsequent confusion concerning public discourse and behaviour.

One way to rein in the contingencies of modern urban life and to impose a kind of order on the unexpected was to codify public behaviour through street etiquette. Throughout the second half of the nineteenth century hundreds of guides and handbooks to social etiquette were published, with special sections devoted to conduct in the streets. These texts evoke a world of polite, stylised public discourse. In a world of uncertainty, they provide unequivocal instructions for heterosocial propriety on the city streets. The advice offered in the pages of the etiquette handbooks is absolute and conservative. It represents the attempt to codify public respectability and to define behaviour and opinion in the period, rather than to record actual behaviour and relations. The rules in the guides could be accepted and internalised, or they could be rejected and ignored.

Street etiquette is a complex semiotic system of looking and aversion of sight. The etymology of 'respectability' derives from the Latin *respicere*: to look back at, or regard.[98] Although this meaning was quickly obsolete, the word retains the traces of this early definition in the history of its uses and particularly its nineteenth-century definition as a social or moral quality rendering a person worthy of notice or observation. This semantic play on relational looking is recalled in nineteenth-century attempts to codify public respectability in the streets. In one of many anonymously written handbooks, the author is identified as a 'man in the club-window' who, recuperating after a serious illness, has perfected his skills of observation by watching the street.[99] The 'man in the club-window' presents a world of formal propriety and symmetry. In a section on 'the greeting', he reminds his readers that a lady has the privilege of recognising a gentleman, although this should not necessitate close scrutiny of the man concerned. No man should stop to speak to a lady, until she has acknowledged him with a bow. 'The lady, in short, has the right in all cases to be friendly or distant' (p. 275). An illustration from the book shows the author in the background, observing a perfectly synchronised greeting (fig. 33). Heads are inclined, hats are raised; gentlemen and women file past on the pavement in orderly lines and street beggars are segregated in the road.

The author acknowledged the assistance of 'A Matron' in composing his advice for women, and many etiquette guides of the period were addressed exclusively to female readers. The 'cut' was the respectable lady's heavy artillery in her social weaponry. It was a last resource and governed by strict rules of usage. There were degrees of 'cut'; ranging from a stiff bow without a smile, to letting the man see that his approach is noticed and then turning the head away. A gentleman must never cut a lady under any circumstances.[100] Similar advice was reiterated in multiple publications throughout the century; in volumes intended for study at home and in other tiny pocket-books clearly intended for consultation while out in public. The unsuspecting pickpocket might come across a miniature volume of Bijou Books *Etiquette for Ladies*, as well as a gold watch, in the dress pockets of some victims.[101]

The correspondence started by the letter from Paterfamilias to *The Times* in January 1862 articulated the confusion regarding identity and behaviour in the public spaces of mid-Victorian London. Young, respectable women of the middle classes were present on the streets, but new spaces seemed to produce new femininities and no one could be sure how these women would behave. Certainly, the rules of street etiquette could not contain the unpredictable diversity of manners and meetings in the city. Was Paterfamilias's daughter harassed by a strange man; did she respond to his advances; or did she seek and initiate an erotic encounter? The response of the *Saturday Review* was to publish 'The Rape of the Glances'; but was there a violation and whose glances were involved? Taking the prompt of the article's title, however, cultural historians should move away finally from monolithic conceptions of the male gaze and its omnipotence in the nineteenth-century city, towards a far more open and fluid model of looking and walking in urban space.

★   ★   ★

# 5    *A Narrative of Footsteps*

In the Museum of London there is a small archive of unpublished letters, written from around 1840 to 1858. The pages are folded and re-folded into tiny squares and are frequently cross-written; the neat handwriting traversing the pages first horizontally, then vertically, creating a grid of news and narration.[102] The letters are written by a young woman called Amelia Roper, to her close friend, Martha Busher. Roper lived in Walthamstow, a residential, suburban area to the north-east of London; her friend lived south of London in Sevenoaks, Kent, moving between 1855 and 1856 to Woolwich and then to Kenilworth in Warwickshire.

Amelia was the daughter of Edmund Roper, an undertaker, with his own business in London. In 1857, she married Tom Pyle, who was a butcher. Busher worked for a number of years for the Leigh family at Stoneleigh Abbey; first as nursery maid and then as the personal maid and companion to the Hon. Margaret L. Leigh. Although they came from different sections of the middle classes, the Ropers and the Bushers were evidently close family friends and shared a common set of social connections and acquaintances.

Some of the letters are transcribed by the Museum, others are not, and a number are barely legible. Taken together, they offer compelling snatches of ordinary men and women's lives in the middle decades of the nineteenth century. They present a useful, alternative perspective on the use and experience of urban space in this period. Not necessarily more authentic than the published texts considered thus far, they are certainly familiar, colloquial and not intended for publication. The letters are a fascinating blend of formalised greetings and impatient transmission of gossip; of apologies and upbraidings for lapses in communication and of hastily added postscripts conveying last-minute thoughts. These are texts written for the eyes of friends and preserved for the sake of memory. Contents are determined by the priorities of one young woman's life, rather than by the expediencies of official, public discourse. The letters document particular key life events, such as Roper's engagement and first pregnancy, but they also record a multitude of incidental experiences, of journeys, meetings and conversations, which constitute the everyday in any historical period. In these pages there is no mention of international or national news, of the Crimean War, or the Metropolitan Board of Works; there is simply an account of a life led in the prosperous south of England, with regular journeys to London – alone and with friends or family – to see her father at work, or to visit the theatre. Roper did not move widely around London; her use of the metropolis was defined by a limited number of routes, for a specific range of purposes. In relating these journeys in her letters, however, she generates a different story of mid-Victorian London, an account of one woman's experience of gender and space, a narrative of footsteps.

Michel de Certeau's theorisation of urban space and the city streets was introduced earlier, in the discussion of the figure of the blind man. De Certeau's account of the meaning and experience of space is structured around an opposition between the controlling, aerial viewpoint of the city planner and the point of view of the walker at street level. The view from on high, from the panoptic towers of coercive power, turns the heterogeneous world of the city into a text; it renders complexity legible and comprehensible. This is the viewpoint represented in the map and the plan; by the moderniser and the law enforcer. At street level, however, pedestrians trace personal itineraries; they actualise abstract sites through their specific uses and experiences of space. The everyday spaces of the street resist the rational, geometric organisation of the aerial, planner's viewpoint. At street level, space is disorganised and improvised. The detours and deviations of individual journeys represent a form of resistance to the disciplinary power symbolised in the aerial, panoptic view. Whereas the aerial viewpoint captures the city as representation, in maps and plans, walking cannot be graphically pictured. It can be mapped, but this can only ever be a trace of what has been and is lost: 'Traces of a journey lose what existed; *the act of going by* itself.'[103] Rather than an iconography of walking, therefore, de Certeau describes street movement as a form of rhetoric, a 'space of utterance'. Space, at street level, is beyond the discipline of the urban system. It describes an illogical geography, produced through symbolic mechanisms such as the dream and memory.

De Certeau's pedestrian is a romantic, nostalgic figure. A classless, genderless, ill-defined character, whose tricky spatial manoeuvres constitute a form of resistance to an abstract, total power. Kristin Ross has produced a fascinating critique of de Certeau and other French spatial theorists by reading these theoretical texts in the historical context of the revolutionary urban politics of May 1968.[104] For Ross, many of the theorists of the streets, who wrote in the aftermath of 1968, turned away from the concrete historical conditions of those spaces, preferring a city of metaphorical relations and anonymous, heroic urban practitioners.

Although Ross does mount a serious and convincing attack on de Certeau's work, there is still much in his account which, if taken metaphorically, is worth holding on to. The framing structure of his opposition between the aerial viewpoint and the view from the street is an important reminder of the existence of competing histories and experiences of the modern city. To attend exclusively to the official discourses of politicians and engineers, is to produce an oddly one-dimensional urban history. The history of modernity lies also in the experiences and journeys of individual men and women through the city streets, which round out the official story and uncover the contradictions of the streets in this period of improvement and the confusion of urban identities embedded in the processes of modernisation.

'History begins at ground level, with footsteps.'[105] This is the moment, then, to reintroduce two Victorian pedestrians: Amelia Roper, creator of the Museum of London's archive of letters; and Eliza Lynn Linton, novelist and journalist. Linton was one of the most prolific professional women journalists of the mid-nineteenth century. Claimed to be the first woman newspaper writer to draw a fixed salary, she was a regular contributor to some of the century's most distinguished newspapers and periodicals, including the *Morning Chronicle*, *Household Words* and the *Saturday Review*.[106] Linton is probably best remembered now for her social conservatism and, in particular, for her lancing attack on the manners and morals of the 'Girl of the Period', which was published in the *Saturday Review* in 1868. According to Linton, fashionable young women of the middle classes were copying the styles of the *demi-monde*; they had lost their natural purity and beauty and had become creatures of artifice and false morals. Following publication of the articles, the 'Girl of the Period' became a catchword for a new style of brash femininity, figuring in caricatures, comedies and fiction. In the preface to a later collection of her essays, Linton made the most emphatic and conservative statement of her position: 'I think now, as I thought when I wrote these papers, that a public and professional life for women is incompatible with the discharge of their highest duties or the cultivation of their noblest qualities.'[107]

Up to this point, Linton's views may seem rather undistinguished, and to conform dogmatically to conventional definitions of respectable femininity. In most respects, however, Linton's professional and personal life contradicted those conventions. She struggled to establish her writing career, moving at the age of twenty-three from her family home in the north of England to a private boarding-house in central London. Linton loved London. She lived and worked in the city and while not exactly, in Walter Benjamin's memorable image, 'a botaniser of the asphalt',[108] she shared with Benjamin's urban analyst a feeling for the city streets which thrilled and inspired her.

Eliza Lynn Linton was born in Cumberland in 1822. Her mother died shortly after her birth, leaving her father, who was a cleric, to bring up twelve children. Not surprisingly, perhaps, the younger children's education was somewhat neglected, and from the ages of eleven to seventeen Linton was largely responsible for her own education, teaching herself history, geography and languages. Linton's influences and interests in her late teens were eclectic and unconventional. She was a devout Christian, although she subsequently experienced several crises of faith; she was a Republican and had a strong interest in spiritualism and occultism. As a young woman it appears that she had a lesbian romance with a married woman whom she met through her family. In her sixties she represented herself as a male character in a three-volume semi-autobiographical novel, *Christopher Kirkland*.[109] Eliza Lynn Linton was hardly the conventional, self-effacing 'gray moth [*sic*]' whose qualities she praised in *Temple Bar*.

In 1845, at the age of twenty-three, Linton decided to leave home and go to live in London, where she would study at the British Museum and become a writer. After initial opposition, her father agreed to finance her for one year only, at the end of which she had to demonstrate that she could earn a living by writing. Linton took rooms in a private boarding-house at 35 Montagu Place, close to the entrance of the old reading room of the British Museum. During this first year in London, she made regular journeys through London to visit family friends and at the end of the year she had completed her first book.[110] After a brief return to her family home in Cumberland, she came back to London, where she began her career in journalism. In the 1850s she mixed in a radical intellectual circle, which included Robert Owen, Elizabeth Gaskell and James Froude; she was an advanced woman in advanced circles. In 1858, she married William James Linton, a wood-engraver and a radical bohemian. It was his second marriage and the relationship was shaped by the financial difficulties involved in bringing up his children from his first wife. Linton was the main wage-earner in the family and in 1864, when William and the children moved to the Lake District, Linton took rooms in Russell Place, so that she could maintain her social and professional contacts in London. The marriage finally disintegrated when William and his family emigrated to America in 1867. From this time, released from her family responsibilities, Linton's career really took off. In 1868 the *Saturday Review* published her articles on 'The Girl of the Period' and her professional reputation was established. She continued to mix in significant literary circles which included pioneer women medics such as Elizabeth Garrett, Mary Walker and Elizabeth and Emily Blackwell.

The point of rehearsing these details is not just to produce a thumb-nail biography of a distinctive Victorian woman, but to reveal the gap between the representation and the experience of urban space in this period; to map this advocate of 'natural' femininity on to the streets of nineteenth-century London. The metropolis was Eliza Lynn Linton's milieu: 'London is my Home, and there are all my best friends, my work, my Ambition, my surrounding.'[111] It is hard to imagine a more emphatic statement of *belonging* in an urban context. Her response to the city seems to have been immediate: in *Christopher Kirkland*, her autobiographical novel, the author recollects the excitement of receiving a favourable review in *The Times* of her first novel: 'I remember the sunset as I went up Oxford Street, to what was not yet Marble Arch. For I could not rest in the house. I could not go home for dinner. I felt compelled to walk as if for ever.'[112]

Throughout her life and career, Linton drew an energy from the city: 'In London you live; in the country you breathe.'[113] Linton not only knew the topography of the city, but she also had an acute sense of its history, of the changes that were taking place in the middle decades of the century. And yet, in a follow-up essay to 'The Girl of the Period', she berated 'modern maidens' for shamelessly 'beating the pavement of the city . . .'[114] To describe Linton's views as contradictory is to read her position too crudely. At no point in her journalism did she deny lone women the right to be pedestrians in the city; but she imposed exacting limits. What she denied women was the very pleasure and enjoyment that she so clearly derived herself from walking in the city.

The tensions between Linton's writing and her life emerge at every turn. In 1855 she published an article called 'Passing Faces' in Dickens's periodical *Household Words*. The essay takes the form of a street ethnography, in which the author describes the types of people to be observed on a walk through the streets of London. It is, on the whole, a conventional and generic piece of writing, in which London is evoked as a world in microcosm; as the stage for tragedy and farce. Linton runs through racial and social categories and then considers the kinds of women to be seen. It is a familiar enough typology: the young mother; the follower of fashion; the gambler's wife; the housekeeper. But then, her eye is caught by a sweet-looking girl:

> [She] is an authoress; and the man with bright eyes and black hair, who has just lifted his hat to her and walks on, with a certain slouch in his shoulders that belongs to a man of business, is an author, and an editor; a pope, a Jupiter, a czar in his own domain, against whose fiat there is neither redress nor appeal. No despotism is equal to the despotism of an editor.[115]

In 'Passing Faces', Linton maps herself on to the streets of London; she becomes one of the female types in her own, imaginary urban landscape. On the pages of *House-*

*hold Words*, Linton turns herself into her own ideal of demure femininity, for the authoress, she notes, is 'dressed all in dove-colour'.

It is impossible to know what Eliza Lynn Linton would have made of Amelia Roper, had their paths crossed in London in the mid-1850s. Roper also found the city thrilling and wrote in her letters of day and evening trips to London on public transport with her friends.[116] In one particularly excited and idiomatic communication, she told her friend about a visit to the Olympic Theatre, in central London. At this point, Roper was obviously feeling at her most fashionable and modish and confessed she was under the weather: 'being very *Maryannish* and dreadfully "seedy" if you know what that is.'[117] The use of slang terms with specifically working-class associations and connotations of sexual immorality, suggests that at this time Roper was experimenting with risky, metropolitan feminine identities. She went on to give an account of the theatre trip:

> Whatever do you think Mr and Miss Whitaker Fanny and I all went to the Olympic Theatre last Monday fortnight, and it was most lovely I can't describe it to you I wished you could have been with us, they were all quite amused to see my 'greenness' I couldn't keep from saying oh my! now and then it was most affecting in some of the parts. We went full dress I had a *low body* on, we felt quite *screamers* I can assure you . . . [Original emphasis and punctuation]

The Olympic Theatre was in Wych Street, just off Drury Lane, an area notorious for its poverty, drunkenness and immorality. In his *Saunterings In and About London* (1853), Max Schlesinger dismissed the district: 'Most dingy and dirty-looking are the streets which surround the Olympic.'[118] The theatre itself was a respectable establishment, although its performances were usually popular and sensational. Roper's experience of the visit is a revealing combination of naivety and swagger. She admits to being overwhelmed by the place, but also claims that she felt at home, a 'screamer' – a showy, swell figure.[119] The telling of this event points to the ways in which women like Roper may have used and experienced the city. Although she lived some distance from the centre, her visits to town enabled her to play with and explore different feminine identities. The city allowed Roper to move between different parameters of respectability.

This process is reiterated in another anecdote she told her friend. In a postscript to a letter dated 4 January 1856, she revealed: 'When I got to the station on Tuesday, the train had gone so I walked to town. I had not gone far when a gentleman in a 4 wheel chaise offered me a ride but I was like you bashful and said no If you had been [there] I should [have] said yes.'[120] What does this brief account reveal and hide? It shows a young woman who travels alone and who takes decisions about her journey. It also describes an encounter with a male stranger; an exchange, a rejection and a reflection on the alternative outcomes. It speaks of embarrassment, apprehension and fantasy. The urban context is one of continuous possibilities and of a new configuration of gender and sexual relations.

It is possible to see the discourses of the 1860s about men, women and the streets of London as part of a repatterning of sexuality in the spaces of the city; but the codes were as yet ill-defined and ambiguous. To reach beneath the surface of official public discourses and to attempt to understand the feelings and desires, the fears and fantasies of urban experiences in the nineteenth century is a risky business. It is necessarily speculative and allusive, but the voices of Eliza Lynn Linton and Amelia Roper begin to reveal the tensions between official and private responses to the city and the range of behaviours and personae from which women drew in their occupation of the mid-nineteenth-century streets.

# 6    *A Balloon Ascent*

In 1862 Henry Mayhew described his flight above London in a hot air balloon.[121] Having conducted his social and moral archaeology of the streets of the city in *London Labour and the London Poor*, he now wanted to contemplate the great metropolis from above. To ascend in the car of the Royal Nassau Balloon was to leave behind a confusion of individuals and particularities and to embrace the whole, the unity of the city in a single glance:

> We had dived into the holes and corners hidden from the honest and well-to-do portion of the London community. We had visited Jacob's Island . . . in the height of the cholera, when to inhale the very air of the place was to imbibe the breath of death . . . We had examined the World of London below the moral surface, as it were; and we had a craving, like the rest of mankind to contemplate it from above. (p. 8)

As the gun was fired to signal the release of the balloon, Mayhew watched the earth sink down and the upturned faces of the crowds disappear. As the balloon rose, the cries of the voices below faded and the city was transformed into a panorama. Smells, infections and noise were left behind and the city became an exclusively visual experience:

> For it is an exquisite treat to all minds to find that they have the power, by their mere vision, of extending their consciousness to scenes and objects that are miles away; and as the intellect experiences a special delight in being able to comprehend all the minute particulars of a subject under one associate whole, and to perceive the previous confusion of the diverse details assume the form and order of a perspicuous unity; so does the eye love to see the country, or the town, which it usually knows only as a series of disjointed parts – as abstract fields, hills, rivers, parks, streets, gardens, or churches – become all combined, like the coloured fragments of the kaleidoscope, into one harmonious and varied scene. (p. 7)

As the balloon ascends, there is a sense of acute relief in Mayhew's account of the scene. But the image constantly threatens to dissolve, to return to its fragmented elements. Mayhew may have left ground level, but he could not leave behind his knowledge of the streets, of their disorder and unpredictability. Many attempts were made to contain the processes of growth and modernisation taking place in mid-Victorian London. The city was mapped and improved; its diverse routes were re-presented through tourist itineraries and in travel fiction. Its wayward pedestrians could even be managed through the codes and customs of street etiquette. Ultimately, however, Victorian Babylon resisted these attempts at spatial ordering. Mayhew, the balloonist, had to descend once more to street level.

PART 2

# GAS AND LIGHT

# Introduction

By the early years of Victoria's reign, gas lighting had converted London nights into day, and to many writers in this period it seemed that London was the most illuminated capital city in Europe. Gas, as a source of street lighting, had been introduced in the city at the beginning of the nineteenth century. Its social advantages and economic possibilities were soon realised and gas rapidly replaced oil as the main form of illumination in the public spaces of the city. As the demand for gas grew, so too did the companies that produced and supplied it. London was mapped by the boundaries of the competing gas companies, whose contours joined with those of the postal districts, railways and sewers to define modernising London.

The organisation and regulation of the London gas companies in the mid-nineteenth century is a story of modern industrial capital set in the heart of the metropolis. The monopolies of the private gas companies were contained by state regulation and challenged by consumer organisation. By the 1860s a vast industry had been built up and the architecture of gas manufacture had become part of the new urban landscape. The unmistakable circular forms of the Blackfriars gasholders are as much a part of the panoramic view in John O'Connor's 1874 *Embankment* (fig. 29) as the rounded dome of St Paul's.

In the age of the Metropolitan Board of Works, therefore, gas was in its heyday; but it was also on the brink of being superseded by electricity. The first incandescent electric lamp was displayed at an industrial exhibition in Newcastle in 1861 and electricity was first used for public lighting on the Embankment in 1878. So, by the 1860s contemporaries were no longer amazed by gas illumination, but were complaining about prices and standards of supply. They were no longer dazzled by its brightness, but were equally struck by its dimness and unreliability. To many, the muted, golden glow of gaslight seemed dull and dirty compared to the blue-white glare of limelight and, later, of electricity.

Gaslight created patches of light interspersed with pools of darkness. Gas seemed to have the power equally to create illumination and to cast shadow. The chiaroscuro of gaslight, its transitional passages from light to dark, created in mid-Victorian London a poetics of gas. Gas does not destroy the night; it illuminates it. Its unsteady flame flares and wanes, giving objects and places an aura of perceptibility, without total, destructive visibility. Gas lights darkness; whereas electricity annihilates it. Cities are defined by temporal as well as by spatial geographies and mid-Victorian London was seen to have a distinctive character by day and by night. Gas bore witness to night scenes, to aspects of the city that were hidden by day. Street lamps represented the intrusion of daytime order and the rational space of the improved city into the darkness of the city at night. Gaslight never fully conquered the night city, however, but was also absorbed by its poetry, evil and irrationality.

Detail of fig. 44.

If the aesthetic of metropolitan improvement was based upon the principles of circulation and movement and the aim to open up the blocked city to light and air, then it was an aesthetic that contained at its heart the presence of darkness and obscurity. London could be mapped and regulated, but it still retained forgotten alleys and dark courts. Gaslight seemed at times to display rather than to eradicate the threat of urban space.

Gaslight in Victorian London was industrial and metaphorical; it had an economics and a poetics. The supply of gas was a product of modern industry and sophisticated commercial organisation; but the gaslight itself was represented as organic and bewitching, with the power to render familiar daytime places strange and unfamiliar. London in this period produced an immense and varied literature dedicated to night-time London. Books and pamphlets recorded Christian rescue missions. Guide-books specialised in tracing the particular attractions of London by night and the eighteenth-century genre of 'fast' guides to city night-life continued throughout the nineteenth century. Leisure was a growing commercial venture in this period; attracting and requiring creativity, investment and labour, but offering the promise of substantial financial returns. Gaslight gave a new vitality to leisure after dark. The spectacle of brightly illuminated shop windows, dance-halls and supper rooms was a distinctive feature of the metropolis during Victoria's reign and attracted large, mixed audiences into the city throughout the night hours.

The story of Cremorne Pleasure Gardens, located in the suburbs of London on the River Thames, encapsulates the themes of gas, light and leisure. One of the main attractions of the Gardens in the 1860s was the giant dancing-platform; a glittering spectacle of cut-glass and gaslight. The sensory cornucopia of Cremorne's music and dancing, food, wine and lights seemed an enchantment and turned the Gardens into a commercial fairyland. To many, however, fairyland was also a source of corruption and a public nuisance, and in the late 1870s Cremorne succumbed to the combined pressures of magistrates and moralists. Constrained by the whimsical renewal and refusal of licences and leases, the spaces of Cremorne finally became unproductive and gave way to the irresistible force of metropolitan property development.

## I        *A Night Ascent*

When Henry Mayhew turned from his investigation of the streets of London and went up in a hot air balloon, he described the experience as exhilarating and sublime. The balloonist's gaze was no longer diverted by troubling, individual details but was able to absorb the extent of the metropolis in a single glance. The bird's-eye-view enabled a momentary, mental control of the city, which surpassed any possibilities for visual authority offered at ground level.[1] But at night, the view of London from a balloon became more fantastic and took on a magical dimension. Familiar landmarks could still be discerned, but they appeared by gaslight as though on fire. A night ascent was less concerned with a utopian sensation of absolute control than with the dazzling transmogrification of the city through the combined effects of elevation and light.

In 1865 the *Illustrated London News* published an account of a night balloon ascent conducted for scientific purposes.[2] The balloonist described the impact of the view as the balloon reached one thousand feet; at this height the scene became more fascinating than science and seemed to exceed description. London is redrawn by gaslight; the codes of the paper map are replaced by alternating lines of light and passages of darkness. The main thoroughfares from the east to the centre of the city appear like 'lines of brilliant fire' and the gas lighting surpasses the natural light of the moon. The map of light creates a mass of illumination that rivals the Milky Way and for a moment perception is disoriented, as though the view is not of the earth but of the sky:

> It seems to me to realise a wish I have often felt when looking through a telescope directed to the milky way, when the whole appeared covered with gold dust, to be possessed of the power to see those many spots of light as brilliant stars; for certainly the intense brilliancy of London this night would have rivalled the brilliancy of such a telescopic view of brilliant clusters of stars.

If a form of power is being invoked here, it is the power of vision and of the imagination. Beyond London, the balloonist is blinded by darkness; the earth is a black obscurity which not even the moon can illuminate.

Balloon ascents were a regular feature in every season's programme of entertainments at Cremorne Gardens. Ascents were made on an almost daily basis in daylight hours and, less often, at night. Written accounts of these night ascents reiterated the powerful spectacle of London enflamed by gaslight: 'it was as if a mass of burning sparks had fallen in regular forms and shapes.' The physical geography of the city was redrawn in lines of artificial light and the entire view was 'like some gigantic fire map'.[3] The 'fire map' of London is articulated equally in terms of light and of darkness. What signifies is not only the lines and spots of illumination, but also the patches of black. The river and parks are dark, so too are the spaces between the brilliant points of the gas lamps. The widespread provision of public gas lighting extended the hours of social life in the city and magnified the symbolic significance of those sites of darkness.

The mid-Victorian period was characterised by an ongoing debate concerning the appropriate temporality of urban life; between, for example, supporters of the long nights of leisure at Cremorne Gardens and the campaigners of the Early Closing Movement. Interest groups such as these wrestled with the attractions of the gaslit, night-time city, against the employment conditions of shopworkers and the neglect of domestic space caused by the extension of the life of the city into the hours of darkness. Gaslight produced the conditions for both the extension of and the resistance to the night-side of London.

Early Victorian London was a late-night place. West End shops were commonly open until at least 8.00 p.m. and City and suburban shops kept even later working hours.[4] The Early Closing Movement was formed in 1842 to campaign for earlier closing of shops and for the Saturday half-holiday.[5] By the 1850s it was attracting court patronage and was achieving significant success in curtailing the opening hours of West End retailers. The Queen and Prince Albert confessed that they were compelled to take an interest in the Movement and, in a letter of support, observed the benefits to customers: 'particularly females, who would probably be thus inclined to spend at home the time now employed in traversing the streets to make late purchases.'[6]

The Early Closing Movement blamed gas for the late hours kept in towns and cities. This night-time, commercial world had, it seemed, created a new type of urban pedestrian and shopper; men and women of the middle classes who consumed the sights and goods of the gaslit city. Reporting in 1858 on the progress of the Early Closing Movement, the *Daily Telegraph* applauded its successes and continuing struggle against late hours and night-work. Nevertheless, the late hour system still prevailed in the metropolis and the paper described the types who constituted the social life of the city at night and who derived their pleasures from its gaslit scenes:

> Now we are disposed to make every allowance for the feelings of those who are amateurs of the picturesque; and we can sympathise with the disappointment of those peripatetic philosophers – those citizens of the world – whose delight it is to wander about the streets of crowded cities at nightfall, and moralise upon the rich contents of gas-lit shop-windows, and the motley crowd of vendors and purchasers. When, as we sincerely hope will speedily occur, the shops in the most busy and overcrowded thoroughfares in London shall, as a rule, be closed after seven o'clock in the evening, we can imagine the rueful glances which the habitual *flâneurs* – the inveterate 'mooners' of the metropolis – will cast upon the hermetically-sealed panelled and iron-ribbed shutters. No seductive linendrapers' and haberdashers', and milliners', and perfumery, and glove, and fancy stationery, and point-lace, and bronze kid boots, and mantle, and Talma, and parasol, and feather-fan shops open in Regent-street![7]

This is a world of strolling, looking and contemplating; a world of commodities – and primarily, of women's luxury goods – transformed into a dazzling, seductive spectacle. The inhabitants of these night streets are 'mooners', whose pleasures are primarily visual and superficial. Early closing produces ocular deprivation, sealed panels and shutters as opposed to brilliant gas, glass and goods. Without its night-time display, London is rendered 'sightless'; it offers nothing to the eye and its inhabitants are blinded. The newspaper sympathised:

> We are very sorry for the peripatetics; there are many of us, indeed, who will regret the kaleidoscopic changes of the night shop-life of London; but health is better than chiaroscuro; the relaxation and recreation of thousands of over-worked young men and women are better than effects rivalling the canvases of a REMBRANDT or a SCHALKER, which every shop-front in a crowded street presents by night; common justice to our brothers and sisters is better than the indulgences of a frivolous system pursued by many couples in London, married as well as unmarried, of 'night shopping', of gallivanting about the streets after nightfall, and

making purchases which there is no earthly reason for them not to have made hours before.

The attractions of night-time shopping are expressed here almost entirely in visual terms – picturesque, kaleidoscopic, chiaroscuro, Rembrandt – and were evidently a feature of metropolitan, bourgeois leisure. The *flâneurs* by moon – men and women, married and unmarried – are drawn to the particular pleasures of the city at night, when the streets themselves become a glittering gallery of images and goods. The fascination of this urban space is implicit within the text of the article, and the newspaper's support for early closing is compromised by its lingering descriptions of night shopping and gaslit streets.

Women of the middle classes and aristocracy were strategic players in this struggle over the temporality of the city. They were identified as key consumers of the pleasures of the streets at night and were influential converts to the Early Closing Movement. In 1860 the Movement succeeded in creating a volunteer list of titled ladies who undertook to abstain from late shopping hours and by the mid-1860s the Saturday half-day holiday was common practice throughout London.[8]

Gaslit shop windows supplemented public lighting in the city streets. They offered a superabundance of illumination. In the shop-fronts gas lighting was more than functional, it was magical and transformed the experience of city space into a mode of visual desire. When the shops closed, the spell was broken; as one newspaper observed, the streets seemed dark and dangerous: 'especially now that the early-closing movement has left the streets to the dim and insufficient light of the ordinary gas-lamps.'[9]

## 2     *Daylight by Night*

The history of public lighting is an essential aspect of the history of cities. In London in the eighteenth century property owners had to bear the cost of lighting. All housekeepers whose house or gateway was next to the street had to provide lighting on dark nights, with sufficient wick to burn until 11.00 p.m.[10] It was not until 1836 that local authorities levied a tax on the householders and undertook the work themselves; gradually this spread until the cost of public lighting became a general charge.

Gaslight is produced through the thermal treatment of coal in retorts and the distribution of the resulting gas through pipes to the point of use. Gaslight is thus created through the projection or transmission of illumination and in this respect it differs from all earlier methods of lighting. With candles and oil lamps, the gases that produce the light are burned on the spot, where the material is consumed; the oil or wax and the light-giving flame are thus in close proximity. With lighting by coal gas, however, gas is transmitted by pipes to any required location and the light is produced at a distance from where the gas is produced in the gasworks. The manufacture of gaslight thus requires a huge initial financial investment to meet the cost of expensive plant machinery for the loading and burning of coal, purifying of gas and laying of pipes.

Gas lighting was introduced to London in the first years of the nineteenth century. In 1805 a length of Pall Mall was lit by gaslights to celebrate the king's birthday. Developments were fast. Gaslight for streets in London was widely advocated; in 1810 the first Parliamentary Act was passed to incorporate a gas company and the London and Westminster Chartered Gas Light and Coke Company began operations in the metropolis. In 1813 Westminster Bridge was lighted by coal gas and from this time the new method of illumination became fully established. Each year a greater number of London streets were lit by gas and by 1823 there were nearly 40,000 public gas lamps, lighting 215 miles of London's streets.[11]

From the start, gas lighting was concerned with more than illumination. The royal birthday exhibit and the lighting of Westminster Bridge established the spectacular potential of gaslight, linking it to a rhetoric of display. Shopkeepers seized immediately on the potential of gaslight to enhance their windows and shop-fronts and London led Europe in the brilliance of its retail displays.[12] By the beginning of Victoria's reign, London had established its reputation as the capital of illumination. In her astute account of London in 1839, Flora Tristan identified the city at night as one of the first sights to strike the visitor: 'But it is especially at night that London should be seen; then, in the magic light of millions of gas-lamps, London is superb! Its broad streets stretch to infinity; its shops are resplendent with every masterpiece that human ingenuity can devise . . . To see all this for the first time is an intoxicating experience.'[13] Wonder, in this case, soon turns to anger. Seen through the filter of Tristan's socialist analysis, the significance of this gaslit display is not pleasure and wealth, but 'arid egotism and gross materialism'.

From around 1840 the use of gas for private house lighting grew in popularity, and gas got its final official stamp of approval when gas lighting was installed in the House of Commons in 1852. As London increasingly became a city of gas, so statistics were ceaselessly compiled to suggest the extent of the provision: 1,900 miles of gas pipes; £4,000,000 spent in the preparation of gas; 360,000 street lights.[14] Little did it matter that these figures did not mean very much; their significance was precisely that they were beyond comparison. London excelled in its consumption of gas. To one German visitor there seemed to be too much gaslight, affording an excess of vision:

> The stairs of every decent London house, have generally quite as much light as a German shop, and the London shops are more strongly lighted up than the German theatres. Butchers, and such-like tradesmen, especially in the smaller streets, burn the gas from one-inch tubes, that John Bull, in purchasing his piece of mutton or beef, may see each vein, each sinew, and each lump of fat. The smaller streets and the markets, are literally inundated with gaslight especially on Saturday evenings. No city on the Continent offers such a sight.[15]

Houses lit like shops, shops lit like theatres and finally streets 'inundated by gaslight' exposing every vein and piece of gristle in a lump of raw meat. For this writer there is a scale of propriety, a kind of etiquette, in the provision of gas lighting; too much gaslight leads to ostentation and disgust. Nowhere is this excess of gaslight displayed more evidently than in the retail outlets of Moses and Son, the Jewish tailors and outfitters and butt of mid-Victorian anti-Semitism. For the continental visitor, the Holborn branch of Moses and Son lit up the London night sky: 'many thousands of gas-flames, forming branches, foliage, and arabesques, and sending forth so dazzling a blaze, that this fiery column of Moses is visible to Jews and Gentiles at the distance of half a mile . . .'[16] The image of vast numbers of gaslights dissolves into an orientalist fantasy and finally an Old Testament vision in the attempt to convey the Jewish merchant's hubristic attempt to 'convert night into day' (p. 18).

For the domestic journalist, also, the ostentatious consumption and display of gas expressed the commercial and moral deviancy of the Jewish trader. Describing the Whitechapel branch of Moses and Son, George Augustus Sala invoked:

> Gas, splendour, wealth, boundless and immeasurable, at a glance. Countless stories of gorgeous show-rooms, laden to repletion with rich garments. Gas everywhere. Seven hundred burners . . . Corinthian columns, enriched cornices, sculptured panels, arabesque ceilings, massive chandeliers, soft carpets of choice patterns, luxury, elegance, the riches of a world . . .[17]

Trade is no longer admirable, but has been perverted by the sinuous lines of the arabesque. The conspicuous merchandising of the Jewish trader, symbolised by the over-ornate, over-bright gas chandelier, turns modern London into an oriental bazaar. It took a fine act of judgement, coupled with social prejudice, to differentiate between the permissible cult of commodities created by gas lighting and the transgressive vulgarity of Moses and Son.

In its proper place, however, gas lighting was an appropriate and visible display of London's 'improvement'. Attention and money were lavished on the provision of street lamps in the new thoroughfares opened by the Metropolitan Board of Works. Southwark Street, which was opened in 1865 and replaced a run-down area on the south side of the Thames, boasted a cast-iron lamp standard designed by Joseph Bazalgette, engineer to the Board of Works. The ornate sandstone base and cast-iron shaft and lamps featured prominently in newspaper coverage of the new street, an unambiguous manifestation of the aims of the new metropolis.[18] Gas lighting provided essential amenities for the modern city. It introduced public order to the streets at night; it made life comfortable and civilised. A strike of gasworks' stokers in 1872 quickly reminded Londoners of their dependency on gas.[19] Street lamps were turned off, theatres closed and London resorted to candles and oil. The *Illustrated London News* visualised a city plunged back into the darkness of seventy years earlier, with urban crime, dark streets and railway stations lit by candlelight (fig. 34). By the 1870s, however, the gas companies were having to face a far more serious threat to their businesses than strikes: the inexorable rise of the electric light. As experiments with electricity developed, it became apparent that it was cheaper and cleaner to produce than gas and had more illuminating power. By the end of the decade, gas and electricity were being described as 'the old light and the new' and the profits of the gas industry were rapidly succumbing to the new competitor.[20]

The London gas industry was at its most powerful in the 1860s, before electricity posed a serious threat as an alternative source of public illumination. In those years central government made repeated attempts to curb the monopolies of the gas companies and a reluctant Metropolitan Board of Works was called upon to take over responsibility for the supply of gas in London. After the creation of the first gas company in 1810, other competitor companies quickly appeared and by the middle of the century there were thirteen companies supplying gas to London.[21] At this time there was free competition between the companies, and the streets of London became the chaotic battlefield for their unregulated practices. Although each company was allocated a particular district beyond which they might not supply gas, these districts overlapped one another and there was no part of London that was not served by at least two companies. Roads were continually being broken up by rival companies because of the several different sets of mains running down the same street and competition between companies was so fierce that it occasionally bordered on the comic. One particular 'stand-off' between two rival companies entered into popular mythology.[22] Workmen from the Great Central Gas Company and the Commercial Gas Company fought a heroic battle over possession of a bridge. Armies of labourers were recruited for the purpose and loss of life was feared. The police were called in and the 'Gas Thermopylae' came to symbolise the ludicrous extremes of the unregulated gas industry.

As well as the nuisance of constant roadworks, the escape of gas was an inevitable consequence of continuous interference with the supply pipes and many critics of the gas companies regarded their practices as dangerous to public health and safety. Quality and cost of gas were equally unregulated. There was no testing of the gas supply and the price of gas varied in different areas of London and even within the same street. In 1857 the Gas Consumers' Mutual Protection Association was formed to agitate for the uniform regulation of the companies supplying gas in the metropolis and for the protection of consumer interests.[23] The Association supported legislation to regulate the companies and also advocated the compulsory public purchase of plant works and pipes to ensure a cheaper and purer gas supply.[24] This call for the public ownership of the London gas supply was made repeatedly throughout the 1860s and 1870s, but was ignored by both municipal and central governments.

In 1860 Parliament responded to the chaotic situation in London and public agitation by passing the Metropolis Gas Act, the first of a number of such legislative moves during the decade. The 1860 Act fixed a maximum price for gas supply in the metropolis and specified a uniform illuminating power and purity for gas. A special area, or 'district', was assigned to each company, within which no other company was allowed to lay its pipes. The power and purity of the gas in each district was to be tested by an Examiner appointed by the local authority. Although the Act put a stop to rival companies competing in the same area, it created the conditions for mini-monopolies in each district. Prices increased; arrangements for testing failed and consumer complaints regarding the illuminating power and quality of the gas supply continued. For the leader-writer of the *Illustrated Times* in 1864, the gas supply in London was so poor that he recommended a return to oil-lamps and candles:

34 'Effects of the Gas Strike in London', supplement to the *Illustrated London News*, 14 December 1872, p. 569.

The monopoly is at present almost intolerable. The price charged for gas is known to be at least twenty-five per cent beyond that which ought to yield a reasonable remuneration. The gas itself is either so scanty in supply or so vile in quality that its advantages in households are daily, or, rather, nightly, becoming more questionable. From a single burner, scarcely two feet from the paper on which we write, we can scarcely obtain the needful illumination, except at such a time as every other jet in the house has been extinguished and the shops in the neighbourhood have all turned off their lights. We draw aside the window-blind, and see the street lamps scarcely, if at all, brighter than in the old days of oil, more than thirty years ago.[25]

With the 1860 Act clearly failing and public demand for gas steadily increasing, a series of Parliamentary Committees was set up between 1866 and 1868 to sort out the London 'gas question'. The 1866 Select Committee found that gas was indeed cheaper and better in the provinces than in London. It recommended that prices should be reduced and illuminating power improved and the adoption of a new and more efficient system for testing. It also advocated the development of the regulated monopolies within the gas districts by amalgamating the companies into bigger units. These recommendations were only partly realised with the passing of the City of London Gas Act in 1868. The legislation applied only to the three City gas companies, but included regulations on pricing and gas quality and the appointment of gas referees. More significantly, the Act set the conditions for the amalgamation of gas companies through private negotiation, and by 1869 one company – the Chartered Gas Company – had acquired a complete monopoly of the gas supply within the limits of the City. By 1871 most of London had been brought under the operation of the 1868 legislation and further company amalgamations had taken place; by the end of the 1870s the thirteen metropolitan gas companies had been reduced to six.

The scale of the monopolies did not alleviate the ferocity of the debates surrounding gas production in the capital. The conflicting interests of the gas companies, the municipal and central authorities and the public continued to be fought out over profits and prices, the quality and power of the gas. The profits of all the London gas companies tended steadily to increase. This was, perhaps, an inevitable consequence of the nature of gas production. After a large initial outlay on gasworks and mains pipes, there was comparatively little additional cost on manufacturing plant. As the cost of production diminished, increased demand was realised more or less directly as profits.

The gasworks were the most distinguishing visual features of the new industry. They were big, they were industrial and they were often on sites close to the centre of London. The most visually striking elements of the process of gas production were the retorts, where coal was loaded and heated to produce gas, and the gasholders, where the gas was stored for subsequent use. By the 1840s the buildings and manufacturing processes of the London gasworks had created a new sublime landscape within the metropolis. The appearance and activities of the retort-house, in particular, seemed like some strange, new version of the eighteenth-century industrial sublime: 'Whoever enters for the first time into a retort-house cannot fail to be struck with its appearance, so different from that of other factories. The iron roof, the iron floor, the absence of windows, the absence of machinery and work-benches . . . the darkness of the place, the appearance of the men – all have an aspect of strangeness.'[26] Periodically, the darkness was interrupted by the startling spectacle of the recharging of the retorts. Explosions occured as the covers of the retort were removed, exposing the intense burning interior where the coke was raked and wetted and fresh coal added. London was greedy for gas and the manufacturing process was interminable:

> No cessation, even for a moment, occurs in the labours. One party of men are engaged at night; another party relieve them after an interval of twelve hours, and are employed by day; but the furnaces are always heated, the retorts always supplied with their fiercely burning contents, the gas always undergoing the purifying processes to its passage into the gasometers.[27]

This was the economics of gas in mid-Victorian London: gasworks covering vast areas of land; intensive use of labour and ceaseless production. The lovers of the night-side of London – its street lamps and dazzling window displays – lived in the shadow of the huge, cylindrical gasholders that punctuated the London cityscape. As demand increased, the gasholders got bigger; the journalist John Hollingshead observed:

> [the gas-holders] stand out boldly, like gigantic iron vats, towering above the walls of the gas-yards. The importance of such reservoirs, containing a night's supply of gas in advance, can hardly be overrated by any man who tries to imagine the condition of London suddenly plunged into total darkness.[28]

Although, Hollingshead conceded, the manufacture of gas might involve beautiful scientific processes, it was on the whole an ugly business and 'what is seen decidedly savours of pandemonium'. The comparison of industrial production and the image of hell was obviously not new. The burning furnaces of eighteenth-century heavy industry were frequently represented and understood in terms of the fires of hell. By the 1860s, however, this imagery had declined as factory production generated a different rhetoric. What is distinctive about the imagery used by Hollingshead and his contemporaries, is that it is revived in order to emphasise the startling visual effects of gas production carried out within the modern metropolis. In his full-page illustration of the 'Lambeth Gas Works', in the 1872 publication *London: A Pilgrimage*, Gustave Doré exploited his characteristic dark engraving technique to convey the hell of the retort-house (fig. 35). The gasworks is not mentioned in the text written by his collaborator, Blanchard Jerrold, but the artist evidently saw some potential in the location. The scene is represented as timeless; only the pipes in the upper right-hand corner indicate that it is contemporary. The dark, huddled figures in the foreground and the teams of men recharging the furnaces evoke paradise lost, rather than London in the 1870s.

The gasworks blighted London. By the beginning of the 1860s there were, within the metropolitan area, twenty-three gas manufacturing works and six gasholder stations used solely for storing gas. Wherever these works were established in the city the land seemed poisoned by pollutants and the stench of gas. To critics of the gas industry, the ground occupied and tainted by gasworks might yield profits for the

35   Gustave Doré, 'Lambeth
Gas Works', from Gustave Doré
and Blanchard Jerrold, *London:
A Pilgrimage* (London: Grant
and Co., 1872), opp. p. 40.

companies, but would fetch much more if the works were removed and the land
regenerated and improved. The situation was clear:

> Wherever a gas-factory − and there are many such − is situated within the metro-
> polis, there is established a centre whence radiates a whole neighbourhood of
> squalor, poverty and disease. No improvement can ever reach that infected neigh-
> bourhood − no new streets, no improved dwellings, not even a garden is possible
> within a circle of at least a quarter of a mile in diameter, and not so much as a
> geranium can flourish in a window-sill.[29]

There was another, even more obvious danger in locating gasworks in the heart of
London − explosions. One of the costs of obtaining daylight by night was constantly
leaking gas pipes and occasional fatal explosions. The coverage of these incidents in
the press created another dimension to the visual language of gas − the drama and
devastation of the metropolitan gas explosion (fig. 36).[30] Excavations for the tangle
of water and gas pipes under London made periodic accidents an inevitable feature
of improving London. London, it seemed, was spontaneously combusting, its houses
and streets continuously on the verge of falling down or blowing up.

One of the worst gas explosions to affect London in this period was at the works
of the London Gaslight Company at Nine Elms, in south-east London. On the afternoon of 31 October 1865, the 'meter-house', next to a huge gasometer, was blown

36 'The Frightful Explosion of Gas in Shoreditch. – Ruins of the Houses in Church-Street', *Penny Illustrated Paper*, 7 June 1862, p. 365.

37 (below) 'The Effects of the Late Explosion at Nine-Elms Gasworks', *Illustrated Times*, 11 November 1865, p. 289 [front page of issue].

down, killing several on the spot and badly injuring many others.[31] The gasworks was wrecked and houses in the neighbourhood were shattered, their windows blown out and doors shaken off their hinges. There were two large gasometers on the site; both were completely filled with gas when one suddenly exploded, filling the air with flames. The second gasometer quickly caught fire, although it did not explode. By the evening nine men were dead and people in streets adjacent to the works had received severe burns from the heat of the flames. During the following days, the newspapers were filled with images of the crumpled ruins of the gasometer (fig. 37). If the sound of the explosion had recalled 'a park of artillery', then the scene of the aftermath is like nothing more than the result of a military bombardment. Engineers and workmen pick over the rubble and twisted metal and only the distinctive circular frame of the gasometer is left standing, its roof collapsed at the bottom of the tank and its sides blown to fragments, bent into various odd shapes and scattered over the ground. This was the consequence of lighting the metropolis.

The question that immediately arose was whether a gasometer could explode without the addition of a certain amount of atmospheric air. Impatient with technical explanations, *The Times* concluded: 'exploded it was if explosion is bursting with violence.'[32] The inquest confirmed that the gasometer had not exploded; that the explosion was confined to the meter-house, the force of which struck the side of the gasometer, caving it in, and driving out a portion of the top. There was an immediate rush of gas, which instantly caught fire. The press was unanimous in its conclusions. The *Penny Illustrated Paper* pointed out:

> This immense reservoir is, like many other metropolitan gasholders, in the midst of a densely-populated neighbourhood; and it is awful to contemplate the dire results of an explosion, which may, apparently, be caused at any moment by the carelessness or ignorance of a labourer . . . these monster eyesores of London should be removed to as great a distance from cities and towns as are gunpowder magazines and manufactories.[33]

On the following page, the paper illustrated the fireworks and burning barrels of 'Fifth-of-November' celebrations at Lewes, above an engraving of the large gasholder belonging to the Imperial Gas Company at Bethnal Green in east London.

London panicked. Newspapers mapped the locations of the metropolitan gasworks and concluded that St Paul's Cathedral, Westminster Abbey and the Houses of Parliament might any day be destroyed by gas explosions.[34] The gasometers at Blackfriars were believed to be particularly dangerous and the *Morning Post* feared that an explosion there might lay 'half London in ruins'.[35] Viewed in this light, O'Connor's panorama of *The Embankment* (fig. 29) might be interpreted not only as representing the new, improved, imperial city, but also the means for razing it to the ground. The *Journal of Gas Lighting*, a specialist publication reporting all aspects of gas manufacture, supply and regulation, was quick to expose the 'nonsensical twaddle' being published by the press and to reassure the public that gasholders were safe. But only up to a point; their safety depended on the care and responsibility taken by the gas companies.

After the Nine Elms explosion the gas industry never recovered its public image. In the years when the entire thrust of public discourse on the metropolis was towards improvement, the gasworks were seen to be wrecking huge tracts of the city. The works were nearly always located in working-class areas of the city and these were often the ones earmarked for improvement, or adjacent to official or bourgeois London. The neighbourhood of the gasworks was the antithesis of the spatial aesthetic of the Metropolitan Board of Works: '[a] muddy and ill-smelling district . . . like a gas city, so beset is it with gas works.'[36]

Mid-Victorian London was defined through a semiotics of gas. Gas was polyvalent; it could signify metropolitan improvement and urban degeneration. It represented the height of modern amenities and metropolitan culture, but was also associated with hellish industrial production and urban blight. Gas also lit up the official rituals of public and royal London. Throughout the period gas lighting was used to provide public displays to celebrate national events.[37] Illuminations were created by moulding wrought-iron pipes into appropriate shapes and then drilling holes in the pipe to create a multiplicity of small gas jets or burners, complete with shades. On major occasions, gas illuminations would be displayed on private houses and shop-fronts, businesses and public buildings. Gas provided the funeral decorations on the death of the Duke of Wellington in 1852; it commemorated peace in the Balkans in 1856; and it celebrated the marriage of the Prince of Wales in 1863.[38] On these nights gas put London on show. It adorned the buildings and was a visual display of the status of the occupants; the bigger and brighter the illuminations, the greater the importance of the individual, corporation or ministry.

Gas articulated social difference. Not only was gaslight a register of economic wealth, but it was also anthropomorphic: its flame took on the human attributes of its user. The two extremes of this process were the over-cultivated gaslights of the Jewish retailer and the raw, unmediated flame of the street butcher. It is important to understand the subtle nuancing of light in the age of gas. Henry Mayhew was able to discern subtle distinctions in the illuminations of a London street market in the 1850s:

> There are hundreds of stalls, and every stall has its one or two lights . . . Some stalls are crimson with the fire shining through the holes beneath the baked chestnut stove; others have handsome octohedral lamps, while a few have a candle shining through a sieve: these, with the sparkling ground-glass globes of the tea-dealers' shops, and the butchers' gaslights streaming and fluttering in the wind like flags of flame, pour forth such a flood of light, that at a distance the atmosphere immediately about the spot is as lurid as if the street were on fire.[39]

Gas reaches the bottom of the social scale with the street butcher, as if there were a reflexive relationship between the raw meat laid out on the market stall and the naked, uncovered flame of the light. The butcher's uncontrollable, unguarded gas flare expresses a form of insanity that is taking place on the streets of the metropolis. In 1861 the *Illustrated Times* ran a series of articles called 'London Sketches'; the fourth in the series described 'Squalors' Market':

> the butcher of Squalors' Market is a madman – a raving lunatic. He unscrews the burners of his gas pipes, and creates great spouts of flame that roar and waver in the wind in front of his shamble-like premises, endangering the hats

of short pedestrians and the whiskers of tall ones; far out from his shop, and attached to roasting-jacks, revolve monstrous pigs' heads and big joints of yellow veal.[40]

By removing the burners, the butcher removes the veneer of civilisation from the gas; what remains are great tongues of flame, shooting out of crazy lamps. The figure of the Drury Lane street butcher and his atavistic gaslight reappeared in the literature of night-time London. George Augustus Sala described 'the gas, no longer gleaming through ground-glass globes, or aided by polished reflectors, but flaring from primitive tubes, [lighting] up a long vista of beef, mutton, and veal'.[41] This is gas and society reverted to a pre-modern, pre-improved state. It is organic and unadorned; it represents the raw and bloody underside of modernity. And it shows too much; illuminating aspects and details of the city that are better not seen. Having thrown light on the base material facts of the city, the scene becomes too much for sight and blindness is the only possible alternative state. The blind man reappears amongst the crowds in the street market. Once again, he is the cipher for the excessive sights of the gaslit streets. Next to the butcher's lurid stall, there is a bookmaker and Mayhew observed: 'to "ensure custom" [he] has illuminated his shop-front with a line of gas, and in its full glare stands a blind beggar, his eyes turned up so as to show only "the whites", and mumbling some begging rhymes.'[42] He stands, too, eyes blank, mouth wide open, at the back of 'Squalors' Market'. He is the symbol of Victorian London's hubristic attempt to turn night into day and his blank stare and mad rantings are the inevitable consequence of the excess of vision produced by the gaslight of the Jew and the butcher.

Gaslight turned the London streets into a stage. Lights in the shop windows and on the streets, provided the winglights, battens and spotlights of everyday life. Is it surprising, then, that viewed by gas, streets seemed like sets, people became characters, and clothes were costumes? For Augustus Mayhew, in his sensation novel *Paved with Gold*, the Haymarket was literally a set for his fictional characters: 'The gas is flaring from the shop windows, and throwing out its brilliant rays until the entire street is lit up as a stage.'[43] People, like moths, are attracted by the glare and, lit by the gas, faces have a hectic, flushed appearance, as though painted with stage make-up. Gas created enchantment and illusion; it made the lives that it illuminated seem 'staged' and unreal.

If gas turned the street into a theatre, then it also enabled the theatre to dramatise the street.[44] London theatres were quick to install the new gas lighting; both in front of stage, in the foyer and auditorium, and on the stage itself. The Olympic Theatre in Wych Street, where Amelia Roper was later to visit and to 'perform' her metropolitan, swell self, had installed gas on stage by December 1817. By the 1820s theatres were using large-scale street lamps to publicise their locations and were advertising the extent and brilliance of their gas lighting. On stage, sensation scenes of London by gas also became part of their seasonal attractions and the gaslit city scene entered into the vocabulary of Victorian drama. The contemporary life of London was one of the dominant themes in the drama of the 1860s. Technical advances in the use of stage mechanisms and gas lighting, enabled an increasingly detailed and realistic depiction of London street life. In 1864, the Princess's Theatre produced a new play, called *The Streets of London*, by the prolific Irish playwright, Dion Boucicault. Boucicault had an astute understanding of the potential of gas lighting to produce sensational effects. His plays were profitable and spectacular pot-boilers, which were popular with audiences if not always with critics. Boucicault's real skill was his creation of sensation scenes, which commonly provided the climax to the drama, and drew on all the resources of the Victorian theatre to produce their effects. Boucicault was not over-concerned with the matter of originality and his career was littered with accusations of plagiarism. This culminated in the copyright action brought against Boucicault by the American author and theatre-manager Augustin Daly, for the theft of his sensation scene set on the gaslit track of an underground railway. The court found that the scene in Boucicault's play, *After Dark*, had indeed been taken from Daly's melodrama, *Under the Gaslight*, and the action established the extension of copyright law to include stage business and the style of staging.[45]

The sensation scene in *The Streets of London* was not particularly original, but was not actually stolen from another play. It provided the hit of the year's London theatrical season. The play itself received mixed reviews, although critics were unanimous in their praise of the scenery and stage machinery. The sensation scene was a view of Charing Cross at midnight, and was such a triumph of scenic illusion that it seemed to its audiences to be reality itself. The 'Theatrical Lounger' in the *Illustrated Times* admired the scene:

> with its lighted lamps, its Nelson Column, its gleaming windows of Northumberland House, its groups of rich and poor wending their way to club or garret, and its cabs and 'buses in the distance rolling by in quick succession. Here, indeed, is a piece of reality that is not to be questioned for an instant – one whose completeness is so extraordinary and whose impression is so unique that it can scarcely fail to invest the drama with more than ordinary attraction . . . [the scene] is, perhaps, the most real scene ever witnessed on the stage in London . . . Real lamps run down each side of the way; the chemist's shop on the right throws its crimson, violet and green lines of colour across the street . . . In short, the scene is a perfect diorama.[46]

The repeated emphasis on the realism of the scene conveys some of the astonishment that audiences felt as the curtains opened to reveal the crowded, gaslit streets of mid-Victorian London. The scene was topographically correct; buildings and streets were where they should be; objects and people were reduced to their proper perspective. And, above all, there was the gas, burning away in street lamps, shops and houses and offering the ultimate proof of the realism of the illusion. On the preceding page, the paper published an engraving of the scene, complete with crowds, gaslights, omnibus and backdrops (fig. 38). It is hard to distinguish this image of London from other contemporary images of the city, which were carried in every issue of the illustrated press. The familiar landmarks and characters are all there and there is nothing in the image to suggest that this is not another journalistic sketch of an actual scene, observed in London. But this is an illustration of an illustration and even the actuality of the street was experienced as a stage set. The impact of the

38  'Scene from the New Play, "The Streets of London", at the Princess's Theatre', *Illustrated Times*, 27 August 1864, p. 129.

engraving is made by the caption, which informs the reader that the scene takes place not on the street but on the stage. The realistic effect is produced by the recognition of artifice.

Gas created a dream world, which blurred the uncertain boundaries between the real and the imagined and which was encapsulated in the space of the Victorian theatre. Here, audiences entered a gaslit fairyland in order to be astonished by the realism of the scenes on stage. The auditorium was a fantasy created by gaslight: 'everywhere white and gold meet the eye, and about 200,000 gas jets add to the glittering effect . . . such a blaze of light and splendour has scarcely ever been witnessed, even in dreams.'[47] On stage, gaslight created the illusion that 'the action was reality itself',[48] but novelty was the guiding principle of sensation drama and, by the late 1870s, gas had had its day. Electric arc lights had been used on stage some years earlier. Electricity was cleaner and had a lower heat output than gas. As it also became less expensive, entrepreneurial theatre managers began to advertise their conversion to the new light and in 1881 Richard D'Oyly Carte replaced all the gaslights at the Savoy Theatre with electric lights.

Lighting London was a big business. The potential of gas to create daylight by night was quickly exploited and London's reputation as the most illuminated city in Europe was established by the time Victoria came to the throne. Maintaining this demand for light required huge capital investment in a heavy, dirty industry located in the heart of the metropolis. The London gasworks were part of the cityscape and generated a new urban aesthetics: of gas storers and explosions, of ceremonial illuminations and the props of metropolitan improvement. Gas was also a register of social difference and flames, burners and lamps could be read as signs of social and ethnic identities. The economics of gas transformed London into a dramatic spectacle which, in its turn, became a critical part of the business of sensation in the London theatre of the 1860s.

## 3     *Secrets of the Gas*

The Gas has its secrets, and I happen to know them. The Gas has a voice, and I can hear it – a voice beyond the rushing whistle in the pipe, and the dull buzzing flare in the burner. It speaks, actively, to men and women of what is, and of what is done and suffered by night and by day; and though it often crieth like Wisdom in the streets and no man regardeth it, there are, and shall be some to listen to its experiences, hearken to its counsels, and profit by its lessons.

I know the secrets of the gas, but not all of them.[49]

Gas possessed a poetics as well as an economics. For writers in this period, London's temporal geography created two distinct worlds; a daytime world of organisation and commerce and a night-time world of danger and disorder. The street lamps occupied both of these worlds; they kept their place in the city, day and night, lit and extinguished. In the daylight the lamps stood dark and silent, but at night they became animated; not only casting light, but also understanding the scenes which they illuminated. It was at night, when the gas was lit and the flames were burning, that the street lamps became observers of the dark side of London. The gas had eyes; it bore witness to the strange and terrible life of London at night and could testify to those able to hear its quiet, whispering voice. The interpreters of the gas were the journalists and philanthropists who created the literature of the night-walk; who shared the temporality of the gas and who revealed its secrets to an audience eager to share the pleasures and dangers of gaslight and to join authors in their passage through the fictional city.

The belief that the streets at night had a peculiar beauty and poetry was a product of the gas industry and the spread of public lighting to more areas of the city than had been lit by oil. The greater provision of light made the streets safer to move around in at night, but not completely safe. Gaslight made the illuminated night-walk possible; it allowed observers to see the night, to perceive its dangers and its attractions and to fictionalise them. The basic tenet of night-walk fiction is that the reader is safe and warm at home, while the author assumes the mantle of outsider and wanderer. Dickens was quick to exploit this symbiotic, literary relationship and to realise that the bleaker the night setting, the greater the possible pleasures for the domestic reader. 'The Streets – Night', a short essay on a winter's night in London, was first published in *Bell's Life in London* in 1836 and collected in the second series of *Sketches by Boz* in the following year. The first paragraph establishes the literary and aesthetic potential of the London night: 'But the streets of London, to be beheld in the very height of their glory, should be seen on a dark, dull, murky winter's night . . . when the heavy lazy mist, which hangs over every object, makes the gas-lamps look brighter, and the brilliantly-lighted shops more splendid from the contrast they present to the darkness around.'[50]

The rhythmic alternation of light and dark is an essential backdrop to the creation of the attraction and threat of the city at night and the winter mist increases the disturbing ambiguities of the gaslight and its passages between illumination and obscurity. Dickens continued to explore the irrational elements of London at night in his later journalistic writings. By 1861, the date of the publication of 'Night Walks', in *The Uncommercial Traveller*, the trope of the author as homeless wanderer had become firmly established within contemporary fiction and far more developed. Usually the author assumes this identity as a result of a temporary, altered physical state, which forces him out of the conventional temporality of the daytime city and on to the streets at night. Illness, or loss of house-keys might initiate these fictional night wanderings; in 'Night Walks', Dickens referred to a case of temporary insomnia that compels the fictional author to walk the streets, where he experiences the spectral and irrational side of London. Loss of sleep in this case creates a hallucinatory, dreamlike evocation of the city as a phantasmagoria of past and present, inhabited by outcasts, ghosts and traces of previous existences. At one point the author imagines all these lives brought together in the city: 'And indeed in those houseless nightwalks . . . it was a solemn consideration what enormous hosts of dead belong to one old great city, and how, if they were raised while the living slept, there would not be the space of a pin's point in all the streets and ways for the living to come out into.'[51] Possessed by this fantastic image of a city of ghosts, the sleepless author quite literally loses his senses and his perception of physical space:

> When a clock strikes, on houseless ears in the dead of night, it may be at first mistaken for company and hailed as such. But, as the spreading circles of vibration, which you may perceive at such a time with great clearness, go opening out, for ever and ever afterwards, widening perhaps . . . in eternal space, the mistake is rectified and the sense of loneliness is profounder. (p. 195)

The literature of the night-side of London was always linked with the idea of the flight from the familiar, everyday existence of the daytime city. The convention of a temporary hiatus in the author's physical condition allowed him to cross the threshold of the night city and to enter a strange new world; a commingling of ghosts of the past and outcasts of the present. The seduction of the gaslit night lay in its invitation to leave the security of the everyday world behind and to experience the hallucinatory images of illuminated darkness.

In a compelling psychoanalytical study of the meanings of fire and candlelight, Gaston Bachelard has contrasted the poetry of the lamp flame with the mechanistic harshness of the electric lightbulb.[52] For Bachelard, the lamp is humanised and the experience of lamplight is an intense, psychological relationship. Time illuminated by the lamp is solemn and observes a slower tempo than the temporality of daylight or electric light. It is a period of dream, contemplation and reverie. It is what Bachelard calls: 'igneous time', that is 'time that passes by burning' (p. 69). This is the domain of darkness lit by a flame and its poetry is generated by the relationship between the individual subject and the lamplight, and the experience of its sober temporality. According to Bachelard, the perception of lamplight is not only that it casts light, but that it also sees; the illumination that it projects becomes a form of surveillance or gaze: 'This distant lamp is certainly not "turned in" on itself. It is a lamp that waits. It watches so unremittingly that it guards' (pp. 71–2). Bachelard's blend of phenomenology and psychoanalysis offers a helpful model for understanding the poetics of gas. His study is built on an opposition between lamplight (the flame) and electricity; there is no reference to gaslight. But if Bachelard's analysis is extended, gaslight can be understood to occupy a place somewhere between the archaic form of the lamp flame and the crude modernity of the electric light. Although gaslight was produced by means of a heavy, dirty industry, at its point of illumination – the flame in its glass case in the street lamp – it resembled most closely the psycho- logical world of the lamplight. The city at night became the city of gaslight; it took on a different temporality, the temporality of gas, which reigned from the moment the lamps were lit until the break of day, when the flames were extinguished. At night space was rearticulated by gaslight, with its alternating rhythm of seeing illumination and blind shadow. This was London's gas time; the time that passed as the gas burned in the street lamps and when the city became a place given over to imagination, dread and dream.

There can be no doubt that this perception of the night city as the strange, irra- tional other of the daytime city was built upon a strong tradition of religious sym- bolism. The New Testament presents a daylight world of honest labour and a world of darkness inhabited by the vicious and evil: 'Work while it is called Today; for the Night cometh, wherein no man can work.'[53] The Victorian Church seized enthusi- astically upon this biblical language of light and darkness and Nonconformist groups, in particular, drew on its unambiguous moral message to represent their evangelical mission into darkest London. So the Christian missionaries joined the journalists in tramping the streets of night-time London and in their accounts of these midnight missions produced a sub-genre of the literature of the night-walk. London by gaslight produced a dedicated group of Christian missionaries who specialised in night-time rescues and conversions. John Blackmore was probably the most well known amongst this group, a regular figure on the streets at night during his missionary cruises to dis- tribute tracts amongst the fallen of the metropolis. He established two homes for rescued prostitutes, the London Female Dormitory and the Female Temporary Home, and published his accounts of his works on the streets of London. In order to convey the danger and immorality of London at night, Blackmore had, paradoxically, to evoke the seductive attractions of the city and, in this respect, his writing often comes uncomfortably close to the literary sketches of the wandering journalist. In *The London by Moonlight Mission*, published in 1860, each chapter is devoted to the story of a separate 'cruise' in the strange, entrancing world of night-time London. For Blackmore it was a world that was never seen by day and which presented a form of parallel existence, unknown to the honest inhabitants of the daylight world. In the writings of night missionaries such as Blackmore, there is a strong sense that while they have successfully carried out their work among the fallen, they have also succumbed to the bewitchment of the city at night and that they have seen things that they cannot properly recall in the daylight. In his account of *The Night Side of London*, J. Ewing Ritchie described the transformation of the streets in the centre of the city by day and by night. At night they are the scenes of crime and depravity, but in the day they assume an ordinary and decent appearance and Ritchie himself appears to doubt whether he has actually witnessed the events of the night or whether he has imagined them. In one passage, he describes the transitional moment of daybreak and the passage from the world of the night to that of the day:

> As we go up Regent-street we see the lamps being extinguished, and the milk carts going round, and the red newspaper expresses tearing along to catch the early train, and the green hills of Hampstead looking lovelier than ever. In the sober light of day our night in the Haymarket will seem unreal, and when we shall tell our experiences, we shall be told possibly that our picture is overdrawn.[54]

Emergence from the night-time city is symbolised by the extinguishing of the gas lamps and the repetition of the ordinary rituals of everyday life. In this comfortable and familiar world memories of the previous night seem vague and unreal. It is precisely at this transitional moment, when the author moves between the familiar everyday world of daylight and the unfamiliar, spectral scenes of night and when he is most unsure whether what he has experienced is real or imagined, that the night-walk text shares many of the qualities that Freud associated with the notion of the uncanny. Freud's essay, published in 1919, defined the uncanny as a category within the field of what is frightening and which is distinguished by its tendency to lead back to what is 'known of old and long familiar'.[55] In this sense, then, there is a linguistic and psychic bond between the feeling of uncanniness and the familiar. This relationship is established by Freud through etymology, which confirms that the uncanny, the *unheimlich*, is rooted in and comes out of the familiar, the *heimlich*. Definitions of the *heimlich* associate the term with the domestic environment, with familiarity and comfort, but its meanings shade off to include that which is concealed or kept from sight; a usage that it shares with its opposite *unheimlich*. At this point, the *heimlich* and the *unheimlich* become identical and Freud concludes: 'Thus *heimlich* is a word the meaning of which develops in the direction of ambivalence, until it finally coincides with its opposite, *unheimlich*' (p. 226). For Freud the uncanny is much more than a sense of unfamiliarity; it is the tendency of the familiar to become defamiliarised, as in a dream, or in the confusion of dream and reality. The sense of the uncanny describes the return of something familiar and old-established, which has been repressed; it is 'something which ought to have remained hidden but has come to light' (p. 241). The uncanny is a condition of disturbing ambiguity; it is the point of slippage between the real and the unreal, the familiar and the strange, the living and the spectral. It is the condition of the partially illuminated darkness of gaslit London.

Freud offers one instance of his own experience of the uncanny, which occurs in the context of a strange experience of urban space. He recalls a visit to a provincial Italian town. Walking down the deserted, unfamiliar streets, he finds himself in a 'red-light' district:

> Nothing but painted women were to be seen at the windows of the small houses, and I hastened to leave the narrow street at the next turning. But after having wandered about for a time without enquiring my way, I suddenly found myself back in the same street, where my presence was now beginning to excite attention. I hurried away once more, only to arrive by another *détour* yet a third time. Now, however, a feeling overcame me which I can only describe as uncanny . . . (p. 237)

Freud compares the helplessness of his condition with that of being in a dream-state and identifies the element of involuntary repetition as one source of his experience. If, however, the spatial context of Freud's memory is examined, it is surely significant that his experience of the uncanny takes place in sexualised space and that his distress at becoming lost in the labyrinthine streets and of constantly returning to the same spot is directly related to his identification of this area as a site of prostitution. The psychoanalyst shares with the journalist and the missionary a particularly spatialised experience of the uncanny. In all three cases, the writers move from the familiar world into the unfamiliar (the unknown provincial town, or the city at night). They are spaces of commodified female sexuality and, moving through these streets, they are overcome by a sensory disorientation from which they finally re-emerge into the safety of the familiar piazza, or the reassuring routines of daily life. The uncanny effect is produced by a momentary dislocation of the self within urban space and the consequent dissolution of the boundaries between reality and imagination.

Darkness generates the conditions of the uncanny.[56] Gas illuminates the night; a place of secrets and fantasy, in which the familiar is rendered unfamiliar and those things: 'which ought to remain hidden . . . come to light' (p. 241). The discovery of the 'night-walk' is the turning-up of old anxieties in the fabric of the familiar. Gaslight might have been expected to eliminate these spectres, but, instead, it put them on show.

In his fascinating study *The Architectural Uncanny* Anthony Vidler has explored the spatial implications of the Freudian uncanny within the specific historical context of the emergence of the modern city. He identifies a 'recent history of modern space', which emerged with Michel Foucault's work on Jeremy Bentham and the paradigm of the panopticon, of total social control through transparency and complete visibility. Institutions and city plans in the eighteenth and nineteenth centuries were constructed on the principle of the opening up of space to the circulation of light and air: 'Transparency, it was thought, would eradicate the domain of myth, suspicion, tyranny, and above all the irrational.'[57] Following on from the initiatives of Foucault, Vidler suggests that historians have tended to concentrate on the technologies of transparency and have ignored the other side of Foucault's spatial paradigm, the presence and fear of darkened spaces. Any history of space, Vidler suggests, must not only describe the political role of transparent space, but must also provide 'a spatial phenomenology of darkness' (p. 169). Vidler points to the limitations of Foucault's account, which retains a polarised relationship between light and dark, transparency and obscurity and which resists a proper investigation of how the pairing and co-operation of these terms is productive of power. He concludes:

> For it is in the intimate associations of the two, their uncanny ability to slip from one to the other, that the sublime as instrument of fear retains its hold – in that ambiguity that stages the presence of death in life, dark space in bright space. In this sense, all the radiant spaces of modernism, from the first Panopticon to the Ville Radieuse, should be seen as calculated not on the final triumph of light over dark but precisely on the insistent presence of the one in the other. (p. 172)

All of the attempts in the 1860s to map, straighten and light London can be seen, therefore, not simply as a reaction to the fear of darkness, but as always bearing within their urban ideal the presence of obscurity and ambiguity, the presence of the uncanny. If metropolitan improvement was driven by the desire to eliminate disorder and superstition, then the night city represented a return of these old anxieties through the uncertain vision of mist, gaslight or the dream. Night-time London troubled the modernisers because the fears that it recalled could not be kept securely in place but remained a part of the contemporary city, threatening at any moment to invade the bright light of day and to turn the feeling of being 'at home' in the city into an illusion.

These might have been 'the secrets of the gas' whispered to the wandering journalist. George Augustus Sala's vision, however, was far more formulaic and represents a containment and stylisation of the more disturbing associations of the city at night. Sala's contribution to the literature of London was to update and popularise the format of the story of a day in the city; it was to write the temporal geography of London.[58] Sala was one of the most active and successful journalists of the period. He had few literary pretensions, about which he was disarmingly frank. This self-assessment was confirmed by his critics, who regarded him as the embodiment of low, populist fiction.[59] Sala was a Londoner by birth; his father was a dancing instructor and his mother a singer and actress. After his father died, when Sala was a baby, his mother supported the family, in part by performing on stage and, on occasion, in works by Dickens. As a child, Sala met Dickens, who remained a significant literary and professional influence. Sala's first work was in the theatre, as a scene painter; he moved on to book illustration and by the late 1840s he began to publish articles and essays. Between 1860 and 1886 he was the author of a regular column of metropolitan gossip in the *Illustrated London News*, called 'Echoes of the Week'. Sala described himself as a 'true Cockney' and he seems to have prepared himself for his career as London's special correspondent by spending much of his life lounging around the clubs and supper-rooms of the West End. He got his journalistic break-through in 1851 when Dickens accepted an article called 'The Key of the Street' for publication in *Household Words*, and he remained a regular contributor to Dickens's journal throughout the 1850s. Even when Sala was commissioned to work abroad, he took his Cockney identity with him. In one of a series of articles for Dickens on Russia in the aftermath of the Crimean War he declared: 'Wherever I go, civilisation will follow me. For I am the streets, and streety – *eis ten polin* is my haven. Like the starling, I can't get out of cities.'[60] But it was as a sketcher of London that he attracted Dickens's attention. A note from Dickens to his sub-editor in 1851 shows not only his understanding of Sala's particular talent, but also his own confident grasp of the range of London subjects:

> There is nobody about us whom we can use, in his way, more advantageously than this young man . . . Suggest to him Saturday night in London, or London markets – Newport Market, Tottenham Court Road, Whitechapel Road (where there are most extraordinary men holding forth on Saturday night about Corn Plaister – the most extraordinary things sold, near Whitechapel Workhouse – the strangest shows – and the wildest cheap Johns) – the New Cut, etc. etc. etc. I think he would make a capital paper out of it.[61]

Many of these topics were to become part of a litany of locations in subsequent 'night-walk' literature.

All of Sala's books were collections of articles that appeared first in periodicals or newspapers. *Twice Round the Clock: Or the Hours of the Day and Night in London* was originally published as a series in Henry Vizetelly's magazine the *Welcome Guest* in 1858. The idea was to chronicle, hour by hour, the changing panorama of Victorian London. Sala denied any personal originality in choosing this theme, which was suggested to him by an eighteenth-century book lent to him by Dickens.[62] Each of the chapters in *Twice Round the Clock* is devoted to a separate hour of the day and focuses on two themes or locations. Midnight is spent in the Haymarket and in a sub-editor's office; the streets of London and journalism were always closely linked for Sala. The identification of midnight with the hectic night-life of the Haymarket in central London was well established by the late 1850s. Sala presents a gothic scene of the lost souls who emerge on to the street:

> A new life begins for London at midnight. Strange shapes appear of men and women who have lain-a-bed all the day and evening, or have remained torpid in holes and corners. They come out arrayed in strange and fantastic garments, and in glaringly gaslit rooms screech and gabble in wild revelry. The street corners are beset by night prowlers. Phantoms arrayed in satin and lace flit upon the sight. The devil puts a diamond ring on his taloned finger, sticks a pin in his shirt, and takes his walk abroad.[63]

Sala relies as much on auditory as on visual impressions to convey the ghastly spectacle of the street, and both senses are bombarded by excess: clothes are fantastic, gaslight glares and people screech. This use of sounds to evoke the peculiar nature of the London night recurs in most of Sala's journalism: 'the whole Haymarket wakes, lights, rises up with a roar, a rattle, and a shriek quite pantomimic; if not supernatural' (p. 320). And describing London in the early hours of the morning: 'all has a solemn, ghastly, unearthly aspect; the gas-lamps flicker like corpse candles; and the distant scream of a profligate, in conflict with the police, courses up and down the streets in weird and shuddering echoes' (p. 373). Sala's accounts of the look of a place are commonly supplemented by descriptions of sound. The unearthly condition of the city at night is expressed in the first instance by the flickering gaslight, but the effects of this altered and uncertain vision is registered in terms of the distortion of sound and the subsequent confusion of space.

Sala was a prolific and somewhat formulaic writer. His London material offers a theatrical version of the metropolis, which did not always satisfy critics who wanted a more nuanced and realist representation of the night-walk. In a review of the work of Sala and other writers associated with *Household Words*, the *Saturday Review* criticised the coyness of their treatment of London subjects: 'They make a point of conducting us to the very threshold, but they distinctly refuse to go further with us. They lead us to the top of the Haymarket, tell us it is a "wretched street" and a "bad thoroughfare", and lead us home again, discoursing beautifully by the way'.[64] For this critic, Sala's style was too rhetorical for the representation of contemporary London life. It had taken the subjects of the social investigation and had replaced truth with rhetoric. But Sala was not greatly interested in truth; for him, London was two things: geography and journalism, and it is no coincidence that *Twice Round the Clock* begins and ends in the offices of a newspaper and a printing-house.

In Sala's other collection of articles published in 1859, twenty-four hours are reclassified as *Gaslight and Daylight*. In his chapter on 'The Secrets of the Gas', Sala gave full rein to the rhetorical style derided by the *Saturday Review*; but in its fulsome, mannered way the text manages to convey something of the strange presence and symbolism of gaslight in mid-Victorian London. Sala's gaslight has sight and sound; it sees and it speaks. Sala is joined on his night-walk by the 'ever-watchful' gas: 'As I walk about the streets by night, endless and always suggestive intercommunings take place between me and the . . . gas.'[65] Wherever Sala goes in the city – in courts and alleys, in parks and on quays – the gas is there too, as counsellor, guide and 'incorruptible tell-tale'. Sala sees and hears the gas as it moves through the streets in pipes and flares in the burners. Sala was the only writer in this period to represent the sound of gaslight. As so many critics of the gas industry were quick to point out, the gas was impure and supply inconstant, but these industrial limitations gave gaslight a voice and a poetics. Sala hears it whispering, puttering, hissing and telling secrets; it speaks of the other side of daytime London, a dreamworld of sexuality and pleasure, phantoms and superstition. It was a voice that would be recaptured only later, by James Joyce, in a Dublin brothel in *Ulysses*.[66]

★　★　★

# *4     Cremorne Pleasure Gardens*

In July 1861 Edward Tyrrell Smith took over the lease and the management of Cremorne Pleasure Gardens, in west London. Smith had a keen feel for the demand and taste for urban leisure in the mid-nineteenth century. He was involved, at various times, in the management of some of London's most famous theatres and music-halls, and under his entrepreneurial guidance in the 1860s Cremorne entered its most popular and commercially successful period.[67]

The pleasure garden was a form of open-air resort, usually located in the suburbs or on the outskirts of major cities. They first appeared in the metropolis in the late seventeenth century, but became most popular in the eighteenth century, when Vaux-hall Gardens became one of the most fashionable locations for summer evening entertainment. The pleasures offered by these gardens were many and diverse. The visitor could stroll in landscaped gardens and along illuminated walks, eat and drink in supper-rooms, listen to music, watch spectacular entertainments, or, simply, look at the crowds. They were, as one recent source has put it, a 'landscape of commodified consumption'.[68] By the nineteenth century, however, the pleasure garden was part of a more highly developed and complex leisure industry and was having to compete with new and emerging forms of public urban entertainment.[69] Novelty was essen-tial and proprietors had to offer a constantly changing programme of events and attractions, day and night, to keep the crowds interested and paying to enter. The history of Cremorne in the middle of the nineteenth century is the history of the speculative and entrepreneurial management of metropolitan leisure and entertain-ment. The opening hours of the gardens were extended so that visitors could enjoy sunny afternoons, as well as long, gaslit nights and each season the programme offered more extraordinary attractions, which, on occasion, took the management to the brink of legality and social acceptability. Cremorne commercialised gas and light. It exploited the temporality of London, with its shifting representations and meanings, and created a schizophrenic social space, associated equally with peaceful family outings and explicit prostitution and public disturbance.

Cremorne Gardens was located in Chelsea, on a site stretching from the King's Road to the River Thames. Originally part of the private estate of Lord Cremorne, the grounds passed from family ownership and were opened to the public as a type of sports stadium in 1831. In the following years more attractions were added to the programme, including dancing and fireworks displays and the event that was to become synonymous with the pleasures of Cremorne, the balloon ascent. In 1846 the grounds were taken over by new management; the site was extended and refur-bished, and Cremorne Gardens was officially opened to the public. Within a few years, Cremorne had established itself as a popular feature of the London summer season and each May the press enthusiastically reported announcements of the new programme. From its opening in 1846 until its closure in 1877 the price of admis-sion to Cremorne was one shilling, which made it relatively affordable to the middle classes, as well as to the new clerical classes of the metropolis. Transport was also good; the grounds could be reached by cab or omnibus from Charing Cross, or by

Thames steamer from the City to the pier at Cremorne. Few argued with the claim of its proprietor that Cremorne was the best pleasure garden in London and that its dazzling attractions made Vauxhall look dull and faded. When E. T. Smith took over the management in 1861, therefore, the Gardens were already a highly successful enterprise. It was a safe business move made by a man with considerable experience in the entertainment industry.

So what was on offer at Cremorne Pleasure Gardens? What did the visitors see as they strolled round the gardens and what could they do to while away the hours from mid-afternoon until long after midnight? If they came by steamer, they would enter the Gardens by the river-gate at the south-east corner (fig. 39). By day they would immediately be struck by the grounds themselves; by the trees, lawns and flower-beds, punctuated with statues and fountains which, combined with the suburban location, made Cremorne seem like a pastoral retreat from the streets of the city. At night they would see gaslights; strung along the walks and in the trees and blazing around the sites of the main attractions and side-shows. One of the most popular features of Cremorne was the orchestra and dancing-platform in the south-west corner of the Gardens. Here, the visitor could listen to the orchestra, playing in its carved and brightly coloured 'pagoda', or dance on the surrounding circular platform, with up to three thousand fellow visitors. Or they could sit and watch from the tables among the trees on the edge of the dancing area, where they could be served food and drink by waiters who also attended to guests in the tiers of supper boxes that overlooked the scene. The Gardens offered an alternating rhythm of nature and sideshow, display and seclusion, brilliance and shade. North of the dancing and refreshment area there was an avenue of trees, joined by a tunnel of coloured lights and culminating in the Crystal Grotto. On the east side, there was a broad lawn from which the balloon ascents took place, with the popular Marionette Theatre and Hermit's Cave to the north. In the centre of the Gardens was an American Bowling Saloon, and other entertainments included a circus to the west of the grounds, a fireworks temple and a theatre for musical and dramatic performances to the south, by the river (fig. 40).

Cremorne was a complex and multi-purpose space. There was no single version of a visit to the Gardens; it would vary according to the time of day, the weather and which parts of the grounds and which attractions were frequented. It also depended on who else was there. A visit to Cremorne could be a family treat to see the marionettes and a balloon ascent, leaving shortly after the night's fireworks display; or, it could be a drunken cab ride after closing time in central London and a few bottles of champagne at a table by the dancing platform. The management of Cremorne needed to keep the gardens busy throughout the day and night during the season, which meant attracting and facilitating as many different types of visit and visitor as possible. Programmes were carefully planned, varied and advertised, so that the pleasures of Cremorne were addressed to a broad public, embracing diverse social groups and individuals. Within the space enclosed by the grounds, Cremorne had to orchestrate a broad and occasionally incompatible public, through a sequence of distinct temporal zones.

There can be no doubt that the potential financial reward for succeeding in this social management was greater in the second half of the nineteenth century than it

39    Plan of Cremorne Gardens, *c.*1870. Watercolour. Photo: The Royal Borough of Kensington & Chelsea Libraries and Arts Service.

40   Playbill advertising 'Cremorne Gardens Open Daily', c.1850. The Royal Borough of Kensington & Chelsea Libraries and Arts Service.

had ever been before. In this period a new world of mass public leisure emerged; there was more regular leisure time for greater numbers of people, and leisure became 'more visible . . . and more controversial'.[70] In the years of Cremorne Gardens leisure became increasingly commercial in its organisation, calling upon substantial injections of capital and new levels of investment. This was the economic world of

Cremorne in the 1860s. It was a world of leases, wages and licences on the one hand and of novelty, entertainment and spectacle on the other. The pleasure garden in the mid-nineteenth century was a hybrid blend of rural retreat and theme park.

Between seasons the exhausted resources of Cremorne had to be replenished: gardens had to be laid out, woodwork repainted, lamps repaired and attractions replaced. In 1860 the proprietor, Mr T. B. Simpson, proposed an inventive new way of raising the required capital. A shares prospectus was issued, announcing the creation of 'Royal Cremorne Gardens Company, Limited' and twenty thousand shares of five pounds each. The company would purchase the 'Lease, Goodwill and Plant' of the Gardens from Simpson and a substantial profit, equal to 'a dividend of 20% upon the capital employed', was estimated for shareholders.[71] Following this attempt to relieve himself of the direct financial demands and risks of the Gardens, Simpson retired in 1861 and the lease of 'Cremorne Gardens' passed into the entrepreneurial hands of E. T. Smith.

There was something fascinating about the economics of leisure and the seemingly incongruous association of business and pleasure. Writers in the 1860s were keen to investigate the commercial facts behind the landscape of leisure and the glittering attractions at Cremorne. Such revelations did not, it seems, detract from or spoil the pleasures of Cremorne, but gave them another dimension and made them even more breathtaking and spectacular. For the author of one article on 'The Business of Pleasure', published in *All the Year Round* in 1863, Cremorne was a good case for analysis since it combined on a single site the attractions of a number of different establishments: theatre, music-hall and supper-room, and attracted a broad public with a wide range of tastes.[72] First the author considers the gardens, which are such an attraction to daytime visitors. During the season, fifteen gardeners are employed to maintain the lawns and flower-beds, and they are just a small proportion of the huge labour force that maintains the site during the season. There are twenty carpenters, six scene-painters and five house-painters, among those attending to the fabric of the buildings, and twelve gasmen, whose sole concern is the maintenance of Cremorne as a nightly gaslit fairyland. Eight bill-posters are employed to publicise the programme on the streets of London. There are variety performers, fireworks manufacturers and security guards, who all contribute to the huge weekly costs of wages. The statistics of Cremorne – its daily consumption of food, its labour force and capital investment – turn the pleasure garden into a mini-metropolis. This is a serious business which, the article concludes: 'is carried on, with the utmost regularity and precision; with every precaution of check and counter-check, book-keeping, and all the paraphernalia of ledger-demain [sic] which respectability prescribes' (p. 152).

This emphasis on the sober conduct of business at Cremorne was, of course, one way of countering accusations, in this period, about the social and moral impropriety of modern urban leisure. As Peter Bailey has shown, leisure in this period was divided into two distinct categories: amusement and recreation.[73] Amusement was really purposeless leisure; it was concerned with diversion and superficial pleasures. Recreation represented the rational side of leisure and was associated with renewal and improvement. There was not much about the annual programmes at Cremorne that expressed the values and concerns of rational recreation; what rescued it, however, from utter repudiation as purposeless, sensual leisure was a sound economic base and the conduct of its business affairs.

By the middle of the 1860s the business of pleasure was seen to equal the economic and commercial scope of other industries that served the needs of the metropolis. What was so marvellous about the leisure industry, however, was how its business practices were transformed in the production and presentation of entertainment. It was a commercial conjuring trick, in which the dull forms of economy were transmuted into the dazzlement of gaslight and cut glass, music and dancing, sideshow and spectacle. Edmund Yates produced two volumes in his 1865 study of places 'where pleasure is carried on as a regular business and in regular business fashion'.[74] The subject of the first chapter is Cremorne Pleasure Gardens. Yates reported his interview with the manager about 'the internal economy of Cremorne' and presented the predictable range of statistics to demonstrate the extent of the operation. He recalled a visit during the previous week and his thoughts as he walked around the gardens and wandered in and out of the entertainments:

> I began to ponder on the magnitude of the undertaking, and to wonder how the various wheels in the great whole worked with such increasing regularity. Here must be large capital involved, very many people engaged, constant supervision exercised, and all for the production of Pleasure . . . I have no doubt that there is as much labour, capital, and energy employed here as in many establishments whose names are household words in the circle of a mile from the Exchange. Pleasure has its business, which requires to be carried on with as great tact, earnestness, energy, forethought, and exactness as any other; and when patience, prudence and perseverance are brought to bear in carrying on the business of pleasure, the result is Fortune. (pp. 11–12)

Which of the diverse attractions at Cremorne stimulated this emphatic denial of pleasure, cannot be known; all that remains in the text is the re-presentation of the purposeless amusement of sideshow culture through the discourse of rational recreation and the values of productivity and profits. It is hardly surprising that E. T. Smith co-operated with writers such as Yates and the author of the article in *All the Year Round* and supplied them with annual statistics and financial figures. It was helpful publicity and could be used to counter the mounting opposition from coalitions of extreme supporters of rational recreation and property developers. The business of pleasure provided a discourse that organised disorder, anaesthetised sensual experience and defused the dangerous attractions of the pleasure garden.

Cremorne sold novelty. Each season had to excel the last in its provision of spectacles and amenities to a public that was becoming increasingly discerning in its demands for leisure. New technologies were quickly exploited; in 1862 Smith announced that an electric telegraph station had been installed at the Gardens to take reservations for the private rooms and boxes around the dancing platform.[75] Cremorne had become a complex industry, requiring a high level of capital investment for the provision of its diverse pleasures and promising a substantial revenue to a speculative manager who was prepared to take risks. Cremorne relied on being in

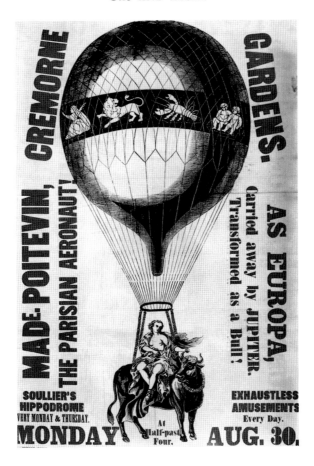

41  Playbill advertising Madame Poitevin's ascent as Europa, 30 August 1852. The Royal Borough of Kensington & Chelsea Libraries and Arts Service.

fashion; on the relentless production of the new, and its inevitable co-production of the old and outmoded. This was the seasonal rationale of Cremorne. It had to provide a constantly changing programme of events while maintaining its popularity as a place with a rustic ambience for public relaxation and casual socialisation.

Balloon ascents were a staple feature of the Cremorne season, but to a knowing public this attraction could appear predictable and old-fashioned.[76] After all, Vauxhall had introduced balloon ascents at the end of the eighteenth century, so Cremorne had to promote new forms of aeronautic spectacle in order to maintain the public's wonder. The balloons got bigger; they flew during the day and the night and the associated stunts became increasingly bizarre. First animals were suspended from the basket, then people, and when the novelty wore off, animals and people were dangled together. One of the more extraordinary versions of this spectacle involved an aeronaut, Madame Poitevin, seated on a bull and, in the mythological guise of Europa, suspended from the basket of an ascending balloon (fig. 41). The prank misfired; the Society for the Prevention of Cruelty to Animals brought a court case against the management of Cremorne, which was fined for the incident. Worse still, the event was interpreted in the newspapers as symptomatic of the lowest tendencies in popular culture, which was rapidly descending to the levels of the Roman circus in its pursuit

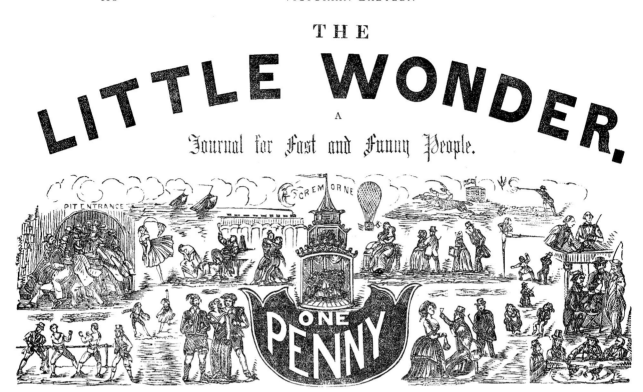

42    *Little Wonder*, no. 4 (24 November 1856), masthead.

of mindless diversion and its display of pointless cruelty. The leader column of the *Illustrated London News* declared:

> it has been reserved for the ingenious managers who cater for the million at public gardens to revive the morbid desire for the cruel, the monstrous, and the terrible – the unfortunate characteristic of a restless populace, eager for novel sensations and strange sights . . . and it is on this unnatural excitement that reckless and greedy managers strive to feed, to the neglect of intellectual and rational amusements.[77]

The image of greedy managers pandering to a mass audience, eager for cruel spectacles and sensory over-stimulation, was not one that Cremorne could afford to be publicly associated with. On the other hand, the playbill promised 'exhaustless amusement' and so the Gardens recovered from this promotional and financial setback and continued in the ceaseless pursuit of novelty. A few weeks later it was hosting Madame Poitevin's night-time parachute descent from a balloon, which the same paper described as 'one of the more daring, reprehensible, and perhaps useless feats ever performed'.[78] The spectacular balloon ascent symbolised the reckless side of Cremorne; the side that understood the drawing power of excitement and terror and provided attractions that indulged those sensations. It is no accident that the masthead of the short-lived, risqué metropolitan paper the *Little Wonder* included a crude representation of the orchestra at Cremorne, flanked by a crescent moon smoking a cigarette, and a balloon in flight (fig. 42). The image is completed by the figures of an embracing couple. This is the Cremorne of the 'Journal for Fast and Funny People', a night-time world of sensation and sensuality.

Promoting the pleasures of Cremorne was a balancing act between the different publics for and uses of the grounds. The gardens had to retain a degree of respectability, without appearing dull and staid; and they had to convey an element of risk and excitement, without becoming infamous. At any time, large sections of its putative public might be attracted to competing venues; Cremorne had to 'stir the nerves' without stirring the nervous.[79]

There were two Cremornes in the mid-Victorian cultural imaginary: the polite, decorous society, the trimmed lawns and neat flower-beds of daytime Cremorne; and the flaunting immorality, dazzling lights and dancing of night-time Cremorne. Representations of Cremorne and its public ricochet between these two extremes; it is imagined equally as a place for families and loungers, clerks and swells, respectable women and screeching prostitutes. From its first years, the beauty of the well-kept grounds was identified as one of the most distinctive features of Cremorne and made the site an attraction during the day as well as at night. The lawns and trees, the statues and fountains, gave the gardens the semblance of a country estate. The *Illustrated London News* commended the 'park-like character of the grounds', which made them 'a delightful resort for a summer's afternoon'.[80] During his period as manager Mr T. Simpson tried to cultivate the image of Cremorne as an English parkland, filled with suitably traditional folk activities. In the 1858 season, the *Illustrated London News* was especially delighted by an afternoon's 'maypole and morris dancing, such as delighted our ancestors . . . in the gardens, which were exquisitely decorated with flags and banners'. The report was accompanied by a full-page illustration of the maypole dancing on the lawn at Cremorne, watched by groups of highly respectable visitors, shaded by the spreading branches of a great elm tree. Cremorne could, when necessary, lend itself to this kind of idealised genre scene, but it was a promiscuous space and could take on many different characters when required.[81]

The attractions of daylight Cremorne were seen to far exceed those of Vauxhall Gardens by day. The experience of a visit to Vauxhall in the daylight was of disenchantment; of an illusion destroyed. Shortly after the closure of Vauxhall in 1859, one commentator described a daytime visit there as: 'the most striking type of all that was tawdry and garish. It was the reverse of a medal; it was the wrong side of a rich piece of tapestry. In traversing Vauxhall by daylight you felt like one who trod alone a banquet-hall deserted: lights fled, garlands dead, and all, save yourself, departed.'[82] Vauxhall by day was the exposure of sham; of false gaiety, faded glitter and trickery. In the daytime the glories of Vauxhall Gardens reverted to the soot-blackened forms of south London. In 1859 Vauxhall was no longer topographically what it had been in 1759. It was no longer a suburban resort; London had grown, the gasworks had appeared and the site was more valuable for property development than as a pleasure garden. In 1859 Cremorne was still a convenient distance from the city; it was easy to reach, but far enough away to be an escape. It would be a few more years before it also succumbed to the inexorable process of metropolitan development.

At various times during his period of management, Simpson succeeded in securing court and aristocratic patronage for the daytime Gardens. In the 1850s a number of floral fêtes were held, which were attended by the queen and members of the royal family, and during these periods the grounds were the popular resort of wealthy, fashionable society. In July 1858 a committee of titled lady patronesses organised an 'Aristocratic Fête' at Cremorne; tickets were one guinea each and vouchers were required for entry. The coup of having such an occasion associated with the Gardens was compromised, however, by appalling weather conditions, which made the event a wash-out. The Aristocratic Fête was a significant failure; it came hard on the heels of the first concerted attempts by the Chelsea Vestry to enforce earlier closing hours at Cremorne, and regular fêtes might have held those local critics at bay. As it was, torrential rain and a concurrent scandal concerning aristocratic ladies turning to Catholicism and the confession-box, made the Aristocratic Fête the butt of jokes about aristocratic femininity, rather than the beginnings of a new daytime niche market for Cremorne.[83]

If daytime Cremorne connoted notions of Englishness in its parklands, fêtes, may-poles and folk dancing, then at night Cremorne became foreign and took on the appearance of a Parisian outdoor ball or a continental pleasure ground. At night Cremorne dazzled, transformed by the effects of gaslight, glass and fireworks displays. At night the focus of attention and imagination was on the dancing platform and surrounding area; on the music of the orchestra and the sight and sound of the dancers. The nucleus of this space was the orchestra in its carved and illuminated pagoda. Since the eighteenth century, chinoiserie had been a conventional style for the design of garden pavilions and was regarded as an appropriate form for build-ings of an informal or frivolous nature.[84] The exotic and extravagant associations of this hybrid style were epitomised in the pagoda, which turned up in private gardens throughout England and at Cremorne. The tiered and fretted pagoda where the orchestra played was at the heart of Cremorne's night life. With its upturned eaves and bracketed balconies, it drew on nearly two centuries of British orientalism to sell the thrills and pleasures of Cremorne after dark. Gaslight performed the final transformation of this space. Globular ground-glass lamps were fitted to the pagoda and to the trees and supper-boxes around the dancing platform and, thus illuminated, it reminded visitors not just of the Orient, but of an enchanted fairyland. In 1847, the year after Cremorne opened, the *Pictorial Times* provided its readers with an engraving of the dancing platform, to accompany its report on the season's attrac-tions (fig. 43). It is a curiously under-populated and demure scene. At the centre is the gaslit pagoda, from which radiate the wooden floor of the dancing platform, the surrounding trees and distant side-shows. This oddly formal image, with its stiff figures, represents a moment before the visual iconography of Cremorne is fully formed. It looks back to the empty urban landscapes of the early nineteenth century, rather than forward to the organised crowds of the Victorian panorama.

The pagoda and dancing platform were frequently refurbished and upgraded. In 1851 the pagoda was enlarged; the ground-level tier was opened up and more ornate fretwork was added to create a rest area at the centre of the circular dancing plat-form.[85] The platform itself was also enclosed by elaborate wrought-iron railings and candelabra around the perimeter of the dancing area. These alterations created a much stronger demarcation between the space of the dancing platform, with the pagoda at its centre, and the surrounding area of strollers and diners. Within its wrought-

43   'The Cremorne Gardens', *Pictorial Times*, 12 June 1847, p. 372.

iron cordon, the dancing became a Cremorne side-show; another of the attractions, like the marionettes or the circus, which visitors could go and watch. And within the enclosure there was another specular economy, as dancers rested and became an 'insider' audience at the base of the pagoda. At the centre of it all and elevated above the crowds, sat the orchestra; their job to accompany this theatre of looks and moves with the latest tunes from the Continent.

An engraving published in the *Illustrated Times* in 1858 shows something of the social dynamic created within the space of the refurbished platform and surrounding area (fig. 44).[86] Here the Cremorne crowd commands the scene. The boundary of the railings creates a perambulatory space between the dancers and the diners, and the performance on the platform is far more enclosed and self-absorbed. At the centre of the platform, in the base of the pagoda, are the Cremorne men, the metropolitan swells and loafers, who were to come to symbolise the manners and morals of night-time Cremorne. They lean against the 'Chinese' columns, idly chat or watch the dancers around them. It is an image of social uncertainties and possibilities. Are people known to each other? Have they met for the first time? How will the crowd behave as the night goes on? In the accompanying article, written by 'The Lounger', Cremorne is described as one of the great innovations of modern life; a distinctly contemporary form of leisure, belonging to the current 'rising' generation, as Vauxhall had belonged to the previous one. The article points out the location of

44   'Cremorne Gardens in the Height of the Season', *Illustrated Times*, 10 July 1858, p. 25.

the engraving: 'the best place for observing the character of the various visitors', and specifically identifies the moment represented as half past ten at night, a key transitional moment in the temporality of Cremorne, when two different kinds of crowd commingle:

> the middle-class visitors have not yet beat a retreat, the 'swells' are just beginning to arrive . . . in all the 'gorgeous array' of evening dress, covered by the large loose-sleeved cape, in all the aristocracy of moustache, beard, and a wing-whisker – in all the easy elegance of toothpick-chewing, hands-in-pocket-holding, and semi-intelligible drawling – wending their sauntering way round the dancing-platform at Cremorne. These young bucks are sources of the greatest delight – of delight mixed with respectful wonder – to the families who have been at the gardens since two p.m. . . . [87]

Cremorne was a testing ground for metropolitan identities and behaviours, for casual socialising in the context of mass urban leisure. Historically, this had taken place before in sites of public leisure; what was distinctive about Cremorne was the scale of the crowd, the range of different social groupings and the unprecedented possibilities for public social contact. People went to Cremorne to look and to be looked at, to dance and to pose, to touch and to flirt. The circular dancing platform was the arena where some of these social manoeuvres and exchanges were played out, and all for the cost of one shilling.

In 1857 another alteration was made to the platform, which was to seal the fantasy image of night-time Cremorne. New wrought-iron lamp standards were added to the perimeter railings, supporting elaborate constructions of garnet- and emerald-coloured cut-glass drops and globes. The standards were joined by arched festoons of gaslights and richly cut glass drops. Now Cremorne was not simply illuminated, it sparkled. It drew on the latest techniques in glass production to transform the dancing area and orchestra into a 'Crystal Platform'.[88] Gaslight and glass altered the space of the dancing platform at Cremorne, enriching its seductive invitation through the play of surfaces, light and reflections. The ornate, glowing forms of the cut-glass enclosed the dancers in a perimeter of luxury and beauty, so that to cross the sparkling threshold on to the platform was to move into a bourgeois utopia of the senses. Other sites of evening entertainment in the metropolis used gaslight and mirrors to embellish their interiors; what was unique about Cremorne was its combination of a rural setting and gaslit sophistication.[89] Surrounded by elm trees, the crystal platform brought fairyland to its visitors; a magic circle, flickering in the light of thousands of gas jets.

The 'gaslit groves' of Cremorne sounded the death-knell for Vauxhall.[90] Unable to compete with the newer venue's non-stop attractions, Vauxhall closed in 1859, and the grounds were divided into building lots. In the 1860s Cremorne was unrivalled in its provision of a multiplicity of entertainments within a single site. It was theatre, music-hall, supper-room, circus, parkland, dance and fireworks display. It was a place of infinite variety where strangers, the thousands of other visitors, were part of the entertainment. Fashion, music and dancing were essential ingredients of the Cremorne experience. People came to Cremorne for its light, popular music and, in turn, these dances and tunes sold Cremorne's image to an extended public. Each season there were new versions of songs and dances to attract visitors to the dancing platform, or to sell to domestic audiences in the form of sheet music. The cover of the sheet music for the *Cremorne Galop* embodies all the elements of the visual iconography of Cremorne in the early 1860s (fig. 45). The image of the orchestra pagoda and dancing platform is placed in a roundel at the centre of the sheet. The scene is framed by tall trees and the shadowy figures of dancers and a couple of swells. In the middle, the familiar form of the illuminated orchestra stands out below a full moon, completing the swirling scene of movement and romance. Supporting the roundel, left and right, and forming a circle around its border, are the distinctive forms of the Cremorne cut-glass lamps and drops, suggesting that the scene of the dancing at their centre is the most glittering illumination of all. The background to the roundel is dominated by the ornate lettering of the title and the name of the composer, and all the other available space is filled with colour and elaborate scrolling, recalling the rich mêlée of styles in the Gardens themselves.

Illustrated sheet music had been sold in England since the seventeenth century. With the introduction of lithography in the nineteenth century, illustrated covers became more complex and a greater 'selling point' for the music inside. At first the lithographed sheets were hand-coloured, but with the development of chromolithography in the late 1830s music publishers were able to use this technique to produce coloured illustrations more cheaply and in greater numbers than had been possible before.[91] Sheet music was sold from the publisher's shop and from the specialist music shops that spread throughout London in the mid-nineteenth century. The windows of the music shops were coated in these covers, so designs were made to be arresting, to stand out and to command attention. Like the managers of Cremorne, therefore, the cover artists sought novelty; images that would advertise themselves and sell. The potential market for the music sheets was large, partly as a result of the introduction of the upright piano and the increased ownership of pianos within the homes of the middle classes from the 1840s onwards.[92] People could purchase the latest waltzes, quadrilles and polkas for performance in their own parlours; they could also take home with them an image of Cremorne for domestic consumption. Sheet-music covers were a direct product of new forms of technology, the growth of urban leisure and the primacy of the visual in the formation of mass markets. In these respects, the illustrated covers and Cremorne had much in common and promoted each other. The music covers drew on the reputation of the Gardens to sell copies, but they also recommodified Cremorne for home consumption. Illustrated covers sold music and dancing, sound and movement, through the visual image, and it is in these images, more than in any other form of visual representation, that the meanings of Cremorne are most powerfully conveyed.

Every season the orchestra at Cremorne played new polkas and galops which the music publishers remarketed on the streets of the city. The galop was probably the simplest dance ever introduced on a dance-floor, requiring a couple to dash down the room, with only the occasional turn. The polka was also a fast and energetic dance, which was adapted from a folk dance and brought to London from Paris.[93] These were the dances of Cremorne, which kept its visitors on the crystal platform during the summer nights. The *Al Fresco Polka* takes the viewer to the steps of the dancing-platform, to the brink of the crystal circle (fig. 46). The surrounding trees and detailed depiction of the lights and dancing area sell the experience of outdoor, evening dancing to a homebound public. Seen here, the polka seems sufficiently polite and restrained to accommodate in a bourgeois parlour. With the cover of the *Cremorne Quadrilles*, the view is on the platform itself, from amongst the dancers (fig. 47). The quadrille was a set dance, with a range of figures that could be used in different combinations. Many of the figures involved changing partners and one of the most popular finales was known as 'The Flirtation', in which the men moved round the floor and danced with each of the women in turn. Concanen's cover for *Marriott's Cremorne Quadrilles* freezes the movement during an exchange of partners in one of the set figures. At the centre, a man and a woman are stopped dead during the moment in which they pass each other and look over their shoulders to exchange a glance. The quadrille encodes the fleeting moment of the street encounter, the flirtatious exchange of looks with a stranger, into the moves of a fashionable dance;

45    Alfred Concanen, music sheet cover *Cremorne Galop*, by Frank Musgrave, *c.*1862. Chromolithograph. The Royal Borough of Kensington & Chelsea Libraries and Arts Service.

46　T. Packer, music sheet cover *Al Fresco Polka*, by C. C. Amos, *c.*1862. Chromolithograph. The Royal Borough of Kensington & Chelsea Libraries and Arts Service.

47  Alfred Concanen, music sheet cover *Marriott's Cremorne Quadrilles, c.*1862. Chromolithograph. The Royal Borough of Kensington & Chelsea Libraries and Arts Service.

48   Phoebus Levin, *The Dancing Platform at Cremorne Gardens*, 1864. Oil on canvas, 66.2 × 107.5 cm.
Courtesy of the Museum of London.

49   Phoebus Levin, *In Cremorne Gardens*, n.d. Grisaille, 45.7 × 62.3 cm. Christie's South
Kensington sale catalogue, 5 October 1989, no. 164. Photo: Courtesy of the Museum of London.

the music cover then completes the process and fixes this ephemeral experience into
the permanent form of the printed illustration. Dancing at Cremorne choreographed
a performance of modern street behaviour; sheet music turned this play-acting into
an icon of contemporary gender relations.

  Respectability in the 1860s was up for grabs; there were different definitions of
what constituted respectable behaviour and of the limits to acceptable public entertainment. Cremorne bred confusion as to the manners and the identities of its visitors. In a satire on the naivety of country visitors, one light-hearted journal published
a sham letter from a female visitor, to her sister in the provinces: 'Ladies don't dance
here, Mr H tells me, or at least only those who belong to the *dummy mund*, whatever that may be.'[94] Did respectable women dance at Cremorne or didn't they? Would
Amelia Roper have danced a quadrille with an unknown gentleman? How many
ways might different visitors interpret the status and identity of the men and women
on and around the dancing platform? High art came up with one relatively unambiguous response to these questions. Phoebus Levin's painting of the dancing platform at Cremorne is a rare example of a fine art treatment of this subject (fig. 48).
In Levin's representation of the scene, the central female figures are sexually aggres-

50   Phoebus Levin, *In Cremorne Gardens*, n.d. Grisaille, 45.7 × 62.3 cm. Christie's South Kensington sale catalogue, 5 October 1989, no. 164. Photo: Courtesy of the Museum of London.

sive and their behaviour indecorous. In the top left-hand corner, a woman located in one of the upper supper-rooms throws a bouquet of flowers to a man below, while her male companion pours the contents of his glass down on to him. In the centre middle-ground, a woman leans over the railings of the dancing platform and knocks off a man's hat with the handle of her umbrella. In the foreground group, a woman gestures with her fan to a man who whispers behind his hand to a companion. In the far right corner, a woman, seated at a table amongst the trees, smiles over her shoulder at the man behind her, and, at a nearby table, a woman slumps in her chair while a waiter pours her another drink. The men and women involved in these anecdotal vignettes represent the wild, illicit Cremorne. Elsewhere in the scene, however, identities become more obscure and behaviour shades off into what might be regarded as legitimate within the context of a night at Cremorne. In two sketches by Levin, related to this painting, the broader style seems to promote a coarser interpretation of the subject. The sketch of the dancing platform is reasonably close to the composition of the central section of the finished painting, although details such as the kissing couple at the table on the left are added (fig. 49). The second sketch represents a scene elsewhere in the Garden, probably near the Grotto (fig. 50). Here, there is a motley crowd of beggars, invalids and diverse other visitors. On the right, a woman breast-feeds her baby; behind her a man leans over to kiss a woman behind her fan. A beggar on crutches solicits a passing gentleman and a woman gives a drink to a man in an invalid chair. Of the many Cremornes circulating in the public imaginary, which Cremorne is this? It is as though the satirical prints of Vauxhall in the eighteenth century have been dragged into the mid-nineteenth century, where they have taken on some of the forms of the Victorian pleasure garden, while retaining aspects of an earlier space and of a different aesthetic. It is hardly surprising that this image did not become the model for the painting; it is a far too uncomfortable and illegible social scene for public exhibition.

Cremorne was a mutable social space. To an extent, it gave people what they wanted to find. It was part of the moral geography of 'fast' London. It was on the circuit of night-spots in bachelors' guides to the city and it turned up regularly in fast-life fiction and journalism.[95] William Stephens Hayward, the author of a number of cheap, risqué 'yellow-back' novels, set the dramatic climax of *London by Night* in Cremorne, with a slanging match between his fallen heroine and her former lover.[96] Cremorne was firmly on the rounds of fictional 'fast' London, where it symbolised a particular kind of modish and indulgent masculinity and an uncontrolled, illicit femininity. This cultural discourse was frequently re-presented in the texts of social investigators. In 1872 Hippolyte Taine claimed to have seen blatant prostitution at a visit to Cremorne: 'the women are harlots . . . and sometimes, in the crowd, they raise terrible cries – the cries of a screech-owl.'[97] Curiously, however, when William Acton, one of the most influential writers on prostitution in the period, visited Cremorne to look for prostitution, he could not find it. Acton dedicated his medical career to the cause of state regulation of prostitution and the creation of a scientific investigation of the subject. His account of Cremorne in a chapter on the 'Haunts of Prostitutes' is an unusual one and expresses something of the illegibility that this space presented to contemporaries. He starts his report with somewhat conventional praise of the beauty of the gardens and the pleasant mix of the crowd in attendance, but then he reminds his readers (and himself) of the purpose of his visit and that he must concentrate on the subject of prostitution. He sets the scene for a visit: it is a pleasant July evening, approaching the time when the character of the crowd begins to change: 'As calico and merry respectability tailed off eastward by penny steamers, the setting sun brought westward Hansoms freighted with demure immorality in silk and fine linen.'[98] There is a shift in class as well as in moral identities here; the jolly, lower middle-class visitors of daytime Cremorne are replaced by the expensively dressed crowds of the night-time Gardens. It is a strange juxtaposition, however, between 'merry respectability' and 'demure immorality' and this image of the grim, determined crowd on the dancing platforms recurs throughout Acton's descriptions. He searches Cremorne for noise, debauchery and bad manners, but finds a peculiar stillness that not even the music of the band is able to penetrate. There is no impropriety and little drinking; there is instead a well-behaved, sober crowd (p. 18). Acton is cautious about classifying the women; at one moment he calls them 'prostitutes more or less *prononcées*', but he also comments on their 'pretty and quiet dressing'. Finally, he hedges his bets and concludes:

Of the character of the female visitors – let me always say *with some exceptions* – I could have little moral doubt, but it was clear enough that self-proclamation by any great number of them was out of the question. It was open to the male visitors to invite attention and solicit acquaintance (p. 18, original emphasis).

The emphasis that Acton places on the exceptions lays open his uncertainty about the moral identities of the women. If they respond to male attention perhaps they are prostitutes; or, perhaps they represent a bold new type of metropolitan femininity; women who dare, rather than women who sell sex. Acton abandoned his visit to Cremorne Gardens and the reader is left with a curiously hesitant and unresolved account of prostitution, but a highly suggestive evocation of the multiplicity of social styles and behaviours in the new leisure spaces of mid-Victorian London.

Cremorne had enemies: moralists and magistrates, local residents and government officials, who, at various moments, formed uneasy allegiances to curb the pleasures and restrict the hours of Cremorne. The charges against Cremorne varied according to the objectives and agendas of the groups and individuals involved. It was morally corrupting; it was a public nuisance; it brought down the surrounding property prices; it was a waste of space. The first attack came at the end of the 1857 season, during which the 'crystal' dancing platform had been opened, with huge success, to the public. The Chelsea Vestry presented the first of many annual petitions against the renewal of Cremorne's licences and called for earlier closing times.[99] Although this action had been initiated by complaints from local residents, the Vestry found itself in the awkward position of having publicly to reassure other ratepayers that it was not trying to force the closure of the Gardens, but simply to secure their greater regulation. In court, Mr Simpson, the manager, pointed out to magistrates that he had invested £30,000 in the improvement of the Gardens, that he was the largest ratepayer in the parish and had made a substantial contribution to the 'Indian fund'. The case against Cremorne failed; it was found that it did not constitute a public nuisance and its licence was renewed. *Punch* magazine celebrated a temporary victory in 'The Battle of Cremorne', but pointed out to its readers that Mr Punch had no experience of the gardens after midnight: 'Any person with the duties of life to do – we don't speak of idle Swells, War Ministers, Members of the Metropolitan Central Board, and other useless beings – must be up at eight o'clock, to be well through his hearty breakfast at nine.'[100] *Punch* places politicians and the magistracy amongst the worldly crowd of late-night Cremorne and thus further compromises the political and moral landscape of contemporary popular leisure. The court officials who decided the future of Cremorne might well be participants in the very pastimes that they were being called upon to combat.

For Cremorne, it was a holding operation, rather than a final victory and moral campaigners continued to create the cultural conditions that made further attacks inevitable. The evangelical writer J. Ewing Ritchie, pointed out that it was the beauty and gentility of the gardens that made them so dangerous: 'they dance along the path to ruin with flowers and music.'[101] Young men who might shrink from entering a gin-shop are seduced by the superficial charms and propriety of Cremorne. The illuminations, the fireworks and the gaslit paths turn the gardens into a fairyland that enchants and corrupts 'inflammable youth' (p. 190). Ritchie's evocation of the male

visitors to Cremorne varies enormously from the late crowds of professional legislators imagined by Mr Punch. They are the new clerical classes of the metropolis;
working in city and warehouse offices and with money to spend, but without the
character to recognise or resist temptation.

Masculinity at Cremorne was confusing and problematic. It represented in micro-
cosmic form, the dazzling range of types that could be seen at any time on the streets
of the city. Cremorne drew the aristocrat and the clerk, the paterfamilias and the
rowdy drunk, each keen to pursue his own objectives and pleasures.

The city streets produced new types of masculine identities, which drew on earlier
forms and styles, but which were articulated according to a different economic and
social register. If the emblematic male figure of the early nineteenth century was the
'dandy' – the aristocratic frequenter of prostitutes and low-life entertainment – then
the emblematic masculinity of mid-nineteenth-century London was the 'lounger',
or 'swell'.[102] The term 'swell' was first used to define a form of masculinity in the
early nineteenth century, when it was used to describe a gentleman of the upper
classes with a taste for smart or fashionable dressing. The term soon took on connotations of a swaggering, showy manner, but gradually, by mid-century, its meaning
changed to a flashily dressed person who apes a higher social position than he actually occupies.[103] Like his predecessor, the dandy, the swell indulges an extravagant
taste for clothes and accessories; he exhibits a lazy informality and is liable to flout
conventional manners and behaviour. But in the 1860s his class identity is unstable;
he could be an aristocrat *manqué*, a middle-class professional, or an upstart clerk, and
this was just one of the problems of masculinity at Cremorne.

The drunken swell is one of the iconic conventions of the mid-Victorian city and
urban entertainment. Moralists and advocates of rational recreation argued that men
were most at risk from purposeless leisure and amusement and that it was male behaviour in the pleasure gardens, as much as female behaviour, that called for regulation.[104] The issue came to a climax at Cremorne in 1863, when there was a 'riot' on
the night of the famous horse race, the Oaks. A group of 'young gentlemen' stormed
and wrecked one of the bars near the dancing platform and a number were caught
and prosecuted. A long court case followed, and finally the jury found all the men
guilty of riotous behaviour.[105] This was exactly the kind of publicity that Cremorne
needed to avoid; it fuelled the campaigns of its enemies and cemented the compelling association of Cremorne with a brash new form of metropolitan masculinity. There is an exquisite irony to be gained from the fact that one of the most
attentive reporters of the 1863 riot was that inveterate 'lounger' George Augustus
Sala, in his weekly columns for the *Illustrated London News*.

The illustrated cover of the music to *The Cremorne Polka* is a celebration of the
Cremorne swell (fig. 51). Three fashionably dressed men link arms and, with their
backs turned to the platform, perform an elegant, drunken saunter towards the
louche, bearded gentleman seated on the right. They seem involved in their own
self-conscious display, with their bodies and behaviour as much part of the spectacle as the dancers in the crystal circle. The polka is dedicated to that symbol of
entrepreneurial masculinity, E. T. Smith Esq., manager of Cremorne. The fast young
Cremorne gentleman became a stock character in popular songs of the period. In

51    Alfred Concanen, music sheet cover *The Cremorne Polka*, *c*.1862. Chromolithograph. The Royal Borough of Kensington & Chelsea Libraries and Arts Service.

52   J. Hamerton, music sheet cover *As Good and a Great Deal Better*, *c.*1862. Chromolithograph. The Royal Borough of Kensington & Chelsea Libraries and Arts Service.

the theatre at Cremorne, variety performers would perform songs enacting the social indeterminacy of the Gardens. In direct competition with the increasing number of specialist music halls springing up in central London, the Cremorne theatre employed rising stars such as Harry Wall to perform hit songs such as *As Good and a Great Deal Better* (fig. 52). The song tells the story of a man who goes to Cremorne, meets a pretty woman, gets drunk and proposes to her. He believes she is an heiress because her address is in Belgrave Square, but the next day he discovers she is a maidservant and he has to pay her to avoid Breach of Promise. The final verse warns:

> So mind all fast young gentlemen, who journey to Cremorne,
> Or any other gardens, or where crinoline is worn,
> Do not propose to wed strange girls, however well they dress,
> Or else like me you perhaps may get in such another mess,
> Be sure you know her station well, before you say you'll wed her,
> A little care is just as good, as good and a great deal better.[106]

The humour is predicated on the young man getting drunk and appearances not being what they seem. The illustration shows an elegant, well-dressed woman and the hero of the song so drunk he can hardly stand.

The 1860s was a critical period in the formation of masculine identities and this had a direct impact on the reputation and regulation of Cremorne. As Gareth Stedman Jones has argued in relation to the late 1860s, the music-halls were the natural habitat of the new metropolitan masculinities. The extension of the franchise in 1867 and the growth of a well-paid working population, produced an audience of 'socially indeterminate single young men', who consumed the pleasures of popular entertainment and who, in turn, became the subjects of acts by leading performers.[107] Stedman Jones suggests that this mass of young men was made up of ' "linen drapers' assistants". "counter jumpers", "city clerks", or "penniless swells" '. The situation at Cremorne in the 1860s was more complicated than this. The men at the Pleasure Gardens certainly included young working men, but they were only one constituency within a genuinely diverse set of economic and social groupings. There were swells, but they were not necessarily penniless and there were professionals, who might subsequently end up adjudicating the renewal of a music or dancing licence. During the summer nights at Cremorne, these and many other types mixed together in the grounds, where they misconstrued the identities of the women in the company. This was what the enemies of Cremorne hated about the place; it was better off closed down.

The most effective way to put a stop to the activities at Cremorne was to intervene in its licences. Each year at the end of the season the manager had to apply to the magistrates at the Middlesex Sessions to renew the licences for music and dancing. This procedure became the focus for alliances of moralists, residents and magistrates, who campaigned against the amusements at Cremorne. During the eighteenth century licences were fairly wide in their scope and did not differentiate particular activities.[108] By the middle of the nineteenth century individual licences were issued for specific activities, such as the sale of alcohol and the provision of music or dancing, which enabled a far more nuanced and sensitive control of the spaces of leisure.

In 1860 the Middlesex Sessions considering the renewal of entertainment licences, received another petition from members of the Chelsea Vestry opposing the late opening hours at Cremorne.[109] After midnight, the petition claimed, prostitutes and crowds of men caused unreasonable noise and disturbance in the surrounding streets and, as a result, the value of property was lowered and many houses were left empty. Simpson denied the allegations and declared in his application that the Gardens were often closed at midnight, that there were no rows, and that Cremorne was the resort of respectable local families. On this occasion the judges agreed to the renewal of Cremorne's licences, but as the 1860s progressed, opposition to the Gardens intensified and became more frequent.

There can be no doubt that the growth in concern about the nature and conduct of public urban entertainment in the second half of the 1860s was, in part, brought about by the development of the music-halls. The range of entertainments on offer at the music-halls could not be contained within the traditional categories of leisure space, such as theatre, pub or restaurant, and demanded new forms of classification and regulation. In 1866 a Select Committee was convened to examine the question of theatrical licences and regulations. One of its main concerns was to define the specific activities carried on within different places of entertainment and to differentiate the functions of the music halls and the theatres. Many witnesses associated with the leisure industry were called before the Committee, including E. T. Smith, manager of Cremorne and associated with such leading West End theatres as Her Majesty's and the Haymarket. Not surprisingly, Smith was keen to defend these more traditional theatres from encroachment by music-halls, and criticised the indiscriminate granting of licences to the new venues. The novelty of the music-halls was that they combined under a single roof eating, drinking, smoking and live performances. No respectable performer, Smith claimed, would work in these conditions and, as a result, the music-hall stage acts were offensive and immoral. Moreover, the metropolitan music-halls did not fall within the jurisdiction of the Lord Chamberlain, who supervised, licensed and censored the major London theatres. At present, therefore, the only way to regulate music-hall performances was to withhold the licences for music and dancing, or for selling spirits.

Cremorne presented a particularly fascinating case to the Committee. It had a licensed theatre, it provided music and dancing, and it sold alcohol and food. The critical factor, however, which differentiated it from the promiscuous blending of functions in the music halls, was the demarcation of space and the separation of activities within the Gardens. The Committee questioned Smith at length and in detail about the locations and proximity of different activities within the Gardens.[110] His responses – occasionally brief, always defensive – present an alternative spatial conceptualisation of Cremorne; one that is predicated on prevailing licensing laws and the growing association of moral regulation with sites of urban entertainment. A Committee member inquired what the first theatrical performance of the season is to be. A ballet, Smith replied. Where will it be performed? In the theatre. How close is the theatre to the dancing platform? Close by. Are there drinking, smoking and eating at Cremorne? Yes, but only in specified areas and not in the theatre. The Committee then turned its attention to the private supper boxes overlooking the dancing platform. The question that most exercised the members of the Committee was whether or not the occupants of the boxes were visible from the ground. Within minutes of questioning, the issue had turned from the conduct of licences to the moral behaviour of the public at Cremorne. Smith countered the suggestion that the supper boxes at Cremorne were the equivalent of Parisian *cabinets*, stating unequivocally: 'I had them built so that everybody could see into them, and so that the magistrates could see that there was nothing immoral possible that the police could not see.'[111] Concealed spaces, or spaces whose functions are multiple or indeterminate were those that troubled the Select Committee. Cremorne at night offered an abundance of brilliant amusements, punctuated with hidden obscure retreats. In the context of the 1866 inquiry, Smith must surely have realised that Cremorne would continue to be the focus of persistent official attention and that his problems were just beginning.

Smith's retirement from the management of Cremorne in 1869 was, therefore, a well-timed move. The new lessee, John Baum, spent much of the 1870s repelling sustained attacks by opponents of Cremorne and fighting to maintain a viable reputation for the Gardens. From 1870 sections of the Chelsea Vestry renewed their

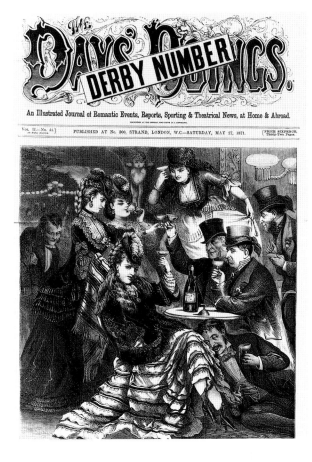

53    'The Derby Night at
Cremorne – Keeping It Up',
*Days' Doings*, 27 May 1871,
p. 273.

campaign to close Cremorne and contested the renewal of its licences on an almost
annual basis. In this atmosphere Baum had to be especially careful about the public
representation of Cremorne. Derby night had always been especially lively at Cremorne. In 1871 the *Days' Doings* carried on its front page an illustration of the crowd
at Cremorne on Derby night (fig. 53). It shows a table near the dancing platform
and a group of gentlemen and extravagantly dressed women drinking and toasting
each other. The accompanying article vividly describes the atmosphere in the Gardens
that night; it is especially 'fast' and crowded and has drawn together all the revellers
of the metropolis. The men are drunk, the women are courtesans and the place has
an air of carnival about it.[112] The *Days' Doings* was a humorous, sometimes risqué,
journal for a middle-class readership. The paper cost threepence and could be bought
by subscription or by single copies from newsagents and railway stations. Like Cremorne, its aims were novelty, sensation and amusement and, like Cremorne, it also
had enemies. Smith and Son, one of the largest retail chains of bookstalls, refused to
sell the journal and the *Leeds Mercury* was one of a small number of regional newspapers that refused to advertise it.[113] So what did it mean to have an image of a
drunken, immoral Cremorne on the front page of a journal like the *Days' Doings* in
1871? In the same issue the paper carried a short article on its inside pages, report-

ing that the management of Cremorne favoured the engraving, but noted that the drunken man slumped under the table would not be allowed in the Gardens in that condition.[114] This brief response suggests how nervous Baum was about Cremorne's public image. In the context of increased opposition and regulation, any hint of impropriety could fuel the case against Cremorne.

The *Days' Doings* was a tireless and vigorous supporter of Cremorne in the early 1870s. In 1871 Canon Cromwell, the principal of St Marks' Training College, which stood almost opposite the entrance of Cremorne, joined allies on the Chelsea Vestry to mount a concerted campaign against the renewal of Cremorne's licences. Their petitions found sympathetic magistrates at the Middlesex Sessions and the licences were refused. The *Days' Doings* raged against Canon Cromwell and the moral hypocrisy of the magistrates.[115] Other licences had also been refused that year and the *Days' Doings* attacked this new severity and intolerance towards popular entertainment. It imagined a world constrained by the refusal of licences, 'If the Autumnal Equinox Does Not Take Care What It Is About the Diddlesex Dogberries Will Remove Its Licences', and the dismal future of Cremorne if the moralists and magistrates had their way.[116] One engraving pictures Cremorne 'Under Future Regulations' (fig. 54). The unattractive and disapproving figures of vestrymen, magistrates and their wives stand at the entrance of Cremorne, appalled by the unac-

54    'Cremorne As It Will Be Under Future Regulations. "No Gentleman Can Be Admitted Unless Accompanied by a Nurse Holding a License [sic] from the Middlesex Bench of Magistrates"', *Days' Doings*, 28 October 1871, p. 216.

55 'A New Occupation for Reverend Preceptors. – What We May Expect to See in the Neighbourhood of Cremorne. "There Shall Be At Least One Place Secure from the Inroads of Women."', *Days' Doings*, 11 November 1871, p. 352.

companied figure of a heavily draped and veiled woman. Notices declare the rules and regulations of the Gardens under the new regime, including no dancing and no flirting. In this environment, the cut-glass drops of the dancing platform in the background symbolise the end of pleasure, rather than its invitation.

There was, undoubtedly, a crackdown on forms of popular urban culture in the early 1870s and Cremorne was only one of the victims. Loose groupings of private anti-vice societies, local officials and moralists succeeded in forcing through restrictions that made the continued existence of a number of institutions untenable.[117] At the beginning of 1872 the *Days' Doings* succumbed to a campaign against immorality in illustrated literature and was forced to reinvent itself for a few last issues as *Here and There*. One of the first issues carried a letter from 'The Ghost of the "Days' Doings"', warning of the threat posed to popular entertainment by the prudery of aldermen, ministers and police inspectors. Dancing is banned at Cremorne, the Alhambra and the Holborn Assembly Rooms, for this is 'the gospel according to the nineteenth century moralists'.[118] A few months later Cremorne's licences were again refused.

It is mistaken, however, to see the campaign against the Gardens in these years as motivated solely by moral values. In 1871, following the refusal of Cremorne's licences, the *Days' Doings* ran an article that identified another element in the campaign: 'Cremorne for years was an isolated spot, until speculating builders leased the ground adjacent at a small rental, ran up rows of houses, and now complain of the very nuisance to which they have come'.[119] There was a powerful economic argument against the continued existence of Cremorne. Like Vauxhall before it, Cremorne had started life on the outskirts of London, but as the city grew so the nature of the location changed. By the 1870s Cremorne was occupying land that had acquired new value for housing; where revellers saw amusement, property developers saw a waste of space. An illustration in the *Days' Doings* inadvertently draws attention to this economic dimension (fig. 55). Reverend Cromwell is shown restraining two women, who are on their way to Cremorne. But at least as significant as the caricature of the round-bellied canon, or the familiar stereotypes of Cremorne femininity, is the land on which they are standing. It is empty and undeveloped and within a couple of miles of central London. This, as much as any moral campaign, was the reason for the end of Cremorne.

In 1873 a licence was granted for music only, and in 1874 the licence for dancing was also restored, but complaints about brothels in the vicinity of the Gardens continued to be made to the Vestry.[120] Cremorne survived through 1875 and 1876. In 1877 Baum once again applied for the renewal of his licences. While awaiting the outcome of this application he was informed that his tenancy at Cremorne would not be renewed as the landowner had decided to lay out the land for building. Baum withdrew his application. Facing huge debts and unpaid rates, the gas was cut off and Cremorne was closed. In its annual report the Vestry noted: 'Cremorne now "a thing of the past", and the site is being cleared for building purposes.'[121]

Cremorne was absorbed by the insatiable metropolis. The Gardens were a large, open space in the midst of a developing residential neighbourhood and, from this perspective, the land was unproductive. The avenues and lawns, supper boxes and dancing platform were more profitable laid out in eligible building lots. Moral campaigners thus fought the battle of Cremorne for property developers; a peaceful, reputable neighbourhood suited the interests of both the local clerics and the speculators.

# 5    *The Last of Cremorne*

In its final months Cremorne was the subject of two distinctive libel actions. The first case involved the unhappy manager of Cremorne, John Baum. At the end of 1876 a pamphlet was distributed around Chelsea, called *The Trial of John Fox, or Fox John, or the Horrors of Cremorne*.[122] The piece was signed 'A. B. Chelsea', who was discovered to be Alfred Brandon, minister of the Chelsea Baptist Chapel. The pamphlet, in verse form, was a crude attack on Cremorne – the 'nursery of every kind of vice' – and its manager. In the context of the recent complaints about brothels in the vicinity of the Gardens, Baum could not afford to ignore such a defamation and in May 1877, he took Brandon to court for libel. The backbone of Brandon's defence was that what he had written was true; that Cremorne was, indeed, a sink of immorality. To justify his position various witnesses were called, including a Cremorne waiter, to testify to the immoral conduct in the Gardens. Baum refuted these claims, arguing that Cremorne was a respectable establishment, in a decent neighbourhood. The jury found for Baum; they awarded him a farthing damages and he had to pay his own costs. It was a legal and moral victory for Baum but, in other respects, irreparable harm had been done. Daily newspapers reported the trial in detail, with the testimonies of Brandon's witnesses and their accusations of immorality and impropriety at Cremorne.[123] For Baum, facing large unpaid bills, a wary Vestry and a hostile landlord, the publicity of May 1877 must have been the final straw.

At precisely the same moment, another situation was developing that was to produce the second libel action involving Cremorne. In May 1877 James McNeill Whistler exhibited eight paintings at the inaugural exhibition of the Grosvenor Gallery in London, including *Nocturne in Black and Gold: The Falling Rocket*, a view of the nightly fireworks display at Cremorne Gardens (fig. 56). The image is dominated by the dark blues and greys of the night sky, which is flecked with the orange and yellow marks of the falling fireworks and the illuminated towers of the fireworks platform. It was not the first painting that Whistler had made of Cremorne; he was a regular frequenter of the Gardens in the early 1870s and it was the setting for several of his 'nocturnes' in this period.[124] The nocturnes are scenes of London at night. They are Whistler's painterly response to the aesthetics of the city's night illuminations; the moonlight, gaslight and fireworks that constituted the visual appeal of the modern metropolis after dark. In these paintings Whistler explored his artistic commitment to the primacy of formal and decorative values. Subject matter and narrative are subordinated in the interest of harmonious composition, and the title 'nocturne', with its musical connotations, was intended to draw attention to the abstract qualities of the art.[125]

Of the eight paintings exhibited by Whistler in the 1877 exhibition, *Nocturne in Black and Gold* was the only one that the artist was trying to sell, and its price was two hundred guineas. John Ruskin's response to Whistler's paintings was published in 1877, in a series of letters bearing the title *Fors Clavigera*. Letter 79, entitled 'Life Guards of New Life', includes Ruskin's remarks on the Grosvenor Gallery exhibition, the artists of the 'modern school' and his brief, but powerful, denunciation of Whistler:

> For Mr Whistler's own sake, no less than the protection of the purchaser, Sir Coutts Lindsay ought not to have admitted works into the gallery in which the ill-educated conceit of the artist so nearly approached the aspect of wilful imposture. I have seen, and heard, much of Cockney impudence before now; but never expected to hear a coxcomb ask two hundred guineas for flinging a pot of paint in the public's face.[126]

Whistler's reasons for suing Ruskin for this attack were complex. As Costas Douzinas has argued in his recent analysis of the action, libel cases are a gamble; they can bestow huge riches on the lucky plaintiff, but they can also incur much greater legal costs and financial ruin.[127] John Baum could have told Whistler this. Whistler's

56   James McNeill Whistler, *Nocturne in Black and Gold: The Falling Rocket*, 1875. Oil on wood, 60.3 × 46.6 cm. Gift of Dexter M. Ferry, Jr. Photograph © The Detroit Institute of Arts.

motives, however, were probably not just financial; a public hearing would also give him an excellent opportunity to present his aesthetic principles in a formal, public setting.

After a number of long delays, the trial finally took place in November 1878. The case is traditionally interpreted by art historians as a key moment in the history of modernism. In his defence of his paintings Whistler invoked the main tenets of modernism: artistic autonomy and liberation from the constraints of mimesis. But the subject of Cremorne was never entirely absent from the proceedings of the court. The trial was a contest of two opposing aesthetic theories and two contrasting and distinctive artistic reputations. Attorney General Holker, lead counsel for Ruskin, defended his client by appealing to the jury's common sense, as opposed to the incomprehensible and fantastic conceits of Whistler and his supporters. Holker invited the jury to join him on an imaginary tour of the Grosvenor exhibition; he overhears the facile comments of the female visitors in the gallery and then reaches the Cremorne nocturne: 'I do not know what the ladies would say to that, because it has an object they would not understand – I hope they have never been to Cremorne – (*Laughter*) – but men will know more about it.'[128]

In *Whistler v. Ruskin* Cremorne was being judged once again. Holker defended Ruskin and dismissed Whistler's work by invoking the male jury's shared cultural knowledge of Cremorne – the Cremorne that had been all over the papers during the weeks of the Grosvenor exhibition, as John Baum defended himself against the libels of Alfred Brandon. To see the relationship between the aesthetic debates generated by *Whistler v. Ruskin* and the definitions of popular urban culture surrounding Cremorne as one of coincidence is to reiterate the formalist values of Whistler's own aesthetic discourse.[129] The Gardens and the painting are both part of a conflict over cultural value in the period. And, in both cases, the law is called upon to adjudicate the question of cultural legitimacy. Whistler drew upon the image of Cremorne as an appropriate, morally ambiguous sign of metropolitan modernity for his own artistic project. Holker invoked the notoriety of Cremorne at night in order to interpellate the jury and to challenge the artistic credibility of Whistler. During the trial, Holker asked Whistler about the subject of *Nocturne in Black and Gold*:

> WHISTLER: It is a night piece and represents the fireworks at Cremorne Gardens.
> HOLKER: Not a view of Cremorne?
> WHISTLER: If it were called 'A View of Cremorne' it would certainly bring about nothing but disappointment on the part of the beholders. (*Laughter*) It is an artistic arrangement.[130]

The nocturne was not a view of Cremorne, but it was certainly about Cremorne. Within public discourse Cremorne was represented in terms of anecdote, character and incident. In Whistler's painting these are condensed to their visual essence, to the darkness and lights that were the enchantment of Cremorne by night.

After a few hours' deliberation the jury returned a verdict, giving a nominal victory to Whistler and damages of one farthing. Libel action proved an expensive business for both Whistler and Baum; but whereas the case had provided welcome publicity for the artist, it had result in damaging attention for the manager of the pleasure

57   'The Last of Cremorne Gardens. April 1878', in 'Papers Relating to the History of Cremorne Gardens, Chelsea. 1831–1878. Volume Two', p. 104. The Royal Borough of Kensington & Chelsea Libraries and Arts Service.

gardens. By the time *Whistler v. Ruskin* came to court Cremorne was closed. The Gardens were dismantled and cleared and an auction of goods was held on 8 April 1878 and on following days. Everything went on sale: mirrors, gas-burners and lamps, plants, trees, garden hoses, the dancing platform, and even 'a large balloon'.[131] The sixth day's sale included the auction of outside gas-lamps with reflectors 'as fitted to the trees', illuminations, statuary and fountains. Piece by piece, the fittings and decorations that had produced the magic of Cremorne were sold to the highest bidder. A cartoon from this period, 'The Last of Cremorne Gardens', commemorates the auctioning of Cremorne (fig. 57). A number of vignettes show the crowds wandering round the Gardens, viewing the lots and attending the sale. In the top right-hand corner there is the dancing platform and a contemplative gentleman whose thoughts are expressed in the caption: 'over the old campaigning ground.' In the bottom left-

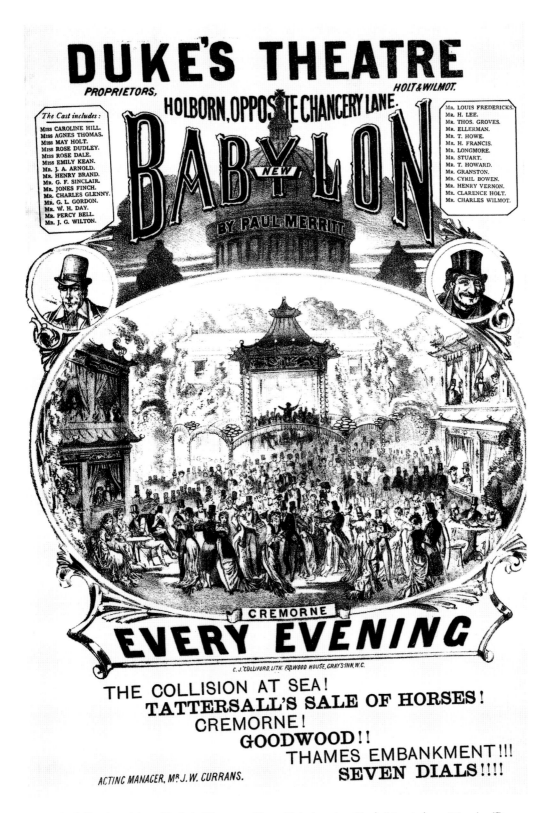

58   Playbill advertising 'Duke's Theatre. New Babylon by Paul Merritt', *c.*1882, in 'Papers Upon the History of Cremorne Gardens, Chelsea. 1840–1878', p. 101. The Royal Borough of Kensington & Chelsea Libraries and Arts Service.

hand corner there is a sale of theatrical props and in the foreground the stereotyped figures of two Jewish merchants. The ostentatious guzzlers of gas, the traders of 'Moses and Son', reappear in the last moments of Cremorne. The poignancy of the image is expressed in terms of the ignominy of the pleasure gardens' ending up in the hands of Jews.

Cremorne was a part of the popular culture and popular memory of mid-Victorian London. Its image symbolised the social and moral ambiguities, the thrilling spectacle of the modern metropolis. By the early 1880s, with houses built on its vacated site, Cremorne had become nothing but image, a stage-set in Paul Merritt's sensation drama *New Babylon* (fig. 58).[132] But this was nothing new; Cremorne had always been a set for the staging of modern identities and modern manners. Long after the disappearance of the physical fabric of the pleasure gardens, the gaslight, music and dancing of Cremorne were still on show 'every evening' to a public eager to share in its sensations and amusements.

# PART 3

# STREETS AND OBSCENITY

# Introduction

Obscenity was the brash, new product of Victorian London. For many legislators and moral campaigners in the period, indecent books and images were a form of cultural poison, deadly to those who came into contact with them and a threat to the very foundations of public order. Obscenity was, however, simply the most explicit and dangerous instance of the many new cultural forms that had emerged within the modern city. For those official and unofficial guardians of public morals, the metropolis had generated a distinctive and degraded form of mass commercial culture, which required new types of surveillance and regulation in order to bring it under control. The problem was not just one of the style and content of these cultural forms, but also concerned the nature of the public for the goods. Cheap literature and images cultivated a new, excited sensibility. They sold sensation and created dangerously motivated and suggestible audiences.

Young, working-class men were believed to be particularly vulnerable to the appeal of penny fiction and the crude performances played out in cheap theatres throughout the metropolis. Over-consumption of these forms of culture, it was claimed, had a direct and pernicious impact on public order, since the delinquent morality often celebrated in these texts fostered a restless and criminalised population. However, it was women, of all classes, who were seen to be particularly susceptible to the appeals of the *visual* image. Drawn by the pictures and illustrations displayed in shop windows, women easily entered a state of heightened daydream and fantasy, which utterly compromised the codes of respectable behaviour advocated for women on the streets of the city. Displays of mass-produced imagery were channels for unregulated fantasy and, within this context, obscene images might create not simply a criminalised audience but, more particularly, a sexualised one. Obscene displays concentrated the erotic possibilities of the city within specific sites of over-absorbed reverie.

The issue of obscenity came to represent a ganglion of concerns about contemporary metropolitan culture. It was cheap, produced on an unprecedented scale, could reach a mass and heterogeneous audience and had the capacity morally to degrade society. Obscenity was also a spatial problem. It was seen to originate in particular locations within the city, which were most resistant to the economic, social and aesthetic ideals of the modernisers. It was sold openly and publicly in shops and on the streets and was part of the visual environment of the city. Most worryingly, obscene images were conspicuously displayed in print-shop windows throughout the metropolis, thus enabling a new form of casual visual consumption among the crowds on the city streets. In the late 1850s and 1860s metropolitan government was driven by the concept of 'improvement'; the modernisation and embellishment of the fabric

Detail of fig. 59.

of the city, which would sweep away the filthy and crumbling passageways of old London and open it up to light and the circulation of traffic, people and goods. Obscenity was an obstacle in the path of improvement. It represented values and desires that were antithetical to those of the modernisers and improvers. The source of this corruption had to be tracked down and destroyed; the shops and streets from which obscene publications emanated needed to be identified and their nefarious trade ended. Coalitions of privately organised vice societies, legislators and officers of the metropolitan police force were created to remove the sites of obscenity from the metropolis. Vice society spies, police officers and members of parliament mingled with the rest of the public on the streets in front of the booksellers' and print-shop windows. Obscenity created a spatial economy in the city, which drew together into a dangerous proximity the centres of official power and their transgressive other. The juridical pursuit of obscenity through the alleys and courts of mid-Victorian London generated a highly focused public contest over contemporary concepts of space, culture and identity.

## *I      Moral Poisons*

On 11 May 1857 John Campbell, the Lord Chief Justice, spoke out in the House of Lords against the trade in obscene publications. The occasion was a debate on legislation to regulate the indiscriminate sale of poisons. Seizing this opportunity, Campbell informed the Lords that a few days earlier he had presided over a trial that had convinced him that there were far greater dangers to society than those presented by the misuse of chemicals:

> he had learned with horror and alarm that a sale of poison more deadly than prussic acid, strychnine, or arsenic – the sale of obscene publications and indecent books – was openly going on. It was not alone indecent books of a high price, which was a sort of check, that were sold, but periodical papers of the most licentious and disgusting description were coming out week by week, and sold to any person who asked for them, and in any numbers . . . He trusted that immediate steps would be taken for stopping the sale of publications of so pestilential a character.[1]

The subject of the exchange was later recorded as 'Sale of Poisons and Poisonous Publications', and the image of obscenity as a social, moral and cultural poison clung tenaciously to subsequent debates on the subject, well into the twentieth century.[2] The power of poison as a metaphor for obscenity is that it describes a substance whose dangers may not be immediately apparent, but which destroys from the inside, as it is consumed. For Campbell, what was most horrifying and distinctive about the current situation was the scale of production and consumption. Obscenity was no longer something contained within the expensive and depraved tastes of collectors of licentious literature, but had become part of the printing revolution; utterly promiscuous and without limits, sold in any number and to anyone who wanted it. It was no longer a small-scale problem, but had become a modern plague.

Within a matter of weeks Campbell again used the opportunity of a Lords debate on the poisons bill, this time to declare his intention to take legislative action against obscenity. The sale of these 'moral poisons' was, he claimed, on the increase. It was flagrant and destructive and, on behalf of the Society for the Suppression of Vice, he had presented a petition to the House of Lords demanding an end to this nefarious trade.[3] The context for the subsequent introduction of Campbell's bill was that in the mid-nineteenth century, culture was becoming one aspect of the problem of metropolitan modernity. It was becoming a thing of the city streets and a matter of public order, and obscene publications crystallised these partially formed fears concerning cultural consumption and public morals. The loose coalition of an innately conservative, but occasionally liberal law lord and a privately run society for the regulation of public morals, typifies the provisional alliances that were formed in this period in order to push legal restraints on mass urban culture through Parliament. There was limited consensus in relation to both the need for legislation and the definition of obscenity. In fact, the 'airing' of the introduction of an obscenity law within the context of a debate on chemical poisons reveals the perplexing problem for legislators of cultural definition. Both bills called for the categorisation of harmful and harmless substances. Some chemicals could be beneficial in small quantities; the harm arose as a side-effect of being absorbed in excess. Campbell's obscene publications were, by definition, consumed in huge numbers; there was no possibility of social benefit from these degraded forms. The problem then arose, when was a text or image classifiable as obscene, rather than as cheap, nasty and plentiful? At what point did a publication become a moral poison, which must be removed from circulation, as opposed to a regrettable, but legitimate, part of modern metropolitan culture? There were no absolute and final answers to these questions; instead the boundary between legitimate and illegitimate culture was constantly reconceptualised within the context of new perceptions of urban space and public behaviour.

The mid-Victorian metropolis was an indulgent host to new forms of visual and literary culture. Technical developments in printing and the introduction of photography; fiscal changes to newspaper and periodical publishing; new forms of spectacular advertising; the rapid expansion of audiences and readerships; and the diversification of sites of urban leisure and entertainment all impacted on the Victorian city in the middle decades of the nineteenth century. The experience of the city streets was shaped, in part, by these new aspects of urban culture. Culture had been revolutionised; it was public, visible and unavoidable, but it was also powerful and potentially dangerous. For critics nostalgic for a slower and more containable world of high art, the commercial street culture of the 1850s and 1860s was an assault on the senses. Ugly images, poorly made, bombarded unsuspecting pedestrians from all directions. Culture was no longer a question of public edification; it had become a public nuisance.

The problem with the new technologies was that they had been harnessed to low, popular taste, and photography seemed like a good case in point. Photography was not innately, or necessarily base, but had been vulgarised by mediocre practitioners, greedy to secure a remunerative market on the streets of the city. Mass-produced imagery – whether photographic or engraved – offered the potential benefit of widening access to visual culture and of bringing art to a broader public. More often, however, it seemed that this noble aim had been perverted by self-interest and aesthetic indifference. For purists such as John Ruskin, photography could never be art. The value of art lay in its expression of the personality and the perception of the human soul, and this distinguished art from the products of all mechanical processes.[4] For Ruskin there was a clear and indisputable hierarchy of technical forms, based on the degree to which mechanical means detracted from the hand of the artist. Pure line engraving was 'the only means by which entire refinement of intellectual representation can be given to the public'.[5] This type of manual engraving was thus superior to any photographic image: 'a square inch of man's engraving is worth all the photographs that were ever dipped in acid . . . only it must be man's engraving; not machine's engraving.'[6] Photography, for Ruskin, had its aesthetic qualities and its uses, but it could never be a work of art. A photograph of a landscape might transcribe the scene, but it was merely an inferior trace of nature. In Ruskin's writings, photography takes on the social and political conditions of the modern metropolis. London is a place where true art cannot thrive and photography is the city's inevitable and appropriate means of artistic expression: 'to a quiet heart, and healthy brain, and industrious hand, there is more delight and use, in the dappling of one wood-glade with flowers and sunshine, than to the restless, heartless and idle could be brought by a panorama of a belt of the world, photographed round the equator.'[7] Ruskin drew on a highly conventionalised language of city versus country to compare the peace, health and industry of nature and the agitation, disease and idleness of the town; but to this he added a visual and cultural register, in which the beauty of nature is contrasted with the meaningless spectacles of urban entertainment. The photographic panorama and its soulless, mass public represented, for Ruskin, the loss of value in the modern city.

Ruskin's lofty dismissal of metropolitan photography had its more popular expression in the leading articles of the daily newspapers. Editors and journalists railed against the inferior and squalid products with which the London public was bombarded. In one particularly irritable leader, the *Daily Telegraph* sniped at a variety of street nuisances, from oriental beggars and black street musicians, to swindlers, thieves and, the most recent form of nuisance, photography. The association of signs of empire and signs of low urban culture recurs in debates in this period concerning the cultural forms of the city. Often, the link is made to seem almost organic, as though the common factor is deeply embedded in the fabric of the metropolis and has generated both debased types of citizen and degraded forms of text and image. Or, perhaps, the implicit assumption is that these colonial intruders have created the conditions in which low culture thrives. These social outcasts of Britain's imperial project represent a throwback to primitive forms of street economy, which involve bartering and harassment and an exchange that is unpleasantly physical, as well as financial. Although the Lascars and Chinese are not explicitly blamed for the production of commercial street photography, the textual conjunction in this leading article poses an association between the trash of the empire and the refuse of the modern city, which is made repeatedly in press repudiations of the cultural environment of the metropolis.

According to the *Daily Telegraph*, mediocre photography had ousted the higher forms of art:

> First-class engravings and handsome lithographs are now almost entirely driven from our print-shop windows; their places are usurped by myriads of stereoscopic slides, showing us interesting duplicates of young ladies trying on crinoline petticoats, exhibiting their ankles to an undue extent while engaged in the arduous occupation of lacing their Balmoral boots, and washing or ironing fine linen. Stereoscopic vignettes . . . exhibiting variations of the domestic mangle and the homely ginger-beer and oyster-stall, will no doubt shortly supersede Turner's 'Venice' and Stanfield's 'Tilbury Port'.[8]

Photography caters to the common and the bathetically familiar. The great works of art of the British School are replaced by low-rate photographic genre scenes of the urban everyday. Print-shop windows, those art galleries of the street in the earlier part of the century, are now little more than lewd displays of clichéd soft porn. But this is only one aspect of the assault of street photography on the visual environment of the city. The photographs spill out of the containing frame of the window display and contaminate the buildings and the space of the street:

> Photographic 'artists' of the lowest grade – in other words, fellows without calling and without character, who have somehow obtained a camera and a few chemicals – have set up in the most populous streets, and in overpowering numbers, their 'operating rooms'. Their door-jambs are hideous with frames filled with vilely-executed photographs of men and women, of squalid and repulsive appearance; the practitioners are ignorant, coarse, and clumsy in manipulation; and the result is a collection of faces and figures that reminds us of the Chamber of Horrors at Madame Tussaud's.[9]

This is a world of ugliness, which spreads from the corrupt workshops of the 'quack' photographers, out on to the buildings and streets. This is not simply an aesthetic assault, however, for the trade uses violent physical assault to waylay pedestrians and to force them to become customers. The distinctions between passer-by and client disappears in the aggressive commercial tactics of the city streets. The article continues:

> Each operator's door has one sometimes two 'touters', men in sordid attire, and of threatening mien – unmitigated ruffians, in a word; in violence of language surpassing omnibus cads, in disgusting importunity equalling Irish beggars. These 'touters' hold tawdry frames in their hands, containing single prices, and they besiege the passers-by, now with entreaties, now with threats, to 'walk up and have their portraits taken' . . . We might smile at the squabbles of such riffraff, but it is impossible to smile at the disgusting language with which they too frequently salute the ears of females. It is no longer a joke, but a nuisance, when the Queen's highway is taken up, when we are jostled, and importuned, and delayed in our lawful business by a pack of impudent and foul-mouthed harpies.

Whatever the reality of running the gauntlet of the photographic touts on the crowded city streets, the article leaves no doubt about the intrusive nature of this new urban culture. This is not a space of quiet display and consumer choice, but of aggressive selling, forcing itself on passers-by and determining the nature and quality of the urban environment. For this reason, the question of culture swiftly moves to being an issue of public order and public safety; a matter not just of the production of ugly images, but of the maintenance of peace on the Queen's highway. Taken out of the hands of art critics and journalists, it requires the law to constrain the most uncontrolled manifestations of this public culture. As the century proceeded, the legal regulation of culture became increasingly enhanced and specialised; not just part of a package of clauses wrapped up in public order and police acts, it earned its own dedicated legislation in Lord Campbell's Obscene Publications Act of 1857.

The enormous expansion and diversity of cultural forms in the city created appalling problems of classification and judgement. Was an image of a woman, dressed only in undergarments and revealing her ankle, an appropriate object for legal intervention? Did it invite an artistic or a sexual gaze and how could such distinctions be guaranteed in the context of the city streets? Was this kind of image democratising art or corrupting morals? What was more certain was that the situation was exacerbated by the huge growth in audiences for these works and that this new expanded public was an urban phenomenon. In the first half of the nineteenth century stamp duty constituted a significant proportion of the price of newspapers. Its abolition in 1855 made possible new, lower levels of pricing and potentially larger audiences for the publications concerned. The abolition of the tax on paper in 1861 also contributed to the economic conditions that made possible the creation of mass circulations.[10] By the mid-nineteenth century the publishing industry was realising huge sales and readerships for particular texts and images. The expansion of this market, however, was not simply through an extension downwards to the less well-off, literate working classes; what was unprecedented about the public for mass culture in this period was its social diversity. As Patricia Anderson has observed in her study of popular culture from 1790 to 1860: 'Such a culture was never exclusively the experience of any one group or class, and for this reason "mass" must be understood to designate multiple social layers . . .'[11] Just as the city streets brought together heterogeneous groups within the entity of the urban crowd, so the new commercial publications gathered diverse social constituencies within the inclusive embrace of their readerships.

Legislators and moralists were torn between seeing these new forms of cheap, commercial culture as a social benefit or as a social harm. The creation of huge publics made texts and images potentially more influential than ever before, but these new audiences were unpredictable; it was unclear how they might respond to narrative, rhetoric, colour and design. The most vehement reactions came from the critics of the new mass culture, who deplored the quality and morality of the publications and warned of the dangers of an over-stimulated and uncontrollable public. According to one article, published in the *British Quarterly Review* in 1859, the huge expansion in cheap literature was one of the great wonders of the age, surpassing the invention of the steam engine, or the telegraph. The marvel lay in its being, unlike other 'discoveries', beyond scientific explanation; but this also constituted its enigma and danger: 'Cheap Literature . . . like the modern Babylon itself . . . no living man has ever been able completely to traverse . . . [it] has sprung up, with the mysterious fecundity of certain fungi, and . . . cannot be accounted for in its volume, variety and universality by any ordinary laws of production.'[12] The new literature shares the characteristics of the modern metropolis and here, the conventional evocation of London as a latter-day Babylon suggests not only the grandeur and scale of the biblical city, but also the Hebraic translation of Babylon as Babel, the site of linguistic confusion and unintelligibility. Modern metropolitan culture is sublime; its limits are not humanly knowable. Its emergence cannot be accounted for in technological terms; instead it is described as an organic entity that grows and spreads in the city streets, beyond the comprehension of measurable economic laws. The new literature is distinguished by its variety and, through this diversity, it has also become a universal feature of the modern city.

The article goes on to examine specific forms of this printed culture and, in particular, cheap, illustrated serial fiction. This form has, necessarily, to excite the curiosity and desire of the reader, to ensure that they buy each subsequent instalment. The narratives are violent, sinister and sensational and these qualities also characterise the accompanying illustrations: 'The art employed upon these pictures is proper to the subject. The effects are broad, bold and unscrupulous. There is an appropriate fierceness in the wild cutting and slashing of the block; and the letter-press always falls short of the haggard and ferocious expression of the engraving.'[13] Although neither text nor image is seen to have any reclaiming aesthetic qualities, the article suggests that there is something about the illustrations that more directly expresses the debased nature of the publication. The engraving technique is an enactment of the types of violence often described in the text. It is murderous and ecstatic and, appropriately, the result is an image that is 'haggard and ferocious', in other words, it has taken on the physical and human qualities of the criminal and the morally dissolute.

Writers and critics were aware of the special relationship between text and image in creating the appeal of the new, mass literature and of the specific and dangerous effectiveness of the visual image. Some years after the publication of the article in the *British Quarterly Review* and just following the passing of the 1867 Reform Act, the *Bookseller* analysed the current forms of 'Mischievous Literature'. In general, the article supported the liberal view that cheap publications were sensational, rather than immoral and doubted whether penny novels relating the adventures of highwaymen and robbers could influence the spread of juvenile crime. It was more concerned, however, about the effects of illustrated broadsheets, whose pernicious contents were exacerbated by being made visual:

> atrocities are rendered more atrocious by means of glaring woodcuts, wherein the worst features of the worst cases are brought before the eye, and rendered plain to the meanest capacities . . . These disgusting pictures of vice in all forms are printed on the outside page of each publication, and every Saturday the windows at which they are exposed are crowded with eager admirers.[14]

Visual images are immediate and involve little mediation by the viewer. They create the visual environment of the streets and can be consumed without purchase, as the audience is constituted around the shop windows where they are displayed. The power of the visual image lies in its immediacy and universality. Style is an expression of immoral content; line is violently drawn or incised and colour is lewd and vulgar.[15]

There can be no doubt that following the 1867 Reform Act, the pattern and nature of concern over the forms of urban culture changed. The extension of the franchise not only signalled an initial triumph of democracy over refined patronage, but, at a cultural level, it also threatened to produce a dangerous levelling out; an inclusion of new sections of society in cultural consumption and an unhealthy commingling of classes in the new forms such as the music-halls and through commercial street culture.[16] After 1867 the anxiety that cheap, commercial culture created a criminalised working-class population became fully installed in the Victorian imaginary. In a passing reference to the subject, the *Illustrated London News* claimed: 'Seldom is a precocious offender brought into the dock but evidence is given that, on searching him or his dwelling-place, a heap of foul fictions is found.'[17] Predictably enough, the books are described as 'moral poisons', the results of which are cities swarming with young criminals and prisons full to overflowing.

Social campaigner and journalist James Greenwood diverted much of his energy to exposing the influence of urban street culture on working-class crime, which he included among *The Seven Curses of London*, published in 1869. In Greenwood's view, the most dangerous time for working boys was between leaving work and going to bed; in other words, their hours of leisure. During this period the boys were prey to various forms of commercial street culture, which Greenwood ranked according to their degree of influence. Although penny fiction could incite an admiration for criminality, its influence was limited and non-existent for the illiterate. How much greater the influence of the visual image in its appeal to this vulnerable group of cultural consumers: 'In the shop window of the newsvendor round the corner, he sees displayed all in a row, a long line of "penny numbers", the mere illustrations pertaining to which make his heart palpitate, and his hair stir beneath his ragged cap.'[18] But this excitement pales at the prospect of seeing these sensational stories acted out in the penny 'gaffs', located throughout the poorer districts of London. In this context, the visual image is merely the advertisement to entice the public to pay to see the live theatrical performance and Greenwood imagined the exploitative proprietor listening at the entrance while an admiring crowd speculates: 'on the pleasures of the night as foretold in glowing colours on the immense placards that adorn the exterior of his little theatre.'[19] Once inside, the audience experiences and is drawn into the sensory phantasmagoria of the pantomimic show.

Greenwood's ranking of affectivity is achieved in terms of the degree of physical presence and proximity involved in the mode of representation. The written text is the most highly mediated and emotionally distant of the new mass cultural forms. The visual image produces a greater dissolution of the boundaries between the viewer and the viewed object; this distinction collapses, however, in the hectic physical performances and responses at the penny gaffs. The visual image stages the transition from mediation to dissolution; it, alone amongst the new forms of commercial culture, moves between interior and exterior, between the gaff, or shop, and the street. The visual image does not 'belong' to a single spatial category. It appears in interiors and in the liminal space of shop windows and its address extends to the city streets in the forms of placards and advertisements and through the wandering commercial exploits of the print hawkers and pedlars.

These were also the urban manoeuvres of obscene images, as they tracked a passage between interior and exterior sites of production and consumption. Henry Mayhew evoked something of the spatial multiplicity of the trade in obscenity in his account, in *London Labour and the London Poor*, of the street seller of sham indecent prints. That he should choose as his subject the seller of sham, rather than genuine obscenity, in itself suggests the complexity and extent of the business on the streets of London by the early 1860s. The street seller described his strategies to Mayhew:

> This street-seller's 'great gun', as he called it, was to make up packets, as closely resembling as he could accomplish it, those which were displayed in the windows of any of the shops I have alluded to. He would then station himself at some little distance from one of those shops, and, if possible, so as to encounter those who had stopped to study the contents of the window, and would represent – broadly enough, he admitted, when he dared – that he could sell for 6d. what was charged 5s., or 2s. 6d., or whatever price he had seen announced, 'in that very neighbourhood'.[20]

The deception is carried out by the street seller being close to, but not part of, the shop selling and displaying obscene publications. In this way, the seller draws on a sexualisation of space in the vicinity of the shop in order to carry out the hoax. It is as though the display of indecent images in shop windows creates a heightened condition of sexual responsiveness, which projects beyond the physical limits of the shop and out on to the city streets. In this environment, if the hawker's packets look as if they might contain the kinds of wares displayed in the shop windows, the punter may be willing to make a hasty purchase and the deception can be successfully concluded.

The spatial mobility of the trade in obscene images made it seem particularly hard to control and its regulation all the more urgent. It was, partly, in response to the spatial promiscuity of obscenity that a key clause in Campbell's Obscene Publications Act stated that, once proven to be obscene, the publications in question should be destroyed; that they should be withdrawn entirely and finally from circulation on the streets of the city. This was one commodity that the improvers did not want to see circulating freely in the metropolis; it had to be stopped and its chain of pernicious influence terminated. The importance of this legislative action was not simply the improvement of morals, but was also a matter of securing the urban environment and maintaining public order. This particular form of poison was not only fatal to moral values, but also destroyed social, political and economic standards. Reviewing the performance of the Act in 1868, over a decade after its introduction, the *Saturday Review* reminded its readers of the significance of obscenity legislation: 'It was not for the purpose of punishing obscenity that Lord Campbell's Act was passed, but because the sale of indecent books not only corrupted private morals, but led directly to breaches of public peace and order.'[21] Private morality, it would appear, might be contained without the intervention of the law; but once morality is defined as a public matter, it becomes an issue of social stability and a legitimate target for official action.

In spite of the association of obscenity with public disorder, it is likely that, without the vociferous campaigning of the Society for the Suppression of Vice, the passing of an obscenity act might have been postponed for some years. At an individual level, Lord Campbell tirelessly steered his legislation through the many stages of its parliamentary progress; but the driving force behind its creation was the Vice Society and its unceasing crusade against all forms of moral poison in modern metropolitan culture.[22] The Society for the Suppression of Vice was founded in London in 1802; its membership was drawn mainly from middle-class, Church of England London. Religious dissenters were ineligible to join and this policy, along with the Society's metropolitan focus, generated subsequent opposition from regional Nonconformists. M. J. D. Roberts has divided the activities of the Society into three main phases: its early years, shortly after its foundation, when it concentrated on issues relating to public standards, such as the observation of the Sabbath; the 1820s and early 1830s, when it was involved in a number of prosecutions against blasphemy, including the case against Richard Carlile; and a third period, from the late 1850s, when it campaigned against prostitution and acted as a pressure group on a range of subjects concerning culture and morality.[23]

Until the passing of Campbell's Obscene Publications Act, the Vice Society played a significant role in initiating private prosecutions for obscene libels. Moreover, as Roberts notes in his account of the passing of the Act, the Society had prepared draft obscenity legislation years before Campbell became involved in the issue and consulted with him on the drafting of his bill and kept up public agitation during its debate.[24] These were busy months for the Society, as it was also campaigning vigorously against London's 'great social evil', prostitution. Obscenity and prostitution were closely linked, both in the Society's literature and within public perceptions more generally; both were seen as products of the modern city and raised issues of public decency and order. Following the passing of Campbell's Act, the volunteers of the Vice Society frequently co-operated with the Metropolitan Police and acted as police informers, supplying evidence of open and clandestine sales of obscene publications. By the 1860s, however, the attention of the Society had turned from obscenity to the more general problem of literary decency and in the 1860s and 1870s the Vice Society joined the voices of campaigners in the popular press, such as James Greenwood, to fight the subversive influence of mass urban culture. By the early 1870s action became focused on the display of and trading in illustrated broadsheets, and a number of titles fell victim to the relentless campaigns of the Vice Society and other cultural and moral purists. It fell to the *Days' Doings*, in a full-page engraving in one of its last numbers before it too folded, to voice the view of many liberal consumers on the subject of modern urban culture (fig. 59). In this wonderful image of a London street at night, three policemen are shown standing around the illuminated window of a bookshop. The window is the brightest element in the scene and is a visual cornucopia, packed with illustrated covers and prints, as well as the legible titles of such reputable journals as the *Graphic*, close to an advertisement for the *Days' Doings*. The point is simply drawn that the richness of metropolitan culture embraces

59  'While the Police are Employed in Examining the Morality of the Illustrated Literature in this Unprotected Neighbourhood, What May Not the Ratepaying Inhabitants be Subjected to Round the Corner?', *Days' Doings*, 17 February 1872, p. 64.

the penny broadsheet and the 'art' engravings of the *Graphic*, and that one of the pleasures of this world is precisely the range of images and texts available to the urban consumer. Through the door, the glowing interior of the shop is revealed, with its shelves of books and the face of the proprietor peering over a half-curtained window at the rear. The shop spills on to the street; it is part of the street furniture, with its wooden advertising figure and window-box put on show by the nearby gaslight and its goods displayed in a box on the pavement. But all this is simply the staging for the cultural politics enacted in the foreground; for the policemen 'inspecting' the images for moral decency are doubled up with laughter and absorbed in the amusement offered by the images. The illustrations might be morally ambiguous, but they are also funny, and humour was not part of Vice Society rhetoric. In the meantime, a street boy thumbs his nose at the backs of the policemen and heads off round the corner to carry out some neighbourhood crime, while the officers of the law are diverted by pointless moral crusades.

Photography did not escape the scrupulous attention of the Vice Society in the years of its campaigns against metropolitan culture, and in 1873 it brought a number of prosecutions against traders for selling indecent photographs. By this time, courts were able to invoke the first legal definition of obscenity to assist in their judgements. This had come out of an 1868 case, *R. v. Hicklin*, in which the then Lord Chief Justice, Sir Alexander Cockburn, stated: 'I think the test of obscenity is this, whether the tendency of the matter charged as obscenity is to deprave and corrupt those whose minds are open to such immoral influences, and into whose hands a publication of this sort may fall.'[25] The significant aspect of this definition is not only the tendency 'to deprave and corrupt', but, more importantly, the specific focus on susceptible audiences; a concern that falls squarely within broader anxieties concerning mass urban culture in this period. Armed with this definition, courts had to tussle over whether prosecuted materials would tend to deprave and corrupt and speculate about the responses of vulnerable minds within the mass of mid-Victorian publics.

The subjects of the prosecuted photographs ranged from portraits of actresses and ballet-girls in various states of dress and undress, to more sexually explicit images, which were generally sold inside the shop and were not displayed in the windows.[26] A common defence was that the photographs were made as study aids for artists and it was perfectly true that daguerreotypes of the human figure had been produced for this purpose since the late 1830s and by the 1850s had become a rapidly expanding market.[27] What courts had to adjudicate was the validity of such claims and the effects of displaying these images in shop windows where they were on public view to all passers-by. One case brought by the Society for the Suppression of Vice was against a shopkeeper in the City of London called Samuel King. The daily newspapers and specialist photographic journals reported the progress of the trial, and it is possible to detect a note of fatigue in the opinions of the judge and the journalists with the whole, endless matter of drawing the line between obscenity and the mass of photographic studies that constituted the everyday signs of metropolitan culture. The judge commented: 'it was very difficult to draw the line where propriety ended and impropriety began, and therefore great allowances should be made in cases like this. Excepting two or three of the pictures seized, all the rest were exhibited, and might be bought, in half the shops in London.'[28]

Even earlier supporters of legal intervention in obscenity, such as the *Daily Telegraph*, saw the prosecution as excessive:

Any one who takes his walks abroad through our streets must be aware that in almost every shop window devoted to the sale of photographic prints there are exhibited . . . a swarm of cartes-de-visite of tenth-rate actresses and fifth-rate ballet girls in an extreme state of picturesque dishabille . . . The real objection to . . . [this] class of pictures is that they are silly and vulgar, and that, whatever may be their effect on public morals, they undeniably deprave the public taste. They belong to the lowest type of low art; still the sale of mere examples of vulgarity should not be sufficient to put the vendor in peril of the treadmill.[29]

A crucial distinction is being drawn, within the context of commercial urban culture, between morality and vulgarity. These are no longer being conflated, but are posed as two discrete orders of offence. The images may represent bad taste, but this is not a criminal offence, or worthy of hard labour. The moment represented by this case does not signal a major sea-change in the campaigns for cultural purity in the late nineteenth century. What it does reveal is that within this period there was a range of different views among conservatives and liberals, secular and ecumenical groupings and that, above all else, the regulation of culture was a spatial and an urban problem, created by the possibilities of indiscriminate viewing and consumption on the streets of the Victorian city.

It is possible to map a geography of London according to the locations of the shopkeepers prosecuted in the early 1870s. This would include parts of central London and Westminster, as well as the City of London. But twenty years earlier, in the period during which Campbell produced his bill, the source of metropolitan obscenity was believed to be highly concentrated and to emanate from one small street in Westminster, which became the focus of public debates on the obscene. This was Holywell Street, the 'London Ghetto', synonymous with the production and consumption of perverse urban culture.

## 2    *Holywell Street: The London Ghetto*

Holywell Street was a narrow, Elizabethan lane extending parallel with and to the north of the Strand and the River Thames, from the churches of St Clement Danes to St Mary-le-Strand, in the parish of Westminster in central London (fig. 60). The Strand at this time was one of the busiest and most important thoroughfares in London. It was one of the few direct routes linking the east and west of the city and had the additional symbolic importance of connecting the financial centres in the City of London with the commercial West End and with government at Whitehall. But frequent bottlenecks limited the Strand's value as a major through-highway, and the site between St Clement Danes and St Mary-le-Strand was a particularly bad traffic bottleneck.[30] At this point, the Strand contracted so that traffic had to be chan-

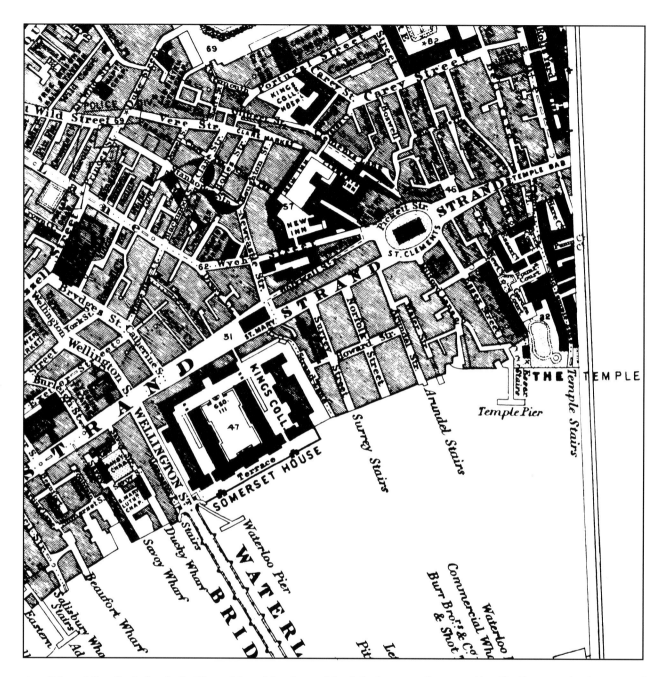

60 Edward Stanford, *Stanford's Library Map of London and Its Suburbs*, 1862, Sheet 10 (detail). Showing the location of Holywell Street. Maps 11.c.5. By Permission of the British Library.

nelled through the nearby narrow old lanes to the north. The *Building News* was expressing general public opinion when it stated its view on the significance of this area and its present disastrous condition:

> The two chief centres of life in London are now the City and Westminster, and the transaction of business – which means the maintenance of the activity of the Empire – depends on the communication between these two centres. At present they are united by an indirect, a tortuous, an obstructed, and a narrow lane, which it is a mockery to call a thoroughfare. If the streets of a city may be compared to the veins of a complex animal, the Strand constitutes a kind of aneurism in the most vital part of the body.[31]

As we have seen, motion and circulation were the two guiding principles of mid-nineteenth-century modernisers, who aimed to create a city on the model of a wholesome body, full of freely flowing conduits through which individuals could circulate like healthy corpuscles.[32] Sewers and drains should carry away the waste of the metropolitan body and streets and subways should facilitate the circulation of trade and production. This metaphor, however, carried with it a constant, fatal threat. Like all bodies, the city could become blocked and a clot in any part of the city's thoroughfares might cause a critical loss of circulation. The alleys and lanes of old London presented just such a possibility. In his series of articles on 'The Streets of the World', George Augustus Sala was appalled by London's:

> abominable little labyrinths of tenements crowded and huddled up together, to the perpetual exclusion of light and air, and the consistent fostering of dirt, disease and vice . . . the stifling courts, lanes, yards, and alleys shouldering one another, and cabining, cribbing, and confining whole nests of poverty-stricken inhabitants.[33]

This is space that arrests movement, holds on to its inhabitants, and is airless, stagnant and claustrophobic. The alley is the spatial and conceptual antithesis of the boulevard. It obeys the logic of the labyrinth; it is illegible and multifarious, as opposed to homogeneous and purposeful. In these areas there is congestion, rather than circulation, and terrible physical proximity. People and houses are crowded together, too close for comfort and physical or moral health; in this tangled knot, disease and sedition spread and threaten the well-being of the entire metropolitan body.

In the terms of this metaphorical language, Holywell Street was a spatial aneurism. It was located on the edge of a dense warren of old streets that supported a variety of street markets, housing and shops. There was even a story about a young man from the country who found himself in this part of London one winter's night, intending to make a short journey of a few yards to the main thoroughfare of the Strand. He soon became lost in the labyrinthine alleyways and it was said that his ghost haunted mid-Victorian London; wandering round and about, constantly returning to the original starting-point of his journey. He never escaped from the narrow, dark, irregular alleyways and never reached the Strand.[34] The legend of the ghost of Holywell Street closely anticipates Freud's strange experience on the streets of the provincial Italian town, which he later recalled in his essay on 'The Uncanny'. Both spatial narratives involve involuntary repetition and a constant return to a place of dangerous and overt sexual desire. Holywell Street was precisely the space of the uncanny, of spatial and psychic disorientation in the heart of the metropolis. At a time when some of the streets in the area were being demolished for the building of new Law Courts, the journalist John Timbs recalled that: 'This strange cluster of wretched dwellings in the heart of the largest capital in the world was in some cases remarkable for picturesqueness; but for the most part presented the miseries of an overcrowded district, and of human beings nestling and huddled up in houses in the last stage of neglect and decay.'[35] But within this topography of ruin and immorality, Holywell Street had a most particular reputation and the specific nature of the blockage with which it threatened London was the collected waste of obscene publications.

For Victorian London, Holywell Street and obscenity were synonymous. In the 1849 edition of his best-selling *Handbook for London*, Peter Cunningham listed the street as 'A narrow, dirty lane . . . occupied chiefly by old clothesmen and the vendors of low publications'.[36] Tradition had it that the street's name referred to a holy well that stood on the spot and at which pilgrims bound for Canterbury may have stopped to take a drink from what were believed to be curative waters.[37] But by the mid-1850s the *Builder* was reminding its readers: 'the place formerly resorted to for its living waters, is no longer the fountain of health or *piety*'. In the 'spirit of improvement', the journal urged large-scale clearance of the area and imagined the creation of a new, straight street that would act as a 'ventilating duct', circulating and cleansing the physical and moral environment of the district.[38] The paradox of Holywell Street's name constantly struck contemporaries. As another writer in *Temple Bar* put it: 'There is no end of streets named after the saints, and of places with holy designations, some of which are among the vilest places I have ever seen. By what strange fatality should a place called Holywell be a fountain of impurity?'[39] But Holywell Street's name was a critical element in the creation of the mythology of the place. It was a name that carried the weight of London's complex history, but its sense had become perverted; it had lost its original meaning and had become, precisely, improper. Michel de Certeau reflects on the role of proper names in mapping the city; he suggests that 'they link gestures and steps, they open up meanings and directions; such words even act to empty and erode their primary function . . . their rich vagueness earns them the *poetic* function of expressing an illogical geography . . .'[40] The name Holywell Street was full of meaning; this was the nature of its poetry. It contained traces of all the archaeological layers of the city, but by the middle of the nineteenth century these had crystallised into the single, mythic entity of obscenity.

In the public debates leading up to the passing of the Obscene Publications Act, the name of Holywell Street was repeatedly invoked. Identified as the central source of modern London's moral and cultural impurities, it poured forth noxious publications which, like infected water, threatened to poison all who came into contact with them. Anyone who doubted the terrible character of the street could take the advice of a correspondent to *The Times* who suggested: 'take a walk through Holywell-street,

Strand – without exception, I should say, the most vile street in the civilised world, every shop almost teeming with the most indecent publications and prints. How such shops exist in such frightful number against the law is to me a marvel . . .'[41] A few months later, in July 1857, a leading article in the newspaper reminded its readers of the significance of the street's location: 'in certain parts of London, and notably in Holywell-street, which is a feeder of the most important thoroughfare of the metropolis, prints, song-books, and other publications of the most disgusting character are exposed to public view.'[42] The obscenities of Holywell Street could not be ignored; they were not hidden away in some remote part of the metropolis, but were close, almost attached, to one of the most important streets in the capital and, indeed, of the empire. It seemed that, as a consequence of *laissez-faire* attitudes in planning and policing, people were being systematically directed through a crumbling, quaint old lane that was synonymous with the dirty book and print industry.

Estimates of the age of Holywell Street and its buildings varied. References to it could be found in the earliest chronicles of the history of London and most nineteenth-century historians agreed that the existing houses had been built in the seventeenth century, perhaps in the reign of Elizabeth I and certainly before the Fire of London.[43] In antiquarian terms, therefore, Holywell Street was highly significant. Its lofty gables, deep bays and overhanging eaves represented some of the oldest remaining lath and plaster houses in Victorian London; they were valuable relics as well as havens of vice and disease. Holywell Street always seemed on the brink of extinction, of crumbling into history, but it clung on tenaciously, curiously resilient to the efforts of man and nature to demolish its old, tottering timbers.

From the first years of Victoria's reign until the end of the century plans were submitted for the demolition of Holywell Street and the neighbouring area, to make way for such metropolitan improvements as the widening of the Strand and the building of the new Law Courts. In 1836 a Select Committee on Metropolis Improvements included the proposal in a number of schemes that it submitted to the House of Commons. The same plan was put forward by the Select Committee again in 1838. In 1847 Strand widening and the demolition of the old streets to the north was again set before the Commissioners as a key element in the improvement of the metropolis. With the establishment of the Metropolitan Board of Works in 1855, the project was made a priority; and in 1889, when the Board was superseded by the London County Council, demolition of the area including Holywell Street became a matter of great urgency. The question of the improvement of the Strand dragged on until the end of the century, when Holywell Street was, at last, pulled down to make way for the construction of Aldwych and Kingsway.[44] These great new imperial thoroughfares tore through such old buildings and incoherent spaces as Holywell Street, carving out a direct route from south to north in central London and enhancing the flow of traffic from east to west.

On New Year's Day in 1853 nature seemed to intervene where local government had thus far failed: the *Illustrated London News* carried a report of a hurricane that had blown down the roof of a house in Holywell Street (fig. 61), but the rest of the street remained secure, surviving occasional, opportunistic calls in the 1850s for its demolition.[45] By the early 1860s, with the approval for massive building works on

**EFFECTS OF THE HURRICANE IN HOLYWELL-STREET, STRAND.**

AMONG the effects of the hurricane on Monday in the metropolis, was the partial destruction of an old house in Holywell-street, Strand. About two o'clock in the morning, the neighbourhood was alarmed by a loud report, produced by a double stack of chimneys falling upon the house No. 37, in Holywell-street, which, and the adjoining premises, are among the oldest houses in the metropolis. The roof was thus driven in, and the lath-and-plaster parapet nearly projected into the street below; whilst

**OLD HOUSE IN HOLYWELL-STREET, PARTIALLY DESTROYED BY THE HURRICANE.**

the floors of the house were displaced, and bricks, plaster, and timber were strewn in all directions. The violence of the wind carried a, great portion of the double stack of chimneys over the house No. 37 (through which the remainder fell) on to the roof of the next dwelling, which is much higher. Of this a portion is left, as it forced it and the back part of the premises away, leaving the roof so neatly severed, that from the street apparently it had received no injury.

61  'Old House in Holywell-Street, Partially Destroyed by the Hurricane', *Illustrated London News*, 1 January 1853, p. 7.

the nearby site of the proposed new Law Courts, the imminent destruction of Holywell Street seemed inevitable.[46] Still it held on, an obstinate and resistant reminder of the past within a modernising present. Holywell Street was pulled between two conflicting impulses within mid-Victorian London. On the one hand, there was the compulsion to pull down and improve; and on the other hand, there was the associated attraction of the metropolitan picturesque. In 1861 the *Builder* responded to a parliamentary bill to clear the area, by publishing an article on 'Elizabethan London'. The article expressed the view that 'Much as we may admire the picturesque and value old structures – landmarks in our history – we can express no sorrow in this case. We have thought it desirable, however, to preserve a memorial of their appearance.'[47] 'One of the views,' it added, 'shows Holywell Street, of evil notoriety.' The accompanying illustration shows three historical locations in the area. The view of Holywell Street includes a number of elements, such as the overhanging eaves, deep bays, high gables, carved crescent moon shop sign and print shops with people gathered round their windows, which recur in most visual representations of this site throughout the century (fig. 62). At times the picturesque character is more strongly emphasised – the roadway is made narrower and the flanking houses taller and more cliff-like – and the nature of the people in the street becomes more or less reputable, or perhaps more difficult to classify, but, in general terms, the visual iconography of Holywell Street remained remarkably consistent and stable.

There are a significant number of pictures of Holywell Street – prints and watercolours, drawings and engravings – recalling the appearance and reputation of

62 'Holywell Street: Looking Towards the East', detail from 'Elizabethan London', *Builder*, 6 April 1861, p. 230.

the ancient street. Artists and collectors were drawn to Holywell Street in the mid-nineteenth century; they wanted to record its eaves, gables and shop-fronts and to preserve its image for posterity. London archives and provenances tell the story of this process; of the interweaving of art and history in the mid-Victorian metropolis. The Department of Prints and Drawings in the British Museum owns the collection of maps and views of London collected, arranged and mounted by Frederick Crace until his death in 1859.[48] Crace was, by profession, an architectural decorator; he was very successful and worked on the royal palaces and other prestigious commissions. He was also a member of the Commission of Sewers, which involved him in consulting old maps and plans of the city and in making decisions concerning London's main drainage and related demolitions. Crace embodied London's dual imperatives, to build and to destroy, and these also drove his ceaseless collection of images of London. Holywell Street was, in the words of an early twentieth-century historian, 'a joy to the artist . . . a sorrow to the sanitarian'.[49] Crace was both connoisseur and hygienist; he could recognise the attraction and the repulsion of Holywell Street, and among the works in his collection are a number of watercolours, many commissioned from his favourite artist, Thomas Hosmer Shepherd, of scenes in Holywell Street (fig. 63).[50] Perhaps as a result of his position as Commissioner of Sewers, Crace, more than others in this period, expected the imminent destruction of Holywell Street. He might even have been involved in one of the several, aborted, plans in these years to pull it down.

As successive plans to rebuild the area failed to be carried out, the picturesque qualities of the housing and streets were increasingly romanticised. By 1870 the *Illustrated London News* began to wonder whether Holywell Street would ever join the rest of disappearing 'Old London'. Imagining the public benefits of the demolition of the area, the paper affirmed the urban ideals of the improvers and modernisers through the familiar mythic figure of the lost stranger:

> The stranger to London, also, whom we meet so often in Lincoln's-inn-fields asking his way to the Strand, will be saved much distress and loss of time when a new street – a wide and straight one – shall be opened through the labyrinth of fetid alleys . . . a thoroughfare not precisely straight, but nearly so, and quite enough for practical convenience.[51]

Seizing the opportunity of a quick dig at the contemporary aesthetics of Baron Haussmann's Paris, with its miles of new, straight boulevards, the article envisages a more liberal and democratic form of modernity than that represented in the autocratic remodelling of Napoleon III's Paris. It imagines the creation of a new kind of urban space, allowing a different form of social circulation. In contrast to the unregulated and purposeless movement symbolised in the meandering lane of Holywell Street, a straight, wide thoroughfare generates order without despotism and circulation with purpose.

Holywell Street was the topographical embodiment of debates throughout the nineteenth century concerning the look of modernity, its spatial articulation and its relationship to the past. Physically, it represented a history that was rapidly disappearing, but not fast enough. As long as Holywell Street resisted and continued to obstruct the course of improvement, the story of London's modernisation

63 T. Hosmer Shepherd, 'Holywell Street, St. Clements. With One of the Old Signs – The Half Moon', 1853. From 'A Catalogue of Maps, Plans and Views of London, Westminster and Southwark. Collected and Arranged by Frederick Crace, Edited by His Son John Gregory Crace' (London, 1878), Portfolio XVII, sheet 66, no. 150. Watercolour, 22.8 × 17.7 cm. © Copyright The British Museum.

64   J. W. Archer, 'Holywell Street, Strand. Drawn March 1862', in 'Drawings of Buildings in London and the Environs', vol. 10-3. Watercolour, 36.9 × 29.6 cm. © Copyright The British Museum.

65 W. Richardson, *Holywell Street*, 1850s. Watercolour, 29.5 × 20 cm. Courtesy of the Museum of London.

66   'Holywell Street, Westminster', n.d. Photograph. © Crown Copyright. NMR.

67　J. W. Archer, 'Old Entrance to Lyon's Inn, Holywell Street, Strand, April 1847', in 'Drawings of Buildings in London and the Environs', vol. 10-4. Watercolour, 24.3 × 33.7 cm. © Copyright The British Museum.

remained unfinished. Holywell Street represented the old within modernity; its appearance was a foil to the creation of an aesthetics of the new (figs 64 and 65). Its narrow pavements, dirty streets, old-fashioned shop-fronts and decrepit housing were simultaneously celebrated and censured in the many watercolour and photographic portraits of the place produced during the nineteenth century (fig. 66). Whether peopled with a disparate crowd of Hogarthian street-types, or eerily depopulated, save for a few ghostly presences caught on a photographic negative, Holywell Street *had to be* represented, for it was a rich and expressive sign of the paradoxes of modernity.

But Holywell Street was not just an image or sign within Victorian discourses on the modern, it was also a place with a history. As the classic writer on urban space, Jane Jacobs, has observed, streets are much more than passageways, more or less congested; they are also environments and localities, with their own, distinctive economic, social and cultural forms.[52] As a site of commerce, Holywell Street was first occupied by mercers, and the carved sign of the Half Moon, allegedly one of the oldest shop signs in London and so loved by antiquarians, was a remnant of this original occupation (fig. 67).[53] As the business in expensive textiles declined, the trade in costume and masquerade dress and second-hand clothes took its place (fig. 68). Holywell Street went down-market and by the middle of the eighteenth century traders in old furniture joined those selling second-hand clothing and the street became the hub of a vivacious trade in cast-off commodities. By the beginning of the nineteenth century, however, the trade in second-hand goods was taken over by a new business, the book trade, and the sale of old and new books, prints, pamphlets, periodicals and broadsheets joined the daily transactions carried out in the confined space of the street. Visual images of commercial life in Holywell Street in the middle decades of the nineteenth century show a world of street retailing; with displays spilling out from interiors on to the walls and pavements, and second-hand clothes, old furniture and print shops trading next door to each other. The caption to Shepherd's watercolour of the block of buildings between Wych Street and Holywell Street, tells a potted history of the site. The text reads 'taken down 1855', but to this has been added an emphatic 'or to be' and a final, later annotation 'taken down 1902'. This sums up Holywell Street's resilience; its continuing survival in the face of imminent destruction.

Some time around the middle of the eighteenth century Holywell Street underwent a significant transformation, from labyrinth to ghetto. The polymorphous space of the street became associated not simply with poverty and criminality, but with a specific ethnic version of these. Holywell Street became a Jewish street and experienced renewed public notoriety in the ugly form of Victorian anti-Semitism. In G. W. M. Reynolds's long-running and popular weekly serial, *The Mysteries of London* (1844–56), the heroine, Ellen Monroe, visits Holywell Street in order to purchase clothing that she can use to disguise herself as a man. According to Reynolds, the old-clothes dealers of Holywell Street were Jewish and their trade was threatened with extinction by the incursion of the booksellers. He described the dilapidated and melancholy appearance of the clothes shops:

> The huge masks, which denote the warehouse where masquerading and fancy-attire may be procured on sale or hire, seem to 'grin horribly a ghastly smile', as if they knew that their occupation was all but gone. The red-haired ladies who stand at their doors beneath a canopy of grey trousers with black seats, and blue coats with brown elbows – a distant imitation of Joseph's garment of many colours – seem dispirited and care-worn, and no longer watch, with the delighted eyes of maternal affection, their promising offspring playing in the gutters. Their glances are turned towards the east – a sure sign that they meditate an early migration to the pleasant regions which touch upon the Minories.[54]

It is possible that around the late 1840s there was a social transformation in Holywell Street, as Jewish traders, ousted by the spread of the bookshops, moved out of Westminster and into the east end of London; but this process was neither sudden nor final. The association of the street with crooked Jewish merchants clung on in the Victorian imaginary. For popular writers such as Reynolds, the Jew was simply

68   T. Hosmer Shepherd, 'Old Houses Between Holywell Street and Wych Street, taken down, 1855 *or to be*',
1855. From 'A Catalogue of Maps, Plans and Views of London, Westminster and Southwark. Collected and Arranged
by Frederick Crace, Edited by His Son John Gregory Crace' (London, 1878), Portfolio XVII, sheet 67, no. 151.
Watercolour, 24.1 × 18.4 cm. © Copyright The British Museum.

69   Anon., 'Vickers – Publisher Holywell St Strand', n.d. Pen and ink, 8.8 × 17.7 cm. B138 Holywell St. (13).
Westminster City Archives.

another type to be mapped on to the literary topography of London that structured
so many of the risqué narratives of contemporary sensation fiction. Reynolds was a
master of the genre; his work often offended conservative taste, but this did not interfere with sales. Reynolds was also personally familiar with Holywell Street; the publisher of *The Mysteries of London*, George Vickers, was located at 28–9 Holywell Street
and the author would certainly have walked through the street, past the old-clothes
dealers, to visit Vickers in his shop (fig. 69).[55] There he would have seen copies of
his own work sold alongside more sexually explicit and tendentious material, which
frequently brought the shopkeeper during this period to the very limits of legality.
This was the murky world of publishing and selling to which Holywell Street played
host in the first half of the nineteenth century. The Jewish traders provided the mythic
dimension of the place; they were ciphers for the dangerous transactions that were
imagined in the dark confines of the narrow lane.

By the middle of the nineteenth century, the association of Holywell Street and
Jews was so deeply embedded that it had become the 'London ghetto', a reeking
alley of shifty Jewish merchants, in Thackeray's anti-Disraeli satire, 'Codlingsby' (fig.
70). The noble Aryan lord, the Marquis of Codlingsby, visits a shop in Holywell
Street:

> The occupants of the London Ghetto sat at their porches basking in the
> evening sunshine . . . every man or maiden, every babe or matron in that English
> Jewry bore in his countenance one or more . . . characteristics of his peerless Arab
> race . . .

70   Illustration to B. de Shrewsbury, Esq. [W. M. Thackeray],
'Codlingsby', *Punch*, XII (1847),
p. 166.

> They passed under an awning of old clothes, tawdry fripperies, greasy spangles,
> and battered masks, into a shop as black and hideous as the entrance was foul.[56]

The link between Holywell Street and Jews was so strong and pervasive in this period,
that in Robert Knox's ethnological study of the 'Jewish race' in *The Races of Man*,
1862, the author ironically invoked the 'beauties of Holywell-street' in his account
of Jewish physiognomy.[57]

There is a clear correspondence between the definition of space and race in this
period. Jewish space is black, ugly and airless. The unkempt exterior world of the
Jewish street terminates in the disturbing, tomb-like interiors of their shops. Jewish
London is dangerous and deceptive, and the ghetto, along with the rest of Holywell
Street's impurities, must come down to make way for the modern metropolis. For
George Augustus Sala, Jewish London described a distinct and subversive topography. Like Reynolds, Sala observed a shift away from the area of Holywell Street
amongst Jewish traders in old clothes but still described in rhetorical detail the Jewish
pubs of the street:

> When Holywell Street was more old clothesy than literary; and, when children of
> the Tribes lay in wait at the shop-doors behind cloaks and patelots, like wild beasts
> in ambush, frousy little public-houses nestled among the old clothes shops pretty
> numerously. They were not cheerful nor gaily-decorated establishments.[58]

The contemporary tourist literature of London endorsed the association of the impurities of Holywell Street and transgressive Jewish trade. The improved 1863 edition of Peter Cunningham's *Handbook to London* also offered simplified diagrams of the city's main thoroughfares. Holywell Street, off the Strand, is the only site given an ethnographic caption: 'Full of Jew-clothesmen and book-stalls.'[59] The nuisances of Holywell Street were twofold; they were, in the words of a columnist in the *Illustrated London News*, '[the] Jews and venders [*sic*] of impure books'.[60] In official metropolitan eyes, this coupling was highly significant. Holywell Street was a double affront to Victorian economic principles: dirty books and Jewish rag traders epitomised the underside of London's commercial and cultural life.

The obscenities of Holywell Street grew out of a radical past.[61] In the first decades of the nineteenth century the street was occupied by radical pressmen: freethinkers, who published tracts on politics, religion and sexuality and who, in the decades following the Revolution in France, were spied on by police informers and prosecuted for sedition, blasphemy and obscenity. This was the home of the literature of radicalism and of a type of bawdy publishing dedicated to exposing the hypocrisy and immorality of the ruling classes. Holywell Street bore the traces of this political radicalism through the nineteenth century, as its activities shifted from freethinking to pornography. Radical politics were part of its history; this was another reason why it had to come down. The street's identity as the main source of indecent and immoral literature was installed around the beginning of Victoria's reign. In *Radical Underworld*, a study of the early nineteenth-century press, Iain McCalman has vividly described the transitional moment during the 1820s when radical pressmen such as the notorious William Dugdale turned their attention in a wholesale way to the production of pornography.[62]

Dugdale's career exemplifies the political and cultural shift in the Holywell Street book trade around the 1820s. In the post-war years Dugdale had been part of a circle of London ultra-radicals, publishing and printing a range of material relating to popular causes of the day. Following severe anti-radical repression around 1820, a contraction in the market for radical publications and a shift in radical ideology towards self-improvement and popular education, Dugdale made an opportunistic move into the lucrative market in obscenity. As McCalman shows: 'an indigenous libertinist canon going back at least as far as the Restoration' had always been an element within the output of the radical press.[63] Dugdale simply shifted the emphasis of his products from radical critique to sex and smut. Operating under his own name and aliases from premises in Holywell Street and the surrounding area, by the mid-1830s Dugdale had become one of the most prolific publishers of pornography in the nineteenth century. Dugdale's industriousness alone might have been sufficient to make Holywell Street and obscenity synonymous, but there were others: friends, relatives and contacts, such as George Vickers – publisher of G. W. M. Reynolds and Dugdale's next-door neighbour – who also moved into the growing market for Holywell Street obscenity. It was on the occasion of one of many prosecutions of Dugdale that the horrified Lord Campbell was stung into introducing his obscene publications legislation in 1857. Dugdale's long career finally ended in 1868, when he died in the Clerkenwell House of Correction, serving a sentence for selling obscene literature.[64]

By the middle of the nineteenth century Holywell Street had accumulated an extra-ordinary degree of symbolic meaning. At the moment of the formation of London's first municipal government, Holywell Street stood as a symbol of old London, against the modernising, improving thrust of the new city. It was disordered, crumbling, labyrinthine, rather than straight, singular and purposeful. Built on the site of an old well, Holywell Street was the physical and moral antithesis of the drive to modernise London through the flow of water, engineered through a complex of drains and sewers. It was stagnant and corrupting, but it was also quaint. A picturesque survival of old London, it would have to come down before the march of modern improvements. Holywell Street symbolised a troubling past that continued to infiltrate and interfere with the clean progress of modernity. It was filthy and poisonous, Jewish and radical, and it lay at the heart of the metropolis, where it inscribed 'the law of the other' and undermined the economic, social and cultural ideals of modern London.[65]

Holywell Street's poisons were not contained within the geographical boundaries of the street; indeed, the real danger was that its corruption was seen to spread, like a disease, into the city and country beyond. During its campaign to support Lord Campbell's legislation through the Houses of Parliament, *The Times* referred to 'the traffic' in obscene publications emanating from Holywell Street; a place 'consisting almost entirely of warehouses in which these abominable commodities are stored for circulation over the metropolis and over the whole kingdom'.[66] Holywell Street sat, like a great, dark spider, at the centre of a web of obscenity. It generated obscene publications; displayed and advertised them and sold them on to other sellers and hawkers (see the shop sign in plate 63).

The trade in obscene publications in the spaces of Holywell Street defies such conventional analytical oppositions as public and private, or interior and exterior. The shop window was a highly permeable boundary, designed to orchestrate a free exchange between shop and street. Through the implicit and explicit display of obscenity, the pleasures of the shop entered the street and the crowds on the street were enticed inside. The pavement 'baulks' of cheap books and prints were a distinctive feature of Holywell Street trading. A watercolour by C. J. Richardson, dated 1871, clearly shows the sales habits of the street's shopkeepers (fig. 71).[67] Wooden trestles lean out from the front wall, and boards on boxes, displaying piles of books and prints, take the space of the shop and its goods far out on to the pavement, creating an environment in which distinctions between street and shop, and passer-by, window shopper and customer are hopelessly blurred.

Holywell Street shops were ostentatiously old-fashioned and out-of-date and presented a stark contrast to the modern styles of retailing displayed in the main thoroughfares of London by the middle of the nineteenth century. New shops were a medley of glass, gas and brass. As the author of one article, published in *Chamber's Journal*, enthused:

> There are few people who have not been struck with the magnificence of London shop-fronts. They form one of the most prominent indications of the grandeur and wealth of the metropolis. Enormous plate-glass windows, gilded or polished brass frames, and all sorts of fancy wood-work; sometimes crystal columns, and generally a singular covering of iron Venetian blinds, which roll up and down by

intricate machinery, like a stage curtain displaying or concealing the gorgeous scenery within – these are the necessary decorations of a fashionable London shop of the middle of the nineteenth century.[68]

Retailing in this period had become an art, borrowing techniques from the theatre in order to create its visual effects. As another writer claimed: 'Picture-galleries and museums present no points of interest that can compete with [London shop windows] in the estimation of the mass of our fellow-creatures.'[69] The shops of Holywell Street, however, belonged to a different era of retailing. The narrow shop windows, fitted with small panes of glass; the wooden 'lean-tos' supporting their packed loads of books and pictures, seemed to belong to another century. The gloomy shops of Holywell Street traded nefarious goods through atavistic styles of retailing.

The shops of Holywell Street traded on the ground floors of the ancient houses. Further inside and on upper floors, an entire obscene publications manufactory was believed to be accommodated. The interiors of Holywell Street houses are seldom represented; when they are, they are described as dirty, cramped and unsafe spaces. One of the most memorable accounts comes from the autobiography of the journalist Thomas Frost, who worked as a compositor for William Dugdale at his premises in Holywell Street and the adjacent Wych Street during the mid-1840s. Frost described following his new employer through the shop, into the printing office:

> we passed through a dark and narrow passage . . . and into a dirty little yard, at the rear of which was a dingy and dilapidated building, the ground-floor of which was closed, and the room above approached by wooden steps from the outside. Following my conductor up the steps, I entered a dirty, cobwebby room, in which seven or eight compositors were at work.[70]

Lord Campbell and his supporters in the Society for the Suppression of Vice might never reach these inner sanctums of obscenity, but in the minds of legislators and moral reformers such as these, the ghastly interiors of Holywell Street found their external expression in the shabby displays and browsing crowds on the street.

In his *Reminiscences* Frost speculated on the identities of the customers for Dugdale's goods. Like others in this period, Frost took the clientele to be rich roués, a type of reworking of the figure of the debauched Georgian or Regency aristocrat. Frost rejected the idea that the works sold by Dugdale were bought by the working classes: 'It is obvious that working-men do not buy guinea books of erotic engravings, imported from Paris, such as were more than once seized on Dugdale's premises.'[71] According to Frost, the evidence provided by the high prices of the publications was corroborated by more anecdotal evidence concerning Dugdale's connections in the Home Office and the suggestion that on one occasion a two-year prison sentence had been prematurely terminated after a couple of months:

> [Dugdale] had been liberated by order of the Home Secretary, on the surgeon of the gaol certifying that his longer incarceration would endanger his life . . . I only know that when I saw him, immediately after his liberation, his sodden and sensual countenance presented its ordinary appearance. No indication of ill-health was

71   C. J. Richardson, 'House in Holywell St, Strand', June 1871. Watercolour, 25.4 × 17.1 cm. B138 Holywell St. (6–7). Westminster City Archives.

visible . . . It would be an instructive lesson in the science of promoting public morality to learn at whose instance the certificate was given, and by whom it was supported when laid before the Home Office.[72]

The implication that Dugdale had influential contacts in high places and that he struck preferential deals during his trials was reiterated by other contemporary observers.[73] Whether or not this was true, there was clearly a niche market for expensive, limited editions of obscene works, the audience for which might well be the circle of powerful and worldly men who also participated in and regulated the pleasures of Cremorne Gardens. As Adrian Rifkin has observed about a similar faction of legislators and civil servants in the context of Parisian entertainment in the first decades of the twentieth century: 'There are the public prosecutors at the Parisian court and legal experts of the Interior Ministry. Very often this personnel is made up of worldly men, who form a bedrock of gallant culture, even while they are responsible for the understanding and implementation of the laws that control and limit it.'[74] But this was not the only group that was identified as the audience for the obscenities of Holywell Street. Public anxiety was also expressed about the cheap goods, the penny broadsheets and papers that were also sold from its shops. And then, there was the spectre of the young, respectable middle classes who were also believed to be amongst the lingering, longing crowds on the street.[75] In fact, what is striking about contemporary definitions of the Holywell Street public is their inclusiveness. Obscenity, it seems, was not selective, but drew all sections of society into its powerful and pernicious embrace.

In *Radical Underworld*, Iain McCalman speculates on the composition of the new mass audience for the publications of William Dugdale and his cronies; he suggests that it 'cut across middle- and working-class boundaries. It included . . . artisans, clerks, army and navy officers, students, journalists, professionals, businessmen, government officials and tourists . . .'[76] While this list evokes something of the social heterogeneity of the public in Holywell Street, the implication is that the audience is male, and that the audience reads rather than views. *Viewing* radically changes the constituency of audiences and the relationship between subject and commodity. Viewing is mapped on to and by the city, so that a passage through Holywell Street is a passage across complex definitions of gender and respectability and the subject's relation to desire, pleasure and power in looking.

Women were present in Holywell Street, both as consumers and as producers of obscene publications. They were part of the streams of pedestrians who passed through the lane, diverted by the blockages and narrowing of the Strand. Women were part of Holywell Street's space, part of its urban discourses: walking, talking, shopping, looking in windows, brushing up against obscenity *and* respectability and forcing a constant renegotiation of modern identities.

The presence of respectable women in Holywell Street alarmed contemporaries and became a central justification for supporters of legislation. The *Daily Telegraph* advocated legal intervention because: 'If this is done with the requisite energy, we are quite sure that Holywell-street will soon be purged of its many abominations, and one source of pollution, which is vitally injurious to the morals – more particularly of the female part of the community – will at once be extinguished.'[77] This can be read in two ways: first, that the greatest harm of obscene publications is their effect on women; and, secondly, that women have a particular disposition or vulnerability towards the harms of obscenity. This association of obscene publications and women consumers recurs consistently throughout the months of debate leading up to the passing of the Obscene Publications Act. Following the bill's third reading, Campbell expressed his hope that it would soon pass into law: 'and that the time would soon come when Holywell Street would become the abode of honest, industrious handicraftsmen, and a thoroughfare through which any modest woman might pass.'[78] Here, there is an interesting shift in the terms of the argument; from women as consumers of obscene materials, to women as pedestrians in Holywell Street. In fact, the two conditions are dependent upon each other. Women are consumers of obscenity *because* they move through the space of the street. As an independent subject within the modern city, woman takes on the mantle of cultural consumer. The significance of the display of obscene publications is that it focuses on the problem of 'seeing'. It generates a specific form of viewing and looking, made possible by mass cultural production and the spaces of the modern city; where the *display* of visual commodities enables their *consumption*, merely by movement through the space of the street. Display and visibility in this context enact the ultimate promiscuity; to pass by, may be to see and to become affected by. If honest women are passing through Holywell Street, they become subject to this chain of possibilities.

This still positions women as the inadvertent victims of the random appeal of obscenity; but what if they are not so innocent? What if the entire public in Holywell Street is a much more confusing and illegible mix of innocence and desire? A leading article, published in the *Daily Telegraph* in June 1857, draws a far more interesting picture of the blurring of social and moral identities in the narrow confines of Holywell Street. It describes the coexistence of respectable and non-respectable booksellers in Holywell Street, which produces an analogous condition in the public who move through the street and browse through the displays. Lawyers from the nearby Inns of Court; professors from King's College on the Strand; medical students seeking second-hand copies of anatomy textbooks; bibliophiles and antiquarians come to Holywell Street for what the paper assumes to be legitimate purposes. But within the public space of the street, they come up against the dissolute and the immoral who are brought there by its trade in dirty books. According to the *Telegraph*, the situation is further complicated by a deliberate misreading of identities amongst this audience. As the professors and lawyers browse through respectable material 'they are elbowed . . . by the dissolute and the brutal, who intentionally misconstrue the purpose of their visit'.[79] The respectable public can visit Holywell Street only 'at the risk of having one's pocket picked, or of being assailed by a volley of ribald jokes'. What we are presented with here is a series of negotiations concerning social identity. Looking, reading, touching, speaking, moving – ways of asserting, transgressing and appropriating identities that testify to the dynamic nature of public life on the streets of the mid-Victorian metropolis. But what if women are part of these exchanges? The article observes:

It is positively lamentable passing down these streets [Holywell Street and Wych
Street], to see the young of either sex – often, we blush to say, of the weaker –
and in many case evidently appertaining to the respectable classes of society,
furtively peeping in at these sin-crammed shop-windows, timorously gloating over
suggestive title-pages, nervously conning insidious placards, guiltily bending over
engravings as vile in execution as they are in subject.

Here we have it, then, evidence of a most fearful situation. Respectable, middle-
class women looking at and consuming the obscenities of Holywell Street. But
in its fiercest denial, the paper articulates an even more dreadful possibility.
What if these women are not timorous, nervous, or guilty, but bold, daring and
desiring?

The case of Holywell Street presents a particular conceptualisation of the relationship of gender and space. The figure of the female pedestrian moving through
the city allows us to think of the built environment and urban space less as a set of
objects and passive backdrops and more as part of an active construction of social
relations and identities. The intermingling and proximity presented by such public
spaces as Holywell Street demanded a continual process of redefinition and renegotiation of self. Neither masculinity nor femininity was fixed; gendered identities could
be adopted or assumed for a time and then relinquished. Appearances, in other words,
could be deceptive. Outward signs of respectability were not stable indices of moral
purity and social manners might mask transgressive dreams and desires. These were
the uncertainties of Holywell Street; uncertainties that were carried over into written
and pictorial representations of the place (fig. 72). In a watercolour dated 1870 the
street is ostensibly well regulated and respectable; but does the woman in blue on
the left peer too closely at the print-shop window; is she too engrossed for her own
good? What is the top-hatted gentleman on the right reading? Is he one of the dissolute, or an innocent lover of books?

The modern city created new forms of mass consumption, in which audiences
could be constituted through occupation of the city streets, rather than through traditional structures of social and cultural distinction. This was part of the city's flow
of activities, in which people not only moved or passed through places, but also
stopped and looked and imagined. Holywell Street was just such a place of stasis and
reverie. Here, people were stopped in their tracks, their passage halted by crowds and
displays of obscenity. But if the new visual forms of the city were perceived as a kind
of moral snare, then it was also believed that women were particularly prone to this
entrapment and dislocated absorption. The windows of print shops and the spaces
immediately in front of them were especially distinctive and dangerous. This was a
new category of urban space; open to the street, but for the indulgence of private
reverie. The display of visual images alone was believed to entrap women and induce
in them a vulnerable state of reverie, but when these images took on the mantle of
obscenity, then the dreams might create sexually entranced women in the middle of
the metropolis. The shop window drew the gaze of the passer-by and projected its
attractions on to the street. The display of sexually explicit, or indecent works could
thus create an eroticised space both behind the glass and in front of it, in the street
beyond. This eroticisation of the space in front of the print-shop window is one

72　Anon., 'Holywell Street. Strand 1870', dated 1870. Watercolour, 28.5 × 17 cm. B138 Holywell St. (8–11). Westminster City Archives.

73   Thomas P. Hall, *One Touch of Nature Makes the Whole World Kin*, 1867. Oil on canvas, 76.2 × 63.5 cm. Private Collection.

element in the modern life narrative represented in Thomas P. Hall's genre painting *One Touch of Nature Makes the Whole World Kin* (fig. 73).[80] Here, the setting is the window of an art dealer and print seller, with the view taken from inside the shop, with the backs of the paintings and prints on display, out to the faces of the crowd on the street gazing at the works in the window. True to its title, the picture shows all classes of society brought together in their fascination with the images in the window; but this unity is compromised by the gaze of the gentleman on the left, which is drawn to the maidservant in the crowd, rather than to the work of art in the window. The woman is vulnerable because she has stopped to look in the window. Hers is not a passing glance, but a long and lingering stare and through her immobility and absorption she becomes subject to the sexual exchanges of the city. In this instance, the attractions of art are seen to have their positive and negative aspects, but as photography and mass-produced engravings were seen to replace high art in the windows of the printsellers, so the effects of the display were believed to be more troubling.

The *Daily Telegraph* observed a correspondence between the shabby quality and the morally dubious content of images in London print-shop windows.[81] These displays of new, cheap, mass-produced images corrupted both the taste and the morals

of the crowds gathered round the packed window displays. For Ruskin, with his suspicion of and distaste for the modern metropolis, the immoral displays in print-shop
windows were a symbolic expression of the economic and social corruption of the
capital city. He imagined a housewife from the north of England, on a visit to
London:

> [she] can indeed get to London cheap, but she has no business there; she can buy
> all the morning's news for a halfpenny, but she has no concern with them . . . she
> can be carried through any quantity of filthy streets on a tramway for threepence;
> but it is as much as her life's worth to walk in them, or as her modesty's worth
> to look into a print shop in them.[82]

In its most extreme form, the space in front of the print-shop window came to represent a space of generalised and indiscriminate sexual desire. In the *Yokel's Preceptor*,
a smutty directory of the brothels, gambling-houses and sexual hotspots of London,
published by William Dugdale, the anonymous author turns, with apparent disgust,
to the subject of the haunts of homosexual men. The text instructs its readers:

> They generally congregate around the picture shops, and are to be known by their
> effeminate air, their fashionable dress &c. When they see what they imagine to be
> a chance, they place their fingers in a peculiar manner underneath the tails of their
> coats, and wag them about – their method of giving the office.[83]

This is a space charged with sexual desire and sexual transgression. It is as though
the sexual values represented in the images behind the window have been projected
beyond the glass barrier and have contaminated the space of the street around. Little
wonder, then, that Eliza Lynn Linton advised modest women in the city to keep
walking; to avoid hanging around the shop windows, and especially the print-shop
windows. Modest women should avoid the urban habits of their curious and
desiring counterparts: 'Lounging round all the shop-windows; scanning *Punch* or the
*Illustrated* as they stand with their faces against the glass; looking at the picture-shops
by the half-hour together . . .'[84]

It is while women stand, absorbed and captivated by the visual image, that they
are at their most vulnerable and suggestible. They do not just dream, they empathise
with the object concerned to the degree that they are able to absorb its emotions
and drives. In the fourth volume of *London Labour and the London Poor*, Henry
Mayhew imagined how the accomplished metropolitan pickpocket worked the
streets:

> A young lady may be standing by a window in Cheapside, Fleet Street, Oxford
> Street, or the Strand, admiring some beautiful engraving. Meantime a handsomely
> dressed young man, with gold chain and moustache, also takes his station at the
> window beside her, apparently admiring the same engraving. The young lady
> stands gazing at the beautiful picture, with her countenance glowing with senti-
> ment, which may be enhanced by the sympathetic presence of the nice looking
> young man by her side, and while her bosom is thus throbbing with romantic
> emotion, her purse, meanwhile, is being quietly transferred to the pocket of this
> elegantly attired young man, whom she might find in the evening dressed as a

rough costermonger, mingling among the low ruffians at the Seven Dials or Whitechapel, or possibly lounging in some low beershop in the Borough.[85]

Although there is no suggestion in this passage that the engraving that the woman is gazing at is an immoral work, she nevertheless enters an excited state and the space in front of the window becomes the site of an erotic encounter with both the visual image and the male stranger.

Women, it seems, were believed to be especially prone to the colour, composition and effects of the images displayed in print-shop windows. Thus arrested, they halted their passage through the city and became absorbed and aroused by the power of the visual. In his study of art and design instruction in mid-Victorian Britain, Rafael Denis has demonstrated the association in this period of colour with sensuality and bodily responses.[86] Drawing on contemporary colour theory and etiquette manuals, Denis shows that colour was thought to be arousing and to induce primitive physical responses rather than intellectual ones. Women, Denis argues, were believed to have a natural affinity for the attractions and pleasures of colour.[87] In this wider context of the gendering of mid-Victorian colour theory, the dangerous attraction for women of print-shop windows takes on an additional dimension. For women, the displays in the shop windows represented the victory of the physical senses over aesthetic judgement; reversing classical accounts of the contemplative experience of the work of art. Moreover, women might be expected to have a particularly immediate and unrestrained physical response to the visual image, witnessed in the hectic flush and heaving bosom of Mayhew's pickpocket victim.

The women described by Linton and Mayhew are in a state of protracted looking and longing. They are curious and desiring and, provoked by the images, they fall into a state of extended daydreaming. In *The Romantic Ethic and the Spirit of Modern Consumerism*, an historical account of modern forms of consumption, Colin Campbell has discussed the significance of the daydream in generating the endless series of new wants that distinguishes modern modes of consumption.[88] Campbell identifies this generation of new desires as a specifically modern form of pleasure-seeking, which he calls 'autonomous, self-illusory hedonism'. What is distinctively modern about this form of hedonism is that it is centred on the indulgence of emotions and sensations that individuals provide for themselves, from an imaginary world that they themselves create. This is the function of the daydream. It is an ideal version of the real, which yields a peculiarly perfect form of pleasure. The daydream thus inevitably leads to dissatisfaction with the limitations and imperfections of reality, generating an endless cycle of longing for the new, consumption, disillusionment and renewed longing. Moreover, although these desires can become attached to specific goods, the daydream is fundamentally the scene of non-specific desires for new experiences and objects. Campbell's argument is concerned specifically with the conditions and forms of modern consumption, however his emphasis on the daydream as a site of self-generated and illusory pleasure and longing bears upon the figure of the woman dreaming in front of the print-shop window. In this context, she becomes a paradigmatic type of the modern city; drawn by and drawing upon the images in the shop window to construct imaginary scenarios for 'covert and pleasurable consumption'.[89] She is in a state of perpetual, unsatisfiable longing; poised on the brink of a consummation of her desires and in a state of pleasurable fantasy, before the disillusionment of reality intervenes once more.

The female consumers of Holywell Street are thus figures of tremendous imminence and potency. In a state of constant potential desire, they respond to the images of Holywell Street and become absorbed creatures of longing and of eventual, inevitable disillusionment. This was the spectre that haunted the dreams of such supporters of moral reform as the *Daily Telegraph*. This was the heart of the fantasy of women: 'furtively peeping in at these sin-crammed shop-windows, timorously gloating over suggestive title-pages, nervously conning insidious placards, guiltily bending over engravings . . .' (17 June 1857). The *Daily Telegraph* might have reason to be worried. These women were not just looking; they were also longing and dissatisfied.

# 3       *From Alleys to Courts:*
## *Obscenity and the Mapping of Mid-Victorian London*

The story of Holywell Street is also the story of the legal pursuit of obscenity from the narrow alleys of pre-modern London to the centres of justice in the City of London. The three players in this metropolitan narrative were the legislators of the House of Lords in the Palace of Westminster, the purveyors of pornography in Holywell Street and the enforcers of the law at the Central Criminal Court at the Old Bailey (fig. 74). Obscenity drew these three elements into a struggle over the legitimate and illegitimate functions of urban space. Obscenity required the law to respond to the changing conditions and forms of mass urban culture in the mid-nineteenth century and to take responsibility for the new types of audiences that were appearing on the city streets. And as the law took up this challenge, it became implicated in the very values and images that it sought to destroy.

The history of the first Obscene Publications Act began on 9 May 1857, when Lord Campbell, the Lord Chief Justice, presided over the trials of two men charged with the sale of obscene publications.[90] The cases clearly had an enormous impact on him. The first case, against William Dugdale of Holywell Street, was a dramatic affair.[91] The defendant entered the court in an excited state, by turns protesting against the conduct of his arrest; proclaiming his innocence; pleading mercy for the sake of his children; and, finally, threatening the court with a knife. The second case, against William Strange, was brought for the publication of two obscene libels, *Paul Pry* (fig. 75) and *The Women of London*.[92] Witnesses were called to vouch for Strange's good character, including George Vickers, the Holywell Street publisher and book-shop keeper. Both defendants were found guilty and given prison sentences. Summing up the case, Lord Campbell expressed his horror that obscene papers, such as those seen in these cases, were sold publicly in the streets of London for as little as one penny.

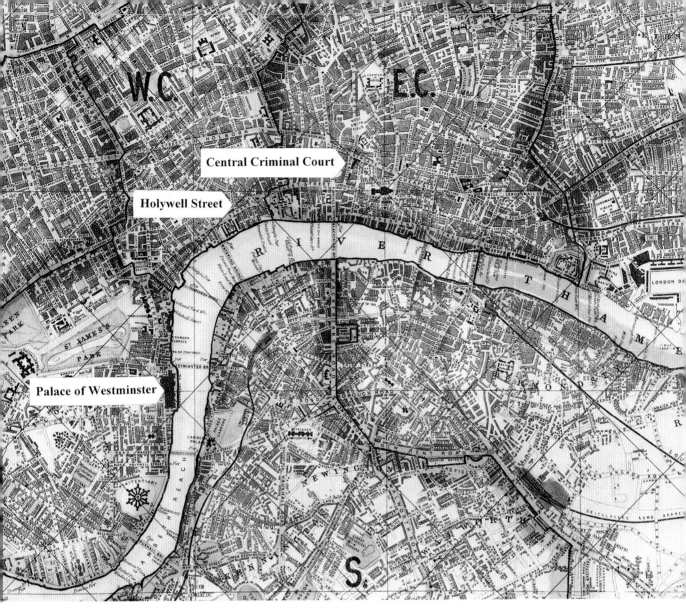

**Central Criminal Court**

**Holywell Street**

**Palace of Westminster**

74  Annotated section of *Whitbread's New Plan of London: Drawn from Authentic Surveys* (London: J. Whitbread, 1857). Showing the topographical relationship of the Palace of Westminster, Holywell Street and the Central Criminal Court. 47 × 65 cm. Maps 3480 (150). By Permission of the British Library.

Hitherto, Campbell argued, there had been some check on the influence of such publications, arising from the high prices that were charged for them; but now, these obscenities were cheap and easily obtainable. They were a source of national disgrace and a pernicious influence on the whole of society.

Campbell took the first available opportunity after the trial to raise the question of obscene publications in Parliament and to demand new legislation to put a stop to them.[93] The major daily and weekly papers were swift in expressing their support for Campbell's proposal; the *Illustrated London News* commented:

# PAUL PRY.

### The Inquisitive, Quizzical, Satirical, and Whimsical Epitome of Life as It Is.

**No. 1.**   PUBLISHED WEEKLY,   **Price One Penny**

## CASINO-TAP, HOLBORN.

TIME, in its mutations, plays sad havoc with houses as well as men. The splendid gin palace of to-day, may, to-morrow, with all its glare and light, be but a sad desert to the pleasure or sight seeker. So the table where once sat the witty, agreeable, and jocund companion, or where the "merriest fellow within the limits of becoming mirth" held court, may now find itself in the receptacle of the low, ill-mannered, and unwashed. There is no accounting for the vagaries of fortune, the jade is so fickle. Bow Street, Brydges Street, and the neighbourhood of Covent Garden, have, within the last few years, shown that their to-day affords but a poor criterion of what they were. But a most remarkable instance of the base use to which we may come is afforded by the past and present *prestige* attached to the Casino-tap, which we have chosen as an illustration to our first number.

For many years, even before Casinos were dreamt of in England, this house was noted for the fast and loose character of its denizens. Under the management of Mrs. Foxall, it was the haunt of all sorts of people—political, literary, and sleight of hand. Here, within the memory of the youngest inhabitant, congregated the Society of Bloaks, which numbered among its members men learned in the law, prize-fighters, swimmers, and downy-blades. In its little oblong back parlour once sat poor O'Flannigan, the legal tout who, under the auspices of Mr. Horry, the Old Bailey advocate, found himself incarcerated in Newgate for a similar offence to that for which that gentleman has now to answer at the bar of public opinion. O'Flannigan was well up in the technicalities of the law, but he was caught at last, and terminated a miserable existence by self-destruction, rather than stand the uncertainties of a trial. His beloved companion and confident, Attorney Jones, was here the observed of all observers; an inveterate punster and gin drinker. Within its hallowed fane the olatile

Jack Grant, son of the pious editor of the *Tap Tub* began his career of dissipation, which ended in emigration to Canada, under the wing of Sir Cusac Roney. At the bar of this house, George Pewtress, the champion swimmer, used to get insensibly drunk ere he condescended to "tread water," and show admiring crowds what he could do on the surface of the placid stream. The genial-hearted Horace Kenworthy—*beau ideal* of "laughter holding both his sides"—on its threshold took his last potation : and here, chewing the cud of dearly bought reflection, has sat many a fast city clerk or merchant's son, ruminating on the folies of the past night. We mind us of Jack Davenport, Tom and Dave Young, the Spider, little Bill, Blackey, Harry Jones, Liverpool Harry, Tom Grant, Bill Fish, Little Jack, and a multitude of others, whose prospects in life were here blighted by women and wine. But few of the old school, and these but wrecks of what they once were, are now left to tell the tale of midnight orgies, which reigned paramount in the Casino Tap.

let us express a hope that some stringent course will be adopted with regard
to the venders [*sic*] of such poison. New shops for its sale spring up every week;
and Holywell-street and its neighbourhood – the heart of the great London
thoroughfare – reeks with vileness . . . Lord Chief Justice Campbell deserves the
gratitude of the public, and we trust he will follow up the crusade against
abomination.[94]

The *Illustrated London News* had a special interest in the matter since its own offices
in the Strand were only a few yards from Holywell Street, but the public debate of
the following months went beyond such neighbourhood struggles and immediately
assumed a much greater national significance.

Within weeks and with the assistance of the Society for the Suppression of Vice,
Campbell introduced his own bill into the House of Lords. In fact, there was some
disagreement over whether existing laws were adequate and needed only stricter
enforcement, or whether new legislation was needed. The question was soon forgotten, however, as the campaign against obscenity took on its own extraordinary
momentum. Until 1857 obscenity had been part of a package of issues contained
within the legal regulation of public order. In the Vagrancy Act of 1824, the public
exhibition of obscene prints was made a summary offence within a range of provisions directed at regulating the public streets. This emphasis on the public display and
sale of obscene matter was reinforced in the Metropolitan Police Act of 1839 and in
the Town Police Clauses Act of 1847, in which obscenity was included alongside
such offences as importuning by prostitutes and indecent exposure.[95] The aim of all
of these laws was to regulate public behaviour and to maintain control of the city
streets. The public display of indecent images was seen as one instance of the transgressive manifestation of sexual desire and the loss of public control. As Beverley
Brown has noted: 'such exhibitions, prints or pictures present the dangers of crowds
out of control. Sexuality was situated as both cause of disorder and one of its forms.'[96]
By removing obscenity from the associated public order issues of earlier legislation
and creating a dedicated obscenity law, Campbell was expressing a broader social
concern about sexuality as a prime cause of public disorder. He was also tapping into
existing unease about the proliferation and influence of new forms of mass culture.
Campbell was not concerned to change the definition of obscenity; he was happy
to continue with the existing common law definition. What he wanted was more
adequate penalties for the dissemination of obscenity and, above all, the destruction
of the obscene goods concerned. He sought to withdraw these rogue commodities
from circulation, both in economic terms and in relation to a visual economy of
public display and viewing. Campbell and his supporters wanted a new law; they
wanted to take on obscenity in the context of new perceptions of metropolitan space.
The introduction of the Obscene Publications Act was, effectively, a struggle over
the nature of modern London. It was a campaign about who occupied the streets,
how they behaved and what they looked at, and it was waged over the symbolic
space of Holywell Street.

Campbell's legislation had a hard time passing through the two chambers of Lords
and Commons. One of the main areas of concern was the possible interference with
private life and individual liberty embodied in the bill's proposed use of search war-

rants. The other problem concerned the generality of the definition of obscenity. Campbell provided the House of Lords with the current test of obscenity, which applied to works with 'the single purpose of corrupting the morals of youth, and of a nature calculated to shock the common feelings of decency in any well regulated mind'.[97] It was not his intention that the legislation should apply to high culture, or to the private consumption of art, but that it should be directed to the public dissemination of mass-produced obscenity. But the question remained, why not? Why should the act not be aimed at obscenity of all kinds that fell within the existing definition; why not the masterpieces of Western culture as well as *Paul Pry* and *The Women of London*? What distinguished sex in high art and sex in mass culture, other than cost? In order to resolve these questions of classification and scope, obscenity had to be recast as a modern phenomenon; the progeny of the city streets, rather than the public art gallery or the private collection.

One of Campbell's chief opponents in the House of Lords' debate was Lord Lyndhurst, whose public career included a period as Lord Chancellor. An aristocratic figure, then in his mid-eighties, Lyndhurst was the son of the American painter John Singleton Copley.[98] The son of the artist faced John Campbell, the son of a Scottish minister and preacher and also nearing his eightieth year, over the benches of the House of Lords, where they battled over the borderlines of art and obscenity. Lyndhurst feared the intrusion of fortified legislation in private and apparently legitimate cultural consumption. As it stood, Campbell's bill allowed intervention in private art collections and legitimised cultural philistinism as under-educated and over-zealous police officers were given greater power to bring offending objects to court. Lyndhurst imagined one such encounter:

> Suppose now a man following the trade of an informer, or a policeman, sees in a window something which he conceives to be a licentious print. He goes to the magistrate, and describes, according to his ideas, what he saw; the magistrate thereupon issues his warrant for the seizure of the disgusting print. The officer then goes to the shop, and says to the shopkeeper, 'Let me look at that picture of Jupiter and Antiope.' 'Jupiter and what?', says the shopkeeper. 'Jupiter and Antiope', repeats the man. 'Oh! Jupiter and Antiope, you mean', says the shopkeeper; and hands him down the print. He sees the picture of a woman stark naked, lying down, and a satyr standing by her . . . The informer tells the man that he is going to seize the print, and to take him before the magistrate. 'Under what authority?' he asks; and he is told – 'Under the authority of Lord Campbell's Act.'[99]

Moreover, Lyndhurst speculated, what was to stop the informant extending his pursuit of obscenity to original paintings held in private collections throughout the country? Campbell hurried to reassure the opponents of his bill that Lyndhurst's fears were groundless. Pictures in private collections were not for sale, but for contemplation. Furthermore, there was a clear and marked distinction between the pictures that Lyndhurst described and the mass of prints that circulated in London shops and possessed no artistic merit whatever. The private possession and enjoyment of explicit works and objects of cultural value were a matter of personal 'taste' and not a subject for legal intervention.[100]

What is evident in this exchange between the two ageing law lords is that obscenity legislation is not only a question of the regulation of social and moral behaviour, but is also to do with the reordering of cultural consumption. The outlawing of obscenity in this period is an attempt to shore up official culture and to redraw the boundaries between the permissible and the forbidden. The new, cheap forms of commercial street culture are legally isolated through the new specialist category of obscenity, but whereas the law judges between art and obscenity in relation to mass culture, the judgement of decency in high culture is a matter of individual taste.

For Campbell's supporters in the press, Lyndhurst's objections were time-wasting sophistry. The *Daily Telegraph* was confident that high culture was safe from interference and that judgements concerning the kinds of objects targeted by the legislation could be left to the 'common sense' of magistrates and juries.[101] For *The Times* the distinction between legitimate and illegitimate culture was also clear. No one was trying to prevent booksellers from supplying their clients with complete editions of the classics (even the licentious ones) but, 'When their works are advertised in low thoroughfares in inflammatory placards, obviously addressed to the young, the ignorant, and the vicious, the law . . . will become applicable to the case'.[102]

The bill scraped through its second reading. Campbell was evidently discouraged by the extent of the opposition, but opened the following debate by saying that letters of public support from doctors, clergymen and fathers of families had made him realise that it was his duty to persevere.[103] He entreated the Lords to treat obscene publications like any other transgressive commodity and to use his bill to give the police the power to handle obscenity in the same way as gambling or contraband goods:

> in Holywell-street the keepers of these abominable publications set decency and law at defiance. If there were the same powers of searching for these books as for 'uncustomed goods' or as in gambling houses for dice and cards, the public might be relieved from these contaminations.[104]

The name of Holywell Street was invoked with greater frequency during the bill's third reading and the street's shopkeepers might have been justifiably nervous as the bill passed through the Lords and on to the Commons. There, similar concerns were raised concerning the definition of obscenity, infringements of privacy and searches of suspected premises; but, by now, the bill's opposition had run its course. By the time Campbell's bill reached the Commons, the Indian Mutiny was reaching a climax. Horrific reports of the siege of Delhi were dominating the press and discussion of the Obscene Publications bill was punctuated with emergency debates about the situation in the Indian Empire. In this context of imperial crisis and colonial resistance, obscenity assumed additional significance as an agent of disruption at the heart of the nation. Obscene publications corroded the moral values of the population on whom the success of Britain's growing imperial project depended. Dissent and disorder had to be eradicated at home and abroad. Delhi and Holywell Street constituted two manifestations of the other for imperial Britain; one, outside the nation, the other, poisonous, within the capital. In the geographical imagination, the regulation of London's unruly spaces had its explicit analogy with the imposition of order in the nation's colonies. The submission of the radical traders of Holywell Street and the rebellious mobs in India were two instances of the triumph of modern, imperial technologies over what were perceived as older and outmoded forms of society and culture.

The Obscene Publications Act was passed in September 1857.[105] It allowed that a search warrant could be issued following sworn information that obscene materials were being sold, distributed or exhibited on the premises concerned. The Act thus relied upon plain-clothed policemen to provide evidence of such transactions. Any obscene publications found as a result of a search could be seized and destroyed unless the owner of the premises could prove, in court, the non-obscenity of the work. As Beverley Brown has shown, this is a reversal of the usual practice in criminal matters, in which the defendant is 'innocent until proven guilty': 'On the contrary, what is required here is that the accused has to show their innocence, i.e. the non-obscenity of the work, which means calling for a trial which otherwise would not occur at all.'[106] Through Campbell's Act, obscenity was routed from the shabby alleys of mid-Victorian London and brought to the heart of the city's legal system. Through the new, fortified powers introduced by the Act, police officers infiltrated the world of Holywell Street and imposed an occasionally violent order on the place. The legislation represented a different perception of modern urban space in which previously tolerated crimes were no longer allowed. Sites of corruption were surveilled, entered and dismantled; goods were destroyed, and traders put out of business. The law thus created its own mapping of the city, as it tracked obscenity from the dark, irregular spaces of Holywell Street through the police courts and subjected it to the ritualised space of the Central Criminal Court at the Old Bailey.[107]

The name Old Bailey applied to the street in which the Court stood and which, through custom, became attached to the session house that stood next to Newgate Prison. The derivation of the name is thought to be either Roman, meaning a defensive wall, or from the Old English bailiff or sheriff. By the mid-nineteenth century, it was housed in a fierce, uncompromising building, erected in the 1770s.[108] Here, British justice supported British democracy. The Old Bailey was to constitute the legal and metaphorical terminus to obscenity's unregulated circulation. If Holywell Street symbolised spatial disorder in mid-Victorian London, then the Central Criminal Court represented the triumph of ritualised order and hierarchical organisation. Within British law, the space of the court and the time of the trial are highly ceremonial and carefully choreographed. Events take place in a set order; seating, appearances and speech are strictly stage-managed and nothing is left to chance.[109] The Central Criminal Court at the Old Bailey was one of the most famous courtrooms in the country; it symbolised the entire ceremonial edifice on which the British law was based (fig. 76). The judge sat, raised above the rest of the court, facing the defendant. To the right of the judge were the jury-box and witness-box and to the left were the seats for witnesses, visitors and the press. The space in the centre, bounded by the judge's bench on one side, the dock on another, the jury-box on the third and the reporters' seats on the fourth, was occupied by counsel and attorneys. Above the dock was the public gallery which, on the occasion of infamous trials, was often full to overspilling. At the start of the trial, the counsel and judge

76    Interior of the Old Bailey, *c.*1865. Photograph. Guildhall Library, Corporation of London.

entered the court. The indictment was read out and the defendant asked to plead; if the plea was not guilty to some of the counts, then the jury would be sworn in. The prosecution then opened the trial, followed by the defence. The judge summed up the case, the jury delivered its verdict and sentence (if guilty) would be passed. This was the familiar and immutable narrative of the time and space of the courtroom. Throughout this process, everything and everyone was in its place. No group encroached on another group's space; the judge stayed behind the bench, the defendant remained in the dock and the jurors never wandered from their box. The conduct of the trial itself symbolised the victory of the space of the courtroom over the space of the street. In Holywell Street the public mingled promiscuously; people touched, stared, spoke. They bought and sold; they wandered and daydreamed. It was a confused and disorderly space, in which meanings and identities were unclear, and intentions misconstrued. The courtroom imposed order on this unruly public and subjected the spatial ambiguities of Holywell Street to the authoritative space of the law. In the courtroom, relations were clarified and identities were confirmed; obscenity's misrule was, momentarily, ended.

   The first arrests under the Obscene Publications Act were made on 22 September 1857. Police executed a number of search warrants on shops in Holywell Street. The occupants, it was claimed, were completely taken by surprise.[110] The police blocked the approaches to the street and closed off access to individual houses in order to prevent any property being removed. Books, prints, photographs and other objects were seized and summonses brought against a number of shopkeepers. Among those first arrested was a certain Mary Elliott, aged forty-nine years, of 14 Holywell Street, on whose premises indecent books and prints were seized by the police. She pleaded guilty, but her defence pointed out that since the charge had been brought, Elliott had closed her shop and had promised never to resume trading in obscene publications again. Elliott was found guilty; the prosecution showed that immediately following the first seizure, a second search had been made of the premises, which revealed a fresh stock of obscene material. The prosecution claimed that the shop was open and trading at the very moment of the trial. In summing up, the judge described Elliott as a defiant and determined pornographer and sentenced her to twelve months' imprisonment with hard labour.[111]

Campbell's supporters in the press were delighted by the action and by the success of the strikes against Holywell Street. The *Illustrated London News* reported:

> Lord Campbell's Act against immoral publications has been put into force, and apparently with skill and completeness, in the abominable *repaire* known as Holywell-street. A strong body of police was drawn round the place, and detectives stormed the warehouses of vice, and carried off masses of their contents to the frenzied wrath of the fellows who live by the foul trade. The razzia must be renewed at intervals, until these pests are convinced that they will not be permitted to live by poisoning the minds of the young, and pandering to the tastes of the corrupt old.[112]

The police assault on Holywell Street made the street's spatial otherness within the modern metropolis more emphatic than ever before. It was like a separate and alien citadel within the city. The police campaign was represented as the reclamation of land occupied by dangerous and 'frenzied' natives and the reimposition of civilised law. The *Daily Telegraph* also reported the arrests under the headline 'The Police Razzia in Holywell-Street'.[113] The term razzia – a nineteenth-century colonial import – summed up the racial and imperial undertones of the police assault on Holywell Street. A razzia is a military expedition. Originally an Arabic term to describe a raid against the infidels, it lost this specific meaning and was absorbed into English to mean any imperial conquest. With its long history of associations with radicalism, Jews and immorality, and in the context of the revolts in India, it was, perhaps, inevitable that the struggle over Holywell Street should assume the significance of a highly concentrated and localised fight over imperial authority.

The Obscene Publications Act was national law, with massive legal implications, which ended up being directed almost entirely at shopkeepers in one small, ancient London street. Following the passing of the legislation, Campbell called for the submission to Parliament of information concerning arrests and trials arising from warrants issued under the Act. With only one exception, all of the warrants issued in the first months of the Act were from Bow Street, the London Police Court responsible for Holywell Street. Other Police Courts responded that no information had been collected and no warrants issued.[114] Holywell Street achieved its full symbolic importance in the singular focus of the Act against its shops and in the subsequent show trials held at the Old Bailey.

The Old Bailey completed the law's line of vision, which was drawn from Parliament Square, along Whitehall and the Strand, to the City of London (fig. 74). It was a mapping of the metropolis that connected legislators and law enforcers in the regulation and suppression of the unruly and transgressive spaces of the city. In the Central Criminal Court, the obscenities of Holywell Street became part of the social organisation of the criminal trial; re-presented as exhibits and evidence, with a given place in the courtroom's predetermined sequence of events. Taken away from the streets and into the courtroom, obscenity took on a new role as part of the public prosecution of corruption and immorality; but even in the courtroom it never entirely surrendered its subversive potential. Records of indictments against Holywell Street shopkeepers summon up an image of extended courtroom recitals of extracts from Victorian soft porn. Prose, verse, photographs and engravings all went on show; nudity, innuendo, puns, coy evasions. The Court procured, exhibited and disseminated the wares of Holywell Street. Only, of course, there was a difference. The distinction between alley and courtroom was made precisely through the law's encounter with and resistance to obscenity; in its being unmoved, or rather, moved only to judgement. But were there no blushes of embarrassment or smiles of pleasure; was the court really able to exclude the responses of the street in its sober, unexcited space of judgement?

Among the first Holywell Street arrests, which included Mary Elliott, was the case of Thomas Bleckter.[115] Bleckter had been found 'caretaking' one of the houses occupied by William Dugdale, during one of his many periods of imprisonment. Thus compromised, the case against Becketer was sealed when the house was searched and found to contain a vast quantity of obscene books and prints. Bleckter pleaded ignorance; claiming that he did not know Dugdale and had been unaware of the nature of the goods kept in the shop. The reading of the indictment would have made the nature of the goods clear to the members of the court.[116] The bill of indictment is read out at the beginning of criminal proceedings, before the assembled participants. It is a formal document; setting out the nature and date of the offences and giving, in detail, all the charges brought against the defendant. Each of the offences is listed as a different 'count' and set out in a separate paragraph. In the case of an obscenity trial, this means not only that lengthy extracts from each printed obscenity have to be written into the indictment, but also that every word has to be read aloud to the court at the beginning of the trial. In the case of visual representations, the images have to be described. The indictment thus contains two types of language: the language of the law and the language of the street. The law frames and seeks to contain the wayward language of commercialised sexuality, as obscenity finds a new audience assembled in the courtroom. So we learn that the third count against Thomas Bleckter was for the dissemination of 'The Wedding Night or Battles of Venus',[117] and are given a long extract from the 'filthy and obscene matter' including:

> All those delicacies of connexion between affection and embrace were dead in
> me. Like a Boarding School Girl, I only now considered the immediate contact

between the sexes. All the remains of the depraved appetite glowed again in my blood and I became eager after sensualities. My husband had left me upwards of a year during all that time I had not been guilty of the least action of irregularity. But I began to be warmed by the kisses of my new suitor . . . and I commenced an intrigue with the Vicar.

The fourth count was for the obscene libel 'The Man of Pleasure's Private Companion', and the fifth count related to 'The Spreeish Spouter or Flash Coves Bang up Reciter'. All counts included long extracts of the publications concerned, including the sixth count, against 'Gems for Gentlemen':

> [in which] there was contained a certain filthy and indecent and obscene picture representing a Man and a Woman in an indecent and obscene attitude position and situation and underneath which said picture there was printed the words following that is to say I'm sure to scream Sir if you do . . .

A significant amount of court time would have been taken up by the reading of the lengthy indictment against Blecketer. The banal rudeness of the charged material clashed with the hierarchical formalities of the court; but it was precisely these instances of cultural trivia that the judge and jury were called upon to adjudicate and, ultimately, to destroy. What is striking about the material charged under the Obscene Publications Act is its low-level smuttiness. These are not the most explicit sexual representations from the period, but are examples drawn from the borderline of Victorian commercial culture; where sensation shades into sex and where the distinction between acceptability and unacceptability must be made most emphatically. This is the borderline that defines the legal and moral limits of mass urban culture. So it was copies of *Paul Pry* (fig. 75), the *Town* and the *Little Wonder* (fig. 42) that were seized during the raids on Holywell Street.[118] These were the 'fast' publications of mid-Victorian London, which combined a mix of anti-official positions in their editorial columns, serialisations, theatrical titbits, agony columns, slang vocabulary and rude jokes. Although there was nearly always agreement about the obscenity of the material, this was not always the case. *Paul Pry* presented a particularly demanding test of judgement. A number of copies of the paper had been seized during the first raids, but following protests by shopkeepers, a few issues were returned to the defendants on the grounds that they were 'not sufficiently indecent' to come within the jurisdiction of the Act.[119] As critics in the House of Lords and the House of Commons had anticipated, Campbell's Act was poorly equipped to decide questions of the definition of obscenity, and juries had to follow the advice of judges such as Mr Justice Coleridge who instructed them: 'Use your common sense . . . and consider what is the general object of any work.'[120]

The Obscene Publications Act brought books, prints, photographs and miscellaneous cheap goods to be judged by the law. In its first months, the Act was evidently used as part of a broad attempt to clean up the mass culture of the city and to rid it of the moral and sexual ambiguities that so troubled mid-Victorian moralists and improvers. Daguerreotypes and photographic slides showing naked human figures, taken from life, were seized. The shopkeeper contended that they were for academic and artistic purposes; the judge ruled that they were low, vulgar and

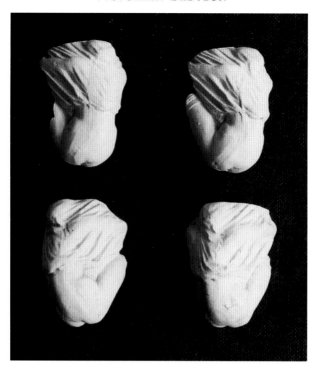

77   Fragments of obscene clay pipes, c.1850–60. Museum of London Archaeological Service. Photo: Birkbeck College.

obscene.[121] In most cases the ruling went against the defendant. One of the most extraordinary cases involved the seizure from premises in High Holborn of pipes, pipe-heads and tobacco-stoppers, said to display various degrees of indecency. The defence argued that the Act did not cover pipes and that the goods were imported and had passed through Customs. The magistrate ordered their destruction.[122] Obscene pipes were surely the nadir of Victorian London's outlawing of obscenity. What did it mean to rule that a pipe had been made with the single purpose of corrupting the morals of the young? In the Archaeology Department of the Museum of London there is an uncatalogued collection of smashed shards of clay pipes and other ceramics, given to the museum by a local collector of the city's ephemera. The pipe-bowls are in the form of veiled, naked female figures, whose legs are wrapped round the stem (fig. 77). All of the pipes are shattered; were these the objects that were ruled obscene and later smashed by some employee of the court? The anthropomorphic pipe-bowls, intended to be cupped in the hands of Victorian smokers, ended up dumped in the mud of the River Thames. The destruction of this kind of mass-produced fairground ephemera symbolised the full extent and concern of Campbell's law. Obscenity, in all its forms, was a dangerous moral poison and the law had to be comprehensive and harsh. Sentences were extreme; in each case imprisonment with hard labour. Thomas Bleckerer was sent down for six months, a lighter sentence than that given to Mary Elliott because he had at least closed his premises following his arrest.[123]

Reviewing the success of the Act in December of 1857, Lord Campbell told the House of Lords: 'This siege of Holywell Street might be compared to the siege of

Delhi. The place was not taken in a day, but repeated assaults were necessary, and at last . . . it was now in the quiet possession of the law.'[124] Holywell Street, he declared, had been successfully cleaned up; goods had been destroyed and shops had ceased trading. In February 1858 *The Times* announced that 'The Royal Academy of Filth in Holywell Street has been shorn of its dirty honours and dirty profits'.[125] In an attempt to signal a clear change in the street's reputation, the Metropolitan Board of Works proposed to alter its name to Booksellers' Row, but the new name would not stick.[126] It is difficult to assess with absolute certainty the extent of the transformation of Holywell Street; many of the shopkeepers continued to trade under the same names and by the late 1860s the *Saturday Review* was describing the Obscene Publications Act as 'a dead letter':

> Holywell Street literature is not only a phrase, but a very visible and palpable fact of the day. At the present moment the dunghill is in full heat, seething and steaming with all its old pestilential fume. It requires but a short walk, and a brief glance at the windows of this unsavoury den, to know what is going on, and in all the rampant insolence of the most extreme publicity.[127]

Holywell Street retained its notoriety until it was finally demolished at the end of Victoria's reign to make way for the new thoroughfares of the Aldwych and Kingsway, and when it finally 'came down', the plans that were circulated showed the densely packed streets of the old city ghosted behind the straight, clean outlines of the new roads of the twentieth-century metropolis (fig. 78). As one nostalgic bibliophile in the 1920s put it: 'careful plans have been made showing at one glance the new streets . . . striding, so to speak, over the prostrate bodies of the old.'[128]

If one of the central ideals of urban improvement in the nineteenth century was the flow of movement, then Holywell Street was an impenetrable congestion, obstructing the main thoroughfare and line of communication between the City of London and Westminster. Just to one side, but not sufficiently out of the way, it was the spatial enactment of the suggested etymology of obscene – that which is off, or to one side of the stage, just beyond visibility. It was also the internal structural link that held together, but fatally compromised the sites of legislation and judgement. Topographically, Holywell Street lay at the mid-point on a route that linked the Houses of Parliament in Westminster and the criminal courts at the Old Bailey in the City of London (fig. 74). These highly symbolic sites marked the spatial beginning and end of law: the place of the framing of legislation and the place of its enactment. Holywell Street's transgressive space interfered with the linear, hierarchical vision of law. It was a place of desire and resistance, in which space itself assumed political dimensions.[129]

In 1868 the Metropolitan Board of Works hit upon a new idea for improving the flow of traffic in London's streets: a fine new thoroughfare, linking in direct communication the Houses of Parliament, the new Inns of Court, planned for a site in Holborn abutting Holywell Street, and the City of London at Temple Bar.[130] The street would be a great arc, following the line of a purified River Thames, with Parliament and Temple Bar at its two extremes. But obscenity had already been there. Official London was simply retracing a route that had already been mapped by the

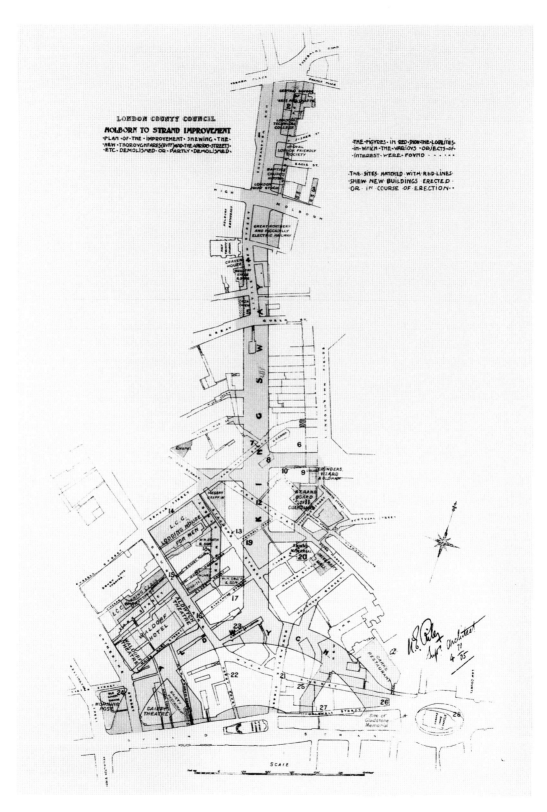

78 Plans for the building of Kingsway and Aldwych, from London County Council, *Opening of Kingsway and Aldwych by His Majesty the King, Accompanied by Her Majesty the Queen. On Wednesday 18th October, 1905* (London: Southwood, Smith and Co., 1905). Guildhall Library, Corporation of London.

production, consumption and regulation of the obscene. Holywell Street may have been to one side of the lines of official London, but its disturbing presence also ensured its centrality within cultural and legal discourses throughout the nineteenth century.

*4       Temple Bar*

> The raw afternoon is rawest, and the dense fog is densest, and the muddy streets are muddiest, near that leaden-headed old obstruction, appropriate ornament for the threshold of a leaden-headed old corporation: Temple Bar. (Charles Dickens, *Bleak House*, 1853)[131]

For hundreds of years Temple Bar was one of the most important landmarks in London, marking the western limits of the City of London and its boundary with the City of Westminster. In terms of the history of London, it was a site of immense symbolic significance, constituting a boundary of jurisdiction between the vested powers and interests of the City of London and those of the monarch, court and government at Westminster. By the middle of the nineteenth century, it stood as a symbol of the problems facing the reform and modernisation of the metropolis and of the persistent, irritating struggles for authority between the Corporation of London, the Metropolitan Board of Works and central government. Temple Bar was a physical expression of the continuing independence of the Corporation of London and of the complex political landscape of London government, which blighted dreams of a total London makeover in the image of Paris and of the creation of a unified modern metropolis. For many contemporaries Temple Bar was the pivot around which London moved; it represented the very heart and centre of the city. But it was also a ghastly old obstacle; a blockage in the free movement of the city between its eastern and western limits. Temple Bar bore the memories of a different, older London; a world of absolute monarchy and of brutal public punishment. In Dickens's memorable description of the impenetrable, atavistic obscurity of London's legal institutions, Temple Bar stands at the heart of the fog and mire. Modern London required light, clarity and coherence, and Temple Bar stood in the way of progress, a barrier to improvement as well as a boundary of authority.

The history of the site at Temple Bar is, effectively, a history of London. First references to a barrier on this spot, separating the liberties of the City of London and the City of Westminster, appear in texts from the twelfth and thirteenth centuries.[132] At first, the Bar was simply an arrangement of wooden posts, with a rail and chain. This was later replaced by a timber building, and in 1670, after the Great Fire, a new stone edifice was built, from designs by Sir Christopher Wren (fig. 79). This was the Temple Bar that still occupied and filled the street of the Victorian city, that channelled traffic in Fleet Street and the Strand into two, congested single lines and squeezed pedestrians under its narrow archways. It was a sold, squat edifice, with a

79   'Temple Bar, *in situ*' (Fleet Street façade, looking west), *c.*1874. Photograph. Guildhall Library, Corporation of London.

central gateway for road traffic and posterns for foot passengers on each side. The upper part of the Bar was flanked with rather theatrical, carved scrolls, either side of an arrangement of Corinthian pilasters, statues in niches and a rounded pediment. The room over the central archway was held by Messrs Child, the bankers, who rented the space from the City of London and kept old account books there. Temple Bar had two façades: one facing east, towards Fleet Street and the City of London, and one facing west, towards the Strand and Westminster. This spatial dualism was both the purpose and the problem of Temple Bar. It was a constant reminder of the historical and political divisions that haunted mid-Victorian London.

Above all else, Temple Bar was a place of ritual and pageantry. When the sovereign visited the City, it was customary to close the gates while the Lord Mayor granted entry; the gates were then reopened and during the visit the Lord Mayor surrendered the city sword to the sovereign who returned it at the end of the visit.[133] All the British monarchs had their historical encounters with Temple Bar, including Queen Victoria who passed through it on her way to a number of judicious ceremonial visits after her accession in 1837. Temple Bar's greatest notoriety arose from the habit, which started at the end of the seventeenth century, of displaying the remains of people executed for treason on iron spikes projecting from the pediment. The spectacle continued into the eighteenth century and earned Temple Bar the unhappy epithet, 'the City Golgotha'. The iron spikes were not removed from Temple Bar until the beginning of the nineteenth century and during Victoria's reign it continued to symbolise the most glorious and the most degraded rituals of British political life.

Temple Bar tracked the highs and lows of court and civic society year by year, through the nineteenth century. On the death and funeral of the Duke of Wellington in 1852 it was draped in deepest, darkest mourning; and on the occasion of the Prince of Wales's marriage in 1863 it bore the greatest number of and brightest gas illuminations in the City.[134] By the 1870s Temple Bar's pageantry was being dismissed as 'ragged and meaningless' and as 'silly mummery', but still it remained a peculiar condensation of the history of London.[135] Throughout the 1850s and 1860s engravings of Temple Bar were on the title-pages of Murray's guidebooks to London and each issue of George Augustus Sala's eponymously named periodical, *Temple Bar*. For Sala, Temple Bar was London's most characteristic monument: it was 'the quaintest, most significant and most impressive'; its gateways a funnel not only for all the traffic of the modern city but also for all of its ghosts.[136] The image that was repeated most frequently was of Temple Bar channelling a tide of humanity that defined the essential character of London. All of these lives left their traces on the worn-out stone of the Bar, which bore witness to the history of the metropolis. A woodcut from the 1870s shows an aerial view of the main east–west arterial route, along Fleet Street and the Strand (fig. 80). From the green outskirts of the city, tiny notations mark the carriages and pedestrians who stream westwards from the City, through the boundary of Temple Bar, on to St Clement Danes and along the Strand, or into the narrow straits of Holywell Street. Everything seems to move to the west, through Temple Bar. As one contemporary history put it, 'more persons pass under Temple Bar than under any archway in the world.'[137]

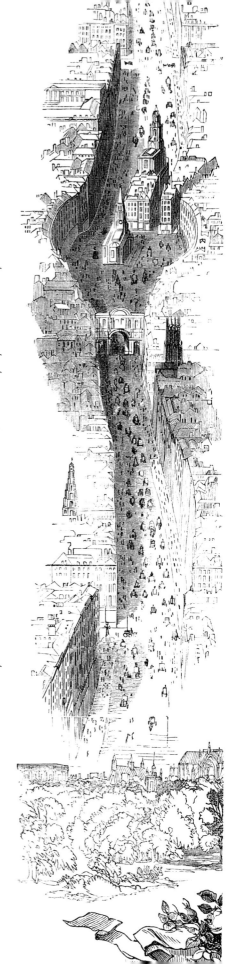

80  'Bird's Eye View of the Strand', n.d. From 'A Catalogue of Maps, Plans and Views of London, Westminster and Southwark. Collected and Arranged by Frederick Crace, Edited by His Son John Gregory Crace' (London, 1878), Portfolio XVII, sheet 76, no. 36. Wood engraving, 29 × 7 cm. © Copyright The British Museum.

When Henry Mayhew went up in his hot-air balloon, he saw London as an entire world, with its opposite poles of east and west, its own vast continents and distinct races. Viewed this way, Temple Bar took on a special geographical significance: 'Of such a world, Temple Bar is the unmistakable equator, dividing the City hemisphere from that of the West End, and with a line of Banks, representative of the Gold Coast, in its immediate neighbourhood.'[138] This was the paradox of Temple Bar in the nineteenth century. It was the heart of the capital of an empire, but it was also a testament to the divisions and conflicting interests within that capital.

By the end of the eighteenth century, it was clear that Temple Bar constituted a public nuisance and was a major obstruction to the flow of traffic in the most important financial and legal district of London. Like the opponents of Holywell Street, critics of Temple Bar engaged in a long campaign for its destruction. From the beginning of the nineteenth century, a number of Acts were passed by Parliament for the widening and improvement of the streets around Temple Bar, but the monument itself was left untouched.[139] The unceasing flow of traffic through the arch grew in volume throughout the first half of the nineteenth century. Citizens of Westminster complained of traffic deadlock, the City aldermen denied any obstruction, and by 1850 the struggle over Temple Bar had settled into a symbolic conflict between the protectionist governors of the City of London and the advocates of modern metropolitan government. In 1853 the *Illustrated London News* responded to the Corporation of London's most recent defence of Temple Bar by proposing a number of compromise plans. Temple Bar did not have to be utterly destroyed, it could stand at the centre of a new, wide roadway at Fleet Street, or it could become pure monument and be re-erected in the grounds of the new Crystal Palace. Finally, the article indulged one envious look across the Channel, where the government of Napoleon III was beginning its massive reconstruction of the centre of Paris. The conclusion was clear; the problem did not lie with Temple Bar but with the government of London: 'The Corporation of London certainly requires repair, reconstruction, and ventilation, new avenues and renewed foundation even more than Temple-bar.'[140]

With the establishment of the Metropolitan Board of Works in 1855 the conflict over the future of Temple Bar became even more polarised and intractable. The Board had been created as the first metropolitan-wide local authority for London, but throughout the period leading up to its introduction the City defended and protected its established rights. The City had fended off earlier attempts at metropolitan incorporation. In 1829 it had been excluded from the area controlled by the newly formed Metropolitan Police Force and it remained autonomous within the new arrangements for the Metropolitan Board of Works.[141] From the second half of the nineteenth century the Corporation of London represented an independent system of local government within the capital, opposed to all attempts at metropolitan unification and centralisation. Moreover, with its financial and business interests, it represented a powerful and influential voice and, not surprisingly, successive governments and commissions endorsed its continued independence. Temple Bar marked the limits of the new Metropolitan Board of Works and the ongoing independence and influence of the City of London. It was an unavoidable reminder of

81 'London a "Slough of Despond": Scene Near Temple Bar on Friday, Jan. 12, 1866', *Illustrated Times*, 20 January 1866, p. 41.

the partial and incomplete nature of London's modernisation. London was not a centralised political entity like Paris but seemed condemned for ever to the fragmentation of competing local vested interests and established rights. This is what its opponents saw in the lines of traffic from the Strand, squeezing together by St Clement Danes and squashing under Temple Bar. The obstacle to open circulation lay in the archaic powers of the Corporation and its aldermen and their unflinching defence of their boundaries and ancient gateways.

Within a few years of its creation, the Metropolitan Board of Works was voting for the removal of Temple Bar. At a meeting on 5 March 1858, the Board resolved *nem. con.*: 'That Temple-bar presents an obstruction to the traffic of the Strand and Fleet-street, and that its removal and the widening of the street adjacent are desirable.'[142] The strangely equivocal language of the resolution expresses the political impotence of the Board when it came to Temple Bar. The Bar did not belong to them and all they could do in the circumstances was write to the Corporation of London and the City Commission of Sewers and request them to consider the Board's resolution. A few letters were sent back and forth between councillors and commissioners, and nothing was done.

In the face of the Corporation's resistance, supporters of unified metropolitan government carried on their campaign against the City of London in printed text and image. In the political context of the early 1860s, pictorial scenes of London street life could be seen as powerful attacks on the City of London's mismanagement, and the site at Temple Bar became an effective shorthand for the diverse obstructions created by the Corporation. The full-page engraving carried in the *Illustrated Times* on 20 January 1866 is not simply a generic scene of a London street in winter (fig. 81). The 'slough of despond' referred to in the title and the chaos of road traffic and pedestrians depicted in the image are framed by the familiar outlines of Temple Bar in the background. The despondency and confusion emanate from its arches and there can be no doubt about the intended message of the image.

The decision to build the spectacular new Law Courts on a site by the Strand just next to Temple Bar, marked the beginning of its inevitable destruction. In 1865 the site was purchased from public funds and the task of demolishing the nearby houses and clearing the ground began. In the midst of this devastation, Temple Bar stood as a shaky marker of the progress of demolition and of its own precarious future. The *Illustrated London News* exploited the visual impact of the scene and showed the gateway surrounded by broken buildings and heaps of debris (fig. 82). Improvement seems to have its own irresistible momentum and in terms of the image it cannot be long before Temple Bar comes down to clear the way for metropolitan improvement. Predictably, as work on the Law Courts progressed and the foundations were laid, Temple Bar began to subside. Surveyors declared it a dangerous structure and wooden scaffolding was erected to shore up the rotting masonry.[143]

Finally, in 1874, the Court of Common Council of the Corporation of London recommended that Temple Bar should be taken down. After even more consultation and prevarication, the Council eventually voted in 1876 for its removal.[144] In the days leading up to the vote the political connotations of Temple Bar were brought out into the open. Sir George Bowyer – baronet, renowned jurist, ex-Liberal Member of Parliament and recently expelled from the Reform Club – wrote to *The Times* defending Temple Bar and turning accusations about its architectural incoherence against the Houses of Parliament and the suite of government buildings on Whitehall.[145] The letter provoked a savage leading article from the *Daily Telegraph* which described Temple Bar as 'absolutely destitute of historic, literary, or picturesque associations of an ennobling kind . . . ancient, decayed, worthless and obstructive'.[146] For the *Telegraph*, the question of the future of Temple Bar was unambiguously a struggle between the Corporation of London and the rest of the metropolis, represented by the district of Westminster:

It is time that the good folks in the City were plainly told that the question of Temple Bar concerns not them alone, but is of equal importance to the inhabitants of Westminster; that what may appear to the citizens as very lovely indeed from the Fleet-street side, is, as seen from the Strand, intolerably ugly; and that the

82   'Forlorn Condition of Temple-Bar', *Illustrated London News*, 14 March 1868, p. 265.

bigoted views of a small section of the community cannot be suffered to weigh against the demand of the metropolis at large.

The removal of Temple Bar began on 3 January 1878.[147] Stone by stone, the gateway was dismantled and painstakingly stored for erection on a new, but as yet undecided, site. *The Times* allowed itself a moment of regret and acknowledged Temple Bar's centrality as a London landmark. Ultimately, however, it was a symbol of archaic local power:

> for no reason whatever, in the pure wantonness of prescription and power, [Temple Bar] bestrid the crowded thoroughfare, and proclaimed to the people that they must creep, crowd, and feel their way under it . . . Self-assertion, as a rule, ought to be very strong, very annoying and injurious, and then it may carry the day.[148]

For *The Times*, the spatial constriction and obstruction caused by Temple Bar was an assertion by the Corporation of London of its power over the rest of the metropolis. It was a 'barricade', rather than a gateway, maintaining the isolation of the City

83   'The Demolition of Temple Bar: Night Scene', *Illustrated London News*, 19 January 1878, p. 56.

of London, as opposed to the free flow of movement throughout the metropolis. But the days of such antiquated insularity were over and Temple Bar had been toppled by the new fluid mobility created by metropolitan improvement, which could not be contained by wooden doors and stone arches. *The Times* suggested:

84   'Temple Bar Re-erected at the Entrance of Theobald's Park', *c.*1910. Photograph. Guildhall Library, Corporation of London.

Possibly its fall has been accelerated by the fact of its being turned on both sides, and even undermined by the spread of improvement. On the south, the Thames Embankment is the best highway to the city, and it is quite guiltless of bar or gate; on the north, Holborn-bars are a thing of the past . . . The Underground Railway knows naught of city boundaries.

For a moment, *The Times* indulges in metropolitan optimism. The new highways of improved London, above and below ground, reclaimed from the earth and the water, have overcome the congestion and obstacles of the old city. The removal of Temple Bar allowed a brief respite of nostalgia and triumph before all the familiar political conflicts and anxieties came back to trouble London's modernisers.

The *Illustrated London News* recorded the last moments of Temple Bar, as workmen and machinery took down the final blocks of stone. A full-page engraving shows the demolition works at night (fig. 83).[149] The half-demolished gateway is dwarfed by the lines and angles of the wooden scaffolding. In order to minimise the disruption to the daytime business of the area, the work goes on through the night, lit by flares and watched by crowds of bystanders. But there is also the sense that this is a night event. That the removal of Temple Bar, that over-determined symbol of the complex and ancient history of London, belongs properly to the night, to the spectral side of the city, and must become another of the whispered 'secrets of the gas'.

In spite of proposals to re-erect Temple Bar in various London parks, the stones were finally purchased by Sir Henry Meux – a wealthy brewer – to stand at the entrance to his private estate at Theobald's Park, north of London (fig. 84). The former symbol of the historic independence of the City of London took on a new role as a gateway to an insignificant personal estate. It now stands on the same site, in what has become a building society conference centre. Abandoned and dilapidated, it is now some distance inside the grounds, surrounded by iron railings, the entrance to nowhere and the boundary of nothing.

# 5          *Reflections on the Ruins of London*

Victorian London was not only haunted by the ruins of its past, it was also possessed by dystopic visions of its future. The projects of metropolitan improvement created a physical environment in which the processes of history were visible and inescapable. The devastation caused by the coming down of old London and by the construction of a new imperial city was vivid testimony to the amalgam within modernity of the past and the future. These dual historical visions drove the modernisers on in their attempts to fashion a strong and stable modern metropolis. It was, however, an impossible goal, for the future itself was already adulterated with spectres of collapse and loss.

Gustave Doré and Blanchard Jerrold's *London: A Pilgrimage* (1872) represents the genre of the textual tour of the city at its most accomplished and resolved.[150] The impact of the book is, without question, a result of the success of the collaboration of writer and artist and of the skilful organisation of text and image. Jerrold's narrative is expanded and enhanced by Doré's engravings, which are placed throughout the text in small vignettes, half-page and full-page illustrations. *London: A Pilgrimage* maps the social life and customs of London at the beginning of the 1870s. It creates a geography of contrasts through its scenes of high life and low life; West End and East End; leisure and labour. It is a place of myth; consumed by the viewer in terms of pleasure and danger, empathy and sympathy. Individual images from the book have, in the twentieth century, been frequently reproduced to illustrate the appearance of mid-Victorian London and to feed our own mythologies of Victorian society and culture. Curiously, though, little attention has been paid to the final full-page illustration of the book. It is not an image of contemporary London, but belongs to a different pictorial register. It is a fantasy image of London's future; of a New Zealander contemplating the ruins of a once great and powerful city (fig. 85).

Jerrold brought his London narration to a close with a final reflection on the importance of the Thames and the iconic significance of the dome of St Paul's Cathedral:

> Now we have watched the fleets into noisy Billingsgate; and now gossiped looking towards Wren's grand dome, shaping Macaulay's dream of the far future, with the tourist New Zealander upon the broken parapets, contemplating something matching –
>
>     'The glory that was Greece –
>     The grandeur that was Rome.'[151]

These are strange, uncharacteristic lines; an uncomfortable combination of hasty conclusion and dense citation. They are, perhaps, simply a formulaic nod to conventional tropes of imperial history, but they are taken by Doré and developed into one of the most dramatic illustrations in the book. It is a dark image, even by the standards of Doré's distinctive style of ruled engraving, with its dense blacks and dark greys. It shows the New Zealand artist, seated on a rock in the foreground and looking across the river to the ruins of London. The buildings are strangely compacted within the ver-

85   Gustave Doré, 'The New Zealander', from Gustave Doré and Blanchard Jerrold, *London: A Pilgrimage* (London: Grant and Co., 1872), opp. p. 188.

tical frame of the picture and recall both the ruins of imperial Rome and a more apoca-lyptic vision of the end of civilisation. The shattered dome of St Paul's and surround-ing desolation might be the consequence of inertia and slow decline, or the result of a sudden and terrible disaster. Victorian Babylon lies at some indeterminate time in the future, wrecked and shattered, under a heavy, foreboding sky. It is a critical con-clusion to this London pilgrimage; it is as though the city's urgency and diversity at the beginning of the 1870s can be understood only in terms of this image of the future. Ruin is the resolution of the contradictory impulses of modernity.

The trope of the native from the New World contemplating the ruins of London was reasonably familiar in the nineteenth century. Edward Gibbon had drawn on this image at the end of the eighteenth century in his account of the genealogy of empires and it took on a renewed vigour in romantic writings on myth and political history.[152]

Macaulay's reference to the New Zealander is in a few almost throwaway lines in an 1840 review of von Ranke's *History of the Popes*. Reflecting on the longevity and resilience of the Catholic Church, Macaulay speculated: 'she may still exist in undiminished vigour when some traveller from New Zealand shall, in the midst of a vast solitude, take his stand on a broken arch of London Bridge to sketch the ruins of St. Paul's.'[153] And there it is left; the vision is abandoned and the historian returns to his views on the power of Catholicism. By 1840 the figure of the New Zealander had both specific and more general connotations. Britain had just annexed New Zealand, so, for Macaulay, the traveller witnessing the ruins of London repre-sented a particularly prescient reversal of imperial fortune. On the other hand, the New Zealander also signified the most extreme position of difference and alterity from which to view contemporary British society.[154] In 1840 the New Zealander sketching amongst the ruins of London represented the most extreme distance of time and place.

By the 1860s, however, things had changed. The Metropolitan Board of Works and the railway companies were re-making London: widening and straightening, levelling and tunnelling, and the image of ruin had become part of the visual vocabu-lary of the historical present. The ruins of London were not just a rhetorical figure for the cyclical evolution of empires, but were a feature of the everyday experience of the modern metropolis. In 1864 a bizarre novel was published called *Archimago*, by the pseudonymous author, Jno.[155] The book is an unpredictable blend of realism and the supernatural. Set sometime in the near future, perhaps in the last decades of the nineteenth century, the novel opens with the author/narrator adopting the position of the New Zealand observer:

> I, Jno., formerly of the U.K. of G.B., – a kingdom scarce a quarter of a century ago the base, or rather the apex, of an Empire which rose over and around it, triangular, precipitous and vast . . .
>
> I sit upon the last crumbling stones of that bridge, – erst the famous London Bridge. Pavement, footway, parapet, abutment, pillar, pier, all, all are gone. A rough, steep bank leads to the water on its northern side . . . and I, on the last few moul-dering stones . . . survey the ruined and desolate city. (p. 1)

The narrator then recounts the events and characters preceding this devastation. In an extended, but incoherent flashback, the author draws the reader back to the

London of the 1860s. Returning after a short break from the metropolis, the narrator describes the transformation of the city landscape:

> I was astounded, on coming into the busy city once more, to observe great changes wrought in its appearance. Some of the bridges over the river, that I had left intact, were nearly demolished, and others were springing up to supplant them. Marketplaces, hotels, and houses, were in ruins, or had put on a new aspect. Arches had risen over many thoroughfares, and steam-trains swept above and between houses, to the jeopardy of upper tenements and tenants. What with digging up and pulling down, building and improving, restoring and adding, I could scarce recognise the old streets, or the old stream . . . In their last days, this people were great changers; their metropolis, indeed, became the Hospital of Cities. (pp. 52–3)

This is a vision of total physical transformation. London has become 'the Hospital of Cities'; an urban environment dominated by sickness and promising in equal measure cure or fatality. The novel sank with hardly a trace; nevertheless, here are all the visual elements of Doré's London, with its emphasis on movement, diversity and change. More than this, however, there is the overwhelming spectacle of ruin, which draws together past, present and future in a physical and psychological continuum. The dystopic vision of the ruins of Victorian Babylon was not just a figure of the possible distant future, it was a cipher for the experience and condition of modernity itself. This was the truth of modernity for London, the 'Hospital of Cities', in the middle of the nineteenth century. London could never cut itself loose from its complex temporality. Modernity was being built upon the image of ruin.

# Notes

*Abbreviations*

CPL          *Chelsea Public Library. The Royal*
             *Borough of Kensington & Chelsea*
             *Libraries and Arts Service*
Hansard      *Hansard's Parliamentary Debates*
ILN          *Illustrated London News*


*Introduction*

1   'London, As It Strikes a Stranger', *Temple Bar*, 5 (June 1862), p. 381.

2   For discussion of the image of Babylon in relation to Dickens's representation of London see Nancy Aycock Metz, '*Little Dorrit*'s London: Babylon Revisited', *Victorian Studies*, 33:3 (Spring 1990), pp. 465–86. On the significance of the Roman Empire within British imperialist ideology see Raymond F. Betts, 'The Allusion to Rome in British Imperialist Thought of the Late-Nineteenth and Early-Twentieth Centuries', *Victorian Studies*, 15:2 (December 1971), pp. 149–59.

3   There are far too many historiographies of modernity to be listed here. A clear and helpful analysis of some recent critical studies of modernity is given in Miles Ogborn, *Spaces of Modernity: London's Geographies, 1680–1780* (New York: Guilford Press, 1998), pp. 1–28. Peter Osborne offered an excellent analysis of the temporal dimensions of the term in 'Modernity is a Qualitative, Not a Chronological Category', *New Left Review*, 192 (1992), pp. 65–84.

4   See, for example, the debate between Marshall Berman, *All That Is Solid Melts Into Air: The Experience of Modernity* (London: Verso, 1983), and Perry Anderson, 'Modernity and Revolution', *New Left Review*, 144 (1984), pp. 96–113; Marshall Berman, 'The Signs in the Street: A Response to Perry Anderson', *New Left Review*, 144 (1984), pp. 114–23.

5   Berman, *All That Is Solid*, pp. 16–17.

6   Ibid., p. 15.

7   For a critique of Berman's periodisation see Osborne, 'Modernity', pp. 67–8. On the colonial dimensions of modernity see Paul Gilroy, *The Black Atlantic: Modernity and Double Consciousness* (London and New York: Verso, 1993).

8   David Harvey has expressed a similar interest in relation to his study of Haussmann's Paris, *Consciousness and the Urban Experience* (Oxford: Basil Blackwell, 1985), esp. p. 168.

9   See, for example, Walter Benjamin, *One-Way Street and Other Writings*, trans. by Edmund Jephcott and Kingsley Shorter (London and New York: Verso, 1979), and the outstanding analysis of Benjamin's concept of history in Susan Buck-Morss, *The Dialectics of Seeing: Walter Benjamin and the Arcades Project* (Cambridge, Mass.: MIT Press, 1989).

10  Walter Benjamin, *Das Passagen-Werk*, as cited in Buck-Morss, *Dialectics of Seeing*, p. 108.

11  For some classic examples of this body of scholarship see David H. Pinkney, *Napoleon III and the Rebuilding of Paris* (Princeton, New Jersey: Princeton University Press, 1958); Anthony Sutcliffe, *The Autumn of Central Paris: The Defeat of Town Planning, 1850–1970* (London: Edward Arnold, 1970); T. J. Clark, *The Painting of Modern Life: Paris in the Art of Manet and His Followers* (London: Thames and Hudson, 1985); and Harvey, *Consciousness and Urban Experience*.

12  Walter Benjamin, 'Paris – the Capital of the Nineteenth Century', trans. by Quintin Hoare, in *Charles Baudelaire: A Lyric Poet in the Era of High Capitalism* (London and New York: Verso, 1973), pp. 157–76. For a critique of the 'saturation' of cultural debates on modernity by Paris see John Tagg, 'The Discontinuous City: Picturing and the Discursive Field', in Norman Bryson, Michael Ann Holly and Keith Moxey, eds., *Visual Culture: Images and Interpretations* (Hanover and London: Wesleyan University Press, 1994), pp. 83–103.

13  The 'spatial turn' in social theory from the late 1960s is discussed in Edward W. Soja, *Postmodern Geographies: The Reassertion of Space in*

*Critical Social Theory* (London and New York: Verso, 1989).

14　Michel Foucault, 'The Eye of Power', in Colin Gordon, ed., *Power/Knowledge: Selected Interviews and Other Writings, 1972–1977* (Brighton: Harvester, 1980), pp. 146–65. See also *Discipline and Punish: The Birth of the Prison*, trans. by Alan Sheridan (London: Allen Lane, 1977).

15　Michel Foucault, 'Of Other Spaces', *Diacritics*, vol. 16 (Spring 1986), pp. 22–7.

16　Michel de Certeau, 'Practices of Space', in Marshall Blonsky, ed., *On Signs* (Oxford: Basil Blackwell, 1985), pp. 122–45, and *The Practice of Everyday Life*, trans. by Steven Rendall (Berkeley, Los Angeles and London: University of California Press, 1984).

17　Michel de Certeau, *Heterologies: Discourse on the Other*, trans. by Brian Massumi (Manchester: University of Manchester Press, 1986).

18　Michel de Certeau, 'Psychoanalysis and Its History', in *Heterologies*, p. 4. For a developed study of the uncanny in relation to architecture and modernity see Anthony Vidler, *The Architectural Uncanny: Essays in the Modern Unhomely* (Cambridge, Mass., and London: MIT Press, 1992).

19　Michel Serres with Bruno Latour, *Conversations on Science, Culture and Time*, trans. by Roxanne Lapidus (Ann Arbor: University of Michigan Press, 1995), p. 60.

**Part 1**

1　For population figures see Francis Sheppard, *London, 1808–1870: The Infernal Wen* (London: Secker and Warburg, 1971), pp. 2, 18. On the growth of statistical studies in the nineteenth century see M. J. Cullen, *The Statistical Movement in Early Victorian Britain: The Foundations of Empirical Social Research* (Hassocks, Sussex: Harvester Press, 1975).

2　Henry Mayhew and John Binny, *The Criminal Prisons of London and Scenes of Prison Life* (London: Griffin, Bohn and Co., 1862), p. 11.

3　John Timbs, *Walks and Talks about London* (London: Lockwood and Co., 1865), p. v.

4　Mayhew and Binny, *Criminal Prisons*, p. 6.

5　*Handbook of London As It Is* (London: John Murray, 1863), p. x. Editions are also known as a *Handbook for Travellers*. The original text was compiled by Peter Cunningham, but later editions are not acknowledged as his.

6　'Echoes of the Week', *ILN*, 28 November 1863, p. 550.

7　Richard Sennett, *Flesh and Stone: The Body and the City in Western Civilisation* (London: Faber and Faber, 1994), esp. Part 3, 'Arteries and Veins'. On the metaphor of circulation and its reworking within the novel see David Trotter, *Circulation: Defoe, Dickens and the Economies of the Novel* (London: Macmillan, 1988).

8　George Augustus Sala, 'The Streets of the World. Paris: The Passage des Panoramas', *Temple Bar*, 10 (February 1864), p. 337.

9　'The Wants of London', *ILN*, 30 September 1854, p. 293.

10　The political debates about the government of London are comprehensively analysed in David Owen, *The Government of Victorian London, 1855–1889: The Metropolitan Board of Works, the Vestries and the City Corporation*, ed. Roy MacLeod, with contributions by David Reeder, Donald Olsen and Francis Sheppard (Cambridge, Mass., and London: Harvard University Press, Belknap, 1982), and in Ken Young and Patricia L. Garside, *Metropolitan London: Politics and Urban Change, 1837–1901* (London: Edward Arnold, 1982).

11　On the history of London's water supply see Anne Hardy, 'Parish Pump to Private Pipes: London's Water Supply in the Nineteenth Century', in W. F. Bynum and Roy Porter, eds., *Living and Dying in London* (Medical History, Supplement no. 11) (London: Wellcome Institute for the History of Medicine, 1991), pp. 76–93.

12　For accounts of Chadwick's work see R. A. Lewis, *Edwin Chadwick and the Public Health Movement, 1832–1854* (London: Longmans, Green, 1952); and Anthony S. Wohl, *Endangered Lives: Public Health in Victorian Britain* (London: Dent, 1983).

13　Full minutes of meetings of the Metropolitan Board of Works are held in the London Metropolitan Archives.

14　'Notes of the Week', *ILN*, 5 January 1856, p. 10.

15　On the Ordnance Surveys of London see the outstanding thesis by Rosa Lynn B. Pinkus, 'The Conceptual Development of Metropolitan London, 1800–1855', PhD thesis, State University of New York at Buffalo, 1975, the whole of which is an invaluable source on Victorian London. Other excellent sources on the mapping of London are Ida Darlington and James Howgego, *Printed Maps of London, c.1553–1850* (London: George Philip and Sons, 1964), and Ralph Hyde, *Printed Maps of*

*Victorian London, 1851–1900* (Folkestone, Kent: William Dawson and Sons, 1975).

16 As quoted in Darlington and Howgego, *Printed Maps*, p. 39.

17 On the symbolic meanings of maps see J. B. Harley, 'Maps, Knowledge, and Power', in Denis Cosgrove and Stephen Daniels, eds., *The Iconography of Landscape: Essays on the Symbolic Representation, Design and Use of Past Environments* (Cambridge: Cambridge University Press, 1988), pp. 277–312, and 'Deconstructing the Map', in Trevor J. Barnes and James S. Duncan, eds., *Writing Worlds: Discourse, Text and Metaphor in the Representation of Landscape* (London and New York: Routledge, 1992), pp. 231–47. See also Denis Cosgrove, ed., *Mappings* (London: Reaktion, 1999).

18 Louis Marin, *Utopics: Spatial Play*, trans. by Robert A. Vollrath (London: Macmillan, 1984), pp. 201–32. See also his 'The King and his Geometer', in *Portrait of the King*, trans. by Martha M. Houle (London: Macmillan, 1988), pp. 168–79. On panoramic views in the nineteenth century see Ralph Hyde, *Panoramania! The Art and Entertainment of the 'All-Embracing' View* (London: Trefoil Publications and Barbican Art Gallery, 1989).

19 Marcia Pointon illustrated the Royal Academician William Dyce's designs for drinking-fountains in *William Dyce, 1806–1864: A Critical Biography* (Oxford: Clarendon Press, 1979), figs. 133, 134.

20 On Bazalgette's plan see Nicholas Barton, *The Lost Rivers of London: A Study of their Effects Upon London and Londoners, and the Effects of London and Londoners Upon Them* (London: Historical Publications, rev. edn. 1992), and Richard Trench and Ellis Hillman, *London Under London: A Subterranean Guide* (London: John Murray, 1984).

21 'The Metropolitan Main-Drainage Works: Machinery for Lifting the Sewage', *ILN*, 21 May 1864, p. 504, full-page diagram.

22 John Hollingshead, *Underground London* (London: Groombridge and Sons, 1862).

23 Ralph Hyde's work on Stanford is invaluable. See Hyde, *Printed Maps*, and his introductory notes to *Stanford's Library Map of London and Its Suburbs* (Lympne Castle, Kent: Harry Margaray in association with Guildhall Library, London, 1980), on which the following account of the 'Library Map' is based.

24 On thematic maps see Hyde, *Printed Maps*, pp. 24–8.

25 George Augustus Sala, 'Travels in the County

of Middlesex', *Temple Bar*, 1 (December 1860), p. 78.

26 'London, As It Strikes A Stranger', *Temple Bar*, 5 (June 1862), p. 382.

27 For Paxton's evidence see 'Report from the Select Committee on Metropolitan Communications', *Parliamentary Papers*, 1854–5, vol. X, pp. 78–90. Paxton's design is illustrated in *Getting London in Perspective* (London: Barbican Art Gallery, 1984), no. 72.

28 'Select Committee on Metropolitan Communications', p. 81.

29 Richard Sennett, *The Conscience of the Eye: The Design and Social Life of Cities* (London: Faber and Faber, 1991), pp. 108, 110.

30 'The Street of Glass, and Metropolitan Communication', *Builder*, 16 June 1855, p. 281. The paper also claimed to have uncovered an 1845 plan for a glass promenade, designed by the director of the Royal Italian Opera: 'Metropolitan Communications: Mr Gye's Plan for a Glass Street', *Builder*, 15 December 1855, p. 603.

31 'Metropolitan Improvements', *Illustrated Times*, 2 June 1866, p. 339.

32 *ILN*, 30 July 1864, p. 114.

33 For further reports in the illustrated press of the 'coming down' of old London see 'Fall of a House near Holborn', *Illustrated Times*, 25 August 1866, pp. 116–17, and 'Fall of a House in Ely-Court, Holborn', *Penny Illustrated Paper*, 25 August 1866, pp. 113–14.

34 *ILN*, 22 August 1868, p. 186, and 10 October 1868, p. 358 respectively. Building works in this year were especially visible to the offices of the paper because of the large-scale demolitions being carried out in the area in preparation for the building of the new Law Courts. See 20 February 1868, p. 195: 'Opposite to the office of this paper is the largest gap that has ever been made in central London since the Great Fire.'

35 Alex Potts referred to the visual drama of construction in the 1820s in 'Picturing the Metropolis: Images of London in the Nineteenth Century', *History Workshop*, 26 (Autumn 1988), pp. 28–56.

36 Caroline Arscott and Griselda Pollock with Janet Wolff, 'The Partial View: The Visual Representation of the Early Nineteenth-Century City', in J. Wolff and J. Seed, eds., *The Culture of Capital: Art, Power and the Nineteenth-Century Middle Class* (Manchester: Manchester University Press, 1988), pp. 191–233.

37 The classic history of the picturesque is Christopher Hussey, *The Picturesque* (London:

G. P. Putnam, 1927). On nineteenth-century developments of the picturesque and its extension to the city see Peter Conrad, *The Victorian Treasure-House* (London: Collins, 1973), chap. 3, 'The City and the Picturesque', and Nancy K. Hill, *A Reformer's Art: Dickens' Picturesque and Grotesque Imagery* (Athens and London: Ohio University Press, 1981).

38   Michel de Certeau, 'The Theatre of the *Quid-proquo*: Alexandre Dumas', in *Heterologies: Discourse on the Other*, trans. by Brian Massumi (Manchester: University of Manchester Press, 1986), pp. 150–55.

39   Ibid., pp. 151–2.

40   On the Society for Photographing Relics of Old London see Mark Haworth Booth, *The Golden Age of British Photography, 1839–1900* (London: Aperture, 1984), and Roy Flukinger, *The Formative Decades: Photography in Great Britain, 1839–1920* (Austin: University of Texas Press, 1985).

41   For a full discussion of the 1884 International Health Exhibition see Annmarie Adams, 'The Healthy Victorian City: The Old London Street at the International Health Exhibition of 1884', in Zeynep Çelik, Diane Favro and Richard Ingersoll, eds., *Streets: Critical Perspectives on Public Space* (Berkeley, Los Angeles and London: University of California Press, 1994), pp. 203–12.

42   For a detailed account of the housing demolitions and related social consequences of railway building see H. J. Dyos, 'Railways and Housing in Victorian London', *Journal of Transport History*, ii (1955–6), pp. 11–21 and 90–100, and 'Some Social Costs of Railway Building in London', *Journal of Transport History*, iii (1957–8), pp. 23–9.

43   Charles Dickens, *Dombey and Son*, first published 1848 (Harmondsworth: Penguin, 1970), pp. 120–21.

44   See also 'Proposed Hampstead and Charing-Cross Junction Railway: Section Showing the New Line, the Metropolitan, and the Pneumatic Railway at the Corner of Hampstead-Road', *Illustrated Times*, 14 January 1865, p. 24.

45   Sheppard, *London 1808–1870*, p. 118.

46   Hollingshead, *Underground London*, p. 205.

47   Ibid., pp. 210–11.

48   'Nothing in the Papers', *ILN*, 7 November 1868, p. 443. Again, the link is made here between women and this form of travel. Three weeks later the column drew attention to the announcement by Stanford of a London railway map that 'appears to be exactly that for which the British matrons are urgent', 28 November 1868, p. 511.

49   See 'A Hard Frost in the Streets of London', 28 January 1865, p. 84; 'A Thaw in the Streets of London', 25 February 1865, p. 184; 'A March Wind', 25 March 1865, p. 277; 'A Spring Shower', 21 April 1866, p. 396. 'A "Block" in Park-Lane' was reprinted in the *Penny Illustrated Paper*, 16 May 1868, p. 316.

50   There is very little analytical literature on Houghton; for biographical details see Paul Hogarth, *Arthur Boyd Houghton* (London: Victoria and Albert Museum, 1975), and Paul Hogarth, *Arthur Boyd Houghton* (London: Gordon Fraser, 1981).

51   As quoted in Hogarth, *Houghton* (1975), pp. 14–15. See also *Old Paris: Twenty Etchings by Charles Méryon*. With an Essay by Philip Gilbert Hamerton (Liverpool: Henry Young and Sons Ltd, 1914).

52   Max Schlesinger, *Saunterings In and About London*, English edn. by Otto Wenckstern (London: Nathaniel Cooke, 1853), pp. 12–13.

53   See also 'Works of the Holborn Valley Viaduct: View Looking West', *ILN*, 30 March 1867, p. 309.

54   'The Queen's Visit to the City', *ILN*, 13 November 1869, p. 494.

55   'A Vision of the Thames Embankment', *Penny Illustrated Paper*, 22 September 1866, p. 182. See also its full-page, cross-section illustration of the site 'Section of the Thames Embankment at Waterloo Bridge, As It Will Be When Completed, Showing the Railway, Subway, Sewers, etc.', p. 181. The opening of the Thames Embankment was anticipated in a full-page engraving 'Opening of the Thames Embankment: Design for Landing-Stairs and Ornamental Gardens Between Hungerford and Waterloo Bridges', 1 August 1868, p. 72. See also 'The Embankment and Pier at Westminster', 29 May 1869, p. 348.

56   'Metropolitan Improvements', *ILN*, 21 April 1866, p. 403.

57   This political reading of the visual differences between Paris and London is made in the *Illustrated London News* as early as 22 October 1853, p. 354. This theme is also explored by Claire Hancock, 'Travellers' Descriptions of Nineteenth-Century Paris and London', unpublished paper given at the Institute of Historical Research, 12 February 1997.

58   'Speaking to the Eye' (from the *Economist*), *ILN*, 24 May 1851, pp. 451–2.

59   'May in Town', *ILN*, 1 May 1852, p. 346.

60   The consumption of the city in travellers' tales

is analysed in Griselda Pollock, 'Vicarious Excitements: *London: A Pilgrimage* by Gustave Doré and Blanchard Jerrold, 1872', *New Formations*, 2: 1 (1988), pp. 25–50.

61  John Tagg, 'The Discontinuous City: Picturing and the Discursive Field', in Norman Bryson, Michael Ann Holly and Keith Moxey, eds., *Visual Culture: Images and Interpretations* (Hanover and London: Wesleyan University Press, 1994), p. 85.

62  John Timbs, *Walks and Talks About London* (London: Lockwood and Co., 1865), pp. v, vi, 39 respectively. Cf. George Augustus Sala's reference to the 'macadamised page' in his account of day- and night-time London, *Gaslight and Daylight: With Some London Scenes They Shine Upon* (London: Chapman and Hall, 1859), p. 2.

63  Schlesinger, *Saunterings*, pp. 20, 23. For a useful general source on Victorian advertising see Diana and Geoffrey Hindley, *Advertising in Victorian England, 1837–1901* (London: Wayland, 1972). On Victorian commodity culture see Thomas Richards, *The Commodity Culture of Victorian England: Advertising and Spectacle, 1851–1914* (London: Verso, 1991).

64  John Urry, *The Tourist Gaze: Leisure and Travel in Contemporary Societies* (London: Sage, 1990), and *Consuming Places* (London and New York: Routledge, 1995).

65  Urry, *Consuming Places*, pp. 132–3.

66  [Peter Cunningham] *Handbook of London As It Is* [Murray's Handbook of Modern London] (London: John Murray, 1863), p. xxx.

67  'How a Blind Man Saw the International Exhibition', *Temple Bar*, 7 (January 1863), p. 228. The figure of the blind man is also a motif of the urban narratives in Charles Dickens, *Barnaby Rudge* (first pub. 1841), and in James Joyce, *Ulysses* (first pub. 1922).

68  Daniel Pick, 'Stories of the Eye', in Roy Porter, ed., *Rewriting the Self: Histories from the Renaissance to the Present* (London and New York: Routledge, 1997), pp. 186–99.

69  Jacques Derrida, *Memoirs of the Blind: The Self-Portrait and Other Ruins* trans. by Pascale-Anne Brault and Michael Naas (Chicago and London: University of Chicago Press, 1993).

70  Michel de Certeau, 'Practices of Space', in Marshall Blonsky, ed., *On Signs* (Oxford: Basil Blackwell, 1985), pp. 122–45.

71  Paterfamilias from the Provinces, 'Cowardly Insult to Ladies', Letter to the Editor, *The Times*, 7 January 1862, p. 7.

72  Puella, 'The Streets of London', Letter to the Editor, *The Times*, 9 January 1862, p. 10.

73  Recent periodisation suggests that young, unmarried middle-class women were chaperoned until the system began to die out in the 1880s. See Leonore Davidoff, *The Best Circles: Society, Etiquette and the Season* (London: Croom Helm, 1973), and Michael Curtin, *Propriety and Position: A Study of Victorian Manners* (New York and London: Garland, 1987).

74  Paterfamilias from the Provinces, 'The Streets of London', Letter to the Editor, *The Times*, 13 January 1862, p. 6.

75  M, 'The Streets of London', Letter to the Editor, *The Times*, 18 January 1862, p. 10.

76  Common Sense, 'The Streets of London', Letter to the Editor, *The Times*, 21 January 1862, p. 10.

77  I have discussed the temporal geographies of prostitution more fully in *Myths of Sexuality: Representations of Women in Victorian Britain* (Oxford: Basil Blackwell, 1988).

78  'The Rape of the Glances', *Saturday Review*, XIII (February 1862), p. 125.

79  E.L.L. [Eliza Lynn Linton], 'Out Walking', *Temple Bar*, 5 (April 1862), pp. 132–9.

80  Separate spheres ideology dominated many feminist accounts in the 1980s of the Victorian middle classes. For a review of this literature and a critique of the model see Amanda Vickery, 'Golden Age to Separate Spheres? A Review of the Categories and Chronology of English Women's History', *Historical Journal*, 36: 2 (1993), pp. 383–414.

81  Because I am trying to develop an alternative model for the gendering of modernity to that derived from these writers I shall not discuss their work in detail here. For a useful account of Simmel and Benjamin see David Frisby, *Fragments of Modernity: Theories of Modernity in the Work of Simmel, Kracauer and Benjamin* (Cambridge: Polity Press, 1985). The experience of the modern crowd is analysed in Richard Sennett, *The Fall of Public Man* (Cambridge: Cambridge University Press, 1977), and Marshall Berman, *All That Is Solid Melts Into Air: The Experience of Modernity* (London: Verso, 1983).

82  Charles Baudelaire, 'The Painter of Modern Life' (first pub. 1863), repr. Jonathan Mayne, ed. and trans., *Charles Baudelaire: The Painter of Modern Life and Other Essays* (London: Phaidon, 1964), p. 9. For a helpful introduction to a range of theoretical and historical issues raised by the *flâneur* see the collection of essays in Keith Tester, ed. *The Flâneur* (London and New York: Routledge, 1994).

83  Baudelaire, 'Painter of Modern Life', p. 9.

84  For a persuasive recent study of nineteenth-century Paris, which draws on the paradigms of Baudelaire, Benjamin and Simmel, see T. J. Clark, *The Painting of Modern Life: Paris in the Art of Manet and His Followers* (London: Thames and Hudson, 1985).

85  Janet Wolff, 'The Invisible *Flâneuse*: Women and the Literature of Modernity', *Theory, Culture and Society*, 2: 3 (1985), p. 37. Wolff re-examined some of the issues raised in this article in 'The Artist and the *Flâneur*: Rodin, Rilke and Gwen John in Paris', in Tester, *The Flâneur*, pp. 111–37.

86  Griselda Pollock, 'Modernity and the Spaces of Femininity', in *Vision and Difference: Femininity, Feminism and Histories of Art* (London and New York: Routledge, 1988), pp. 50–90.

87  Christine Stansell, *City of Women: Sex and Class in New York, 1789–1860* (New York: Alfred Knopf, 1986).

88  Jenny Ryan, 'Women, Modernity and the City', *Theory, Culture and Society*, 11: 4 (1994), p. 47. For a fascinating analysis of the debates concerning gender, respectability and space following the opening of Whiteley's see Erika D. Rappaport, '"The Halls of Temptation": Gender, Politics and the Construction of the Department Store in Late Victorian London', *Journal of British Studies*, 35 (January 1996), pp. 58–83.

89  This periodisation is constructed in Lynne Walker's excellent and innovative work on women in Victorian London, see 'Vistas of Pleasure: Women Consumers of Urban Space in the West End of London, 1850–1900', in Clarissa Campbell Orr, ed., *Women in the Victorian Art World* (Manchester and New York: Manchester University Press, 1995), pp. 70–85.

90  See Jenny Ryan, 'Women, Modernity and the City', p. 52.

91  For discussion of redefinitions of the public sphere see Nancy Fraser, 'Rethinking the Public Sphere: A Contribution to the Critique of Actually Existing Democracy', in Craig Calhoun, ed., *Habermas and the Public Sphere* (Cambridge, Mass.: MIT Press, 1992), pp. 109–42.

92  Mary P. Ryan, *Women in Public: Between Banners and Ballots, 1825–1880* (Baltimore and London: Johns Hopkins University Press, 1990). For an analogous study of early twentieth-century London see Lisa Tickner, *The Spectacle of Women: Imagery of the Suffrage Campaign, 1907–14* (London: Chatto and Windus, 1987).

93  Mary P. Ryan, *Women in Public*, p. 61. It comes as a disappointment in this otherwise exemplary study when Ryan suggests that wives and daughters of the élite were chaperoned, leaving poor and unprotected women prey to upper-class dandies (p. 66). This seems to conform to the urban mythology of planners and reformers, rather than to social-spatial realities. Although class clearly affected women's occupation of public space, the city cannot be neatly segregated in these terms.

94  See Elizabeth Wilson, *The Sphinx in the City: Urban Life, the Control of Disorder, and Women* (London: Virago, 1991); 'The Invisible *Flâneur*', *New Left Review*, 191 (Jan./Feb. 1992), pp. 90–110; and 'The Rhetoric of Urban Space', *New Left Review*, 209 (Jan./Feb. 1995), pp. 146–60.

95  Wilson, 'Invisible *Flâneur*', p. 103.

96  Ibid. p. 109. See also Mary P. Ryan, *Women in Public*, pp. 75–6.

97  Henry Mayhew, *London Labour and the London Poor*. vol. 4 (London: Griffin, Bohn, and Company, 1862), pp. 306–7.

98  My thanks to Lindsay Farmer for drawing this etymology to my attention.

99  *The Habits of Good Society: A Handbook of Etiquette for Ladies and Gentlemen. With Thoughts, Hints, and Anecdotes Concerning Social Observances; Nice Points of Taste and Good Manners; and the Art of Making One's-Self Agreeable. The Whole Interspersed with Humorous Illustrations of Social Predicaments; Remarks on the History and Changes of Fashion; and the Differences of English and Continental Etiquette* (London: James Hogg and Sons, 1859).

100  On the 'cut' see ibid., p. 279; [C. W. Day] *Hints on Etiquette and the Usages of Society: With a Glance at Bad Habits* (London: Longman, Brown, Green, and Longmans, 1849), p. 104; F.W.R. and Lord Charles X, *The Laws and Bye-Laws of Good Society: A Code of Modern Etiquette* (London: Simpkin, Marshall and Co., 1867), p. 39; and 'On Being Cut', *All the Year Round*, 19 (1868), pp. 208–10.

101  *Etiquette for Ladies* (London: Frederick Warne and Co., 1866). The dimensions of this volume are 9 × 6 cm.

102  My thanks to Alex Werner, Curator of the Modern Collection at the Museum of London, for allowing me access to this uncatalogued archive. Biographical details on Roper and Busher are taken from documents

accompanying the archive. The custom of cross-writing, which is adopted in a large number of letters in this collection, was not unusual in this period.

103    De Certeau, 'Practices of Space', p. 129. See also Michel de Certeau, *The Practice of Everyday Life,* trans. by Steven Rendall (Berkeley: University of California Press, 1984).

104    Kristin Ross, 'Streetwise: The French Invention of Everyday Life', *parallax*, 2 (February 1996), pp. 67–76.

105    De Certeau, 'Practices of Space', p. 129.

106    On Eliza Lynn Linton's life see G. S. Layard, *Mrs Lynn Linton: Her Life, Letters, and Opinions* (London: Methuen and Co., 1901); Herbert von Thal, *Eliza Lynn Linton: The Girl of the Period: A Biography* (London: George Allen and Unwin, 1979); Nancy Fix Anderson, *Women Against Women in Victorian England: A Life of Eliza Lynn Linton* (Bloomington, Indiana: Indiana University Press, 1987), on which the following biographical details are based.

107    Eliza Lynn Linton, *The Girl of the Period and Other Social Essays*, vol. 1 (London: Richard Bentley and Son, 1883), p. viii.

108    Walter Benjamin, *Charles Baudelaire: A Lyric Poet in the Era of High Capitalism*, trans. by Harry Zohn (London and New York: Verso, 1976), p. 36.

109    Eliza Lynn Linton, *The Autobiography of Christopher Kirkland*, 3 vols. (London: Bentley, 1885).

110    On her journeys round the West End and north of London see Eliza Lynn Linton, *My Literary Life* (London: Hodder and Stoughton, 1899), p. 15: 'Bayswater was not then the unbroken continuation of Oxford Street that it is now . . . and there was a long stretch of waste land . . . But I thought nothing of the walk from Montagu Place, where I then lived; and I very soon became a constant Sunday visitor at the house.'

111    Letter from Eliza Lynn Linton to Mrs Cooper, 15 September 1869. As quoted in Anderson, *Woman Against Women*, p. 113.

112    Linton, *Christopher Kirkland*, vol. 1, p. 261.

113    E. Lynn Linton, 'Town or Country?', *New Review*, vol. IX (October 1893), p. 383.

114    Eliza Lynn Linton, 'Modern Maidens', in *Ourselves: A Series of Essays on Women* (London and New York: G. Routledge and Sons, 1870), p. 193.

115    [Eliza Lynn Linton], 'Passing Faces', *Household Words*, 263 (7 April 1855), p. 264.

116    See, for example, Amelia Roper, unpublished

letter to Martha Busher, 8 November 1855, Museum of London.

117    Amelia Roper, unpublished letter to Martha Busher, 19 July 1857. Museum of London; original emphasis and punctuation. Contemporary meanings of 'Maryann' and 'seedy' are given in Eric Partridge, *A Dictionary of Slang and Unconventional English* (London, Melbourne and Henley: Routledge and Kegan Paul, eighth edn, 1984), pp. 724–5, 1033. Roper appears to be using the term 'Maryann' very precisely to suggest a working-class woman of dubious morals. The meaning of the term changed later in the century to describe a male homosexual. See also the decision to retitle William Bell Scott's poem about a prostitute, 'Mary Ann' (1854) which is recounted in W. Minto, ed. *Autobiographical Notes of the Life of William Bell Scott and Notices of His Artistic and Poetic Circle of Friends 1830 to 1882*, vol. 1 (London: Osgood, McIlvaine, 1892), p. 135.

118    Schlesinger, *Saunterings*, p. 266. See also the entry on the Olympic Theatre in *The World's Guide to London in 1862, by Day and by Night* (London: Darton and Hodge, 1862), p. 78. For a full discussion of the area around Wych Street in the context of obscene publications see Part 3, 'Streets and Obscenity'.

119    See Partridge, *Dictionary of Slang*, p. 737.

120    Amelia Roper, unpublished letter to Martha Busher, 4 January 1856, Museum of London.

121    Mayhew and Binny, 'A Balloon View of London', in *Criminal Prisons*, pp. 7–10, first pub. by Mayhew in *The Great World of London*, part 1 (London: David Bogue, March 1856).

*Part 2*

1    For a suggestive analysis of the sensations of balloon travellers in terms of Freudian regression see Elaine Freedgood, 'Groundless Optimism: Regression in the Service of Egos, England and Empire in Victorian Ballooning Memoirs', *Nineteenth-Century Contexts*, 20:1 (1997), pp. 61–80.

2    'A Night Balloon Ascent', *ILN*, 14 October 1865, p. 370.

3    'Balloon Ascent from Cremorne, Night of Wednesday July 24th, 1861', 'Papers Relating to the History of Cremorne Gardens, Chelsea. 1831–1878. Volume Two', p. 59 verso, CPL.

4    See Alison Adburgham, *Shopping in Style:*

*London from the Restoration to Edwardian Elegance* (London: Thames and Hudson, 1979), p. 128.

5   For a history of the Movement see Albert Larking, *History of the Early Closing Association and How the Saturday Half-Holiday Was Won* (London and Woking: Unwin Brothers Ltd., 1912).

6   Ibid., pp. 9–10.

7   *Daily Telegraph*, 2 April 1858, p. 5.

8   Larking, *Early Closing Association*, pp. 9, 12.

9   'The Last Omnibus', *Penny Illustrated Paper*, 3 February 1866, p. 75.

10  Many histories of gas lighting are quite old, but informative. See Charles Hunt, *Gas Lighting. Volume III of Groves and Thorp's Chemical Technology or Chemistry Applied to Arts and Manufactures* (London: J. and A. Churchill, 1900); Charles Hunt, *A History of the Introduction of Gas Lighting* (London: Walter King, 1907), and Dean Chandler, *Outline of History of Lighting by Gas* (London: South Metropolitan Gas Company, 1936) on which the following summary is based. William T. O'Dea, *The Social History of Lighting* (London: Routledge and Kegan Paul, 1958), is one of the few social histories of this subject. For more recent cultural analysis of public lighting see Wolfgang Schivelbusch, *Disenchanted Night: The Industrialisation of Light in the Nineteenth Century*, trans. by Angela Davies (Oxford, New York and Hamburg: Berg, 1988), and Joachim Schlör, *Nights in the Big City* (London: Reaktion, 1998).

11  O'Dea, *Social History of Lighting*, p. 98.

12  On early nineteenth-century shop window lighting see Neil McKendrick, John Brewer and J. H. Plumb, *The Birth of Consumer Society: The Commerialization of Eighteenth-Century England* (London: Europa, 1982), pp. 78–9.

13  Flora Tristan, *The London Journal: or, the Aristocracy and the Working Class of England* (first pub. 1842), trans. by Jean Hawkes (London: Virago, 1982), p. 17.

14  Figures drawn from J. Ewing Ritchie, *The Night Side of London* (London: William Tweedie, 1857), p. 5.

15  Max Schlesinger, *Saunterings In and About London* (London: Nathaniel Cooke, 1853), pp. 85–6.

16  Ibid., p. 17.

17  George Augustus Sala, *Gaslight and Daylight: With Some London Scenes They Shine Upon* (London: Chapman and Hall, 1859), pp. 259–60.

18  Full-page illustrations of this view of the street include 'Southwark-street, Borough', *ILN*, 18 February 1865, p. 156, and 'London Street Improvements: Part of Southwark-street', *Penny Illustrated Paper*, 21 March 1868, p. 181.

19  'The Gas Strike in London', *ILN*, 14 December 1872, p. 570.

20  'London Gas', *British Quarterly Review*, LXIX (1879), p. 39. For a cultural analysis of the distinctions between gas light and electric light see Schivelbusch, *Disenchanted Night*, pp. 114–34.

21  Sources on the London gas companies in the nineteenth century include 'London Gas', *British Quarterly Review*, LXIX (1879), pp. 1–39; Laurence W. S. Rostron, *The 'Powers of Charge' of the Metropolitan Gas Companies: A History of the Question of Price in London, from the Introduction of Gas Lighting to the Year 1899* (London: Ernest Benn for the South Metropolitan Gas Company, 1927); Dean Chandler and A. Douglas Lacey, *The Rise of the Gas Industry in Britain* (London: British Gas Council, 1949).

22  'The Battle of the Bridge' is recounted in A. Angus Croll. *The Great Central Gas Company: Its Origin and History* (London: Samuel Harris and Co., 1875), pp. 30–34.

23  See Rostron, *'Powers of Charge'*, p. 8.

24  Publications calling for public ownership include Thomas G. Barlow, *On the Supply of Gas in the Metropolis* (London: W. B. King, 1859), and C. G. Cleminshaw, *A Few Remarks on the Pamphlet Entitled 'Metropolitan Gas Legislation Past and Prospective'* (London: Longmans, Green and Co., 1867), and *The Gas Supply of the Metropolis: A Word to the Public, the Companies, and the Shareholders* (London: Longman, Green and Co., 1868).

25  'The Gas', *Illustrated Times*, 5 March 1864, p. 151.

26  From 'A Day at the Westminster Gas-works', *Penny Magazine*, XI (1842), pp. 81–8, as cited in Chandler and Lacey, *Rise of the Gas Industry*, pp. 146–7.

27  Chandler and Lacey, *Rise of the Gas Industry*, p. 149. See also the account in 'The London Gas Works, Vauxhall', *Pictorial Times*, 8 May 1847, pp. 330–32, and 22 May 1847, pp. 317–8.

28  John Hollingshead, *Underground London* (London: Groombridge and Sons, 1862), pp. 197–8.

29  'The Gas', *Illustrated Times*, 5 March 1864, p. 151. See also 'The Removal of Gasworks', *The Times*, 10 November 1865, p. 7.

30  See also 'Accident at Ratcliff Gas-Works',

*Journal of Gas Lighting, Water Supply, and Sanitary Improvement*, 31 July 1860, p. 528.

31   Accounts of the Nine Elms explosion are given in the *Penny Illustrated Paper*, 11 November 1865, pp. 369–70; *Illustrated Times*, 4 November 1865, p. 286; 11 November 1865, pp. 289–90; *ILN*, 11 November 1865, pp. 463, 465; *The Times*, 1 November 1865, p. 9; 2 November 1865, p. 12, and 3 November 1865, p. 10; *Journal of Gas Lighting*, 14 November 1865, pp. 807–10.

32   *The Times*, 3 November 1865, p. 10.

33   'The Fatal Gas Explosion at Nine Elms', *Penny Illustrated Paper*, 11 November 1865, p. 370.

34   The leading articles of the London journals are summarised in 'The Explosion at the London Gas-Works, at Nine Elms', *Journal of Gas Lighting*, 14 November 1865, pp. 807–10.

35   As cited in ibid., p. 807.

36   'The Gas Explosion at Nine Elms', *The Times*, 2 November 1865, p. 12.

37   Public gas illuminations are discussed briefly in David Gledhill, *Gas Lighting* (Aylesbury: Shire Publications Ltd, 1981) p. 12.

38   See the *ILN*: 'Temple-Bar on the Night Before the Funeral of the Duke of Wellington', 11 December 1852, pp. 525–6; 'The Peace Illuminations', 31 May 1856, pp. 580–81; 'The Illuminations in London on the Night of the Royal Marriage', 14 March 1863, p. 236, and 4 April 1863, pp. 389–93. See also the full-page illustration of the crowds visiting the illuminations 'Street Scene in the Metropolis During the Illuminations on Tuesday Night', *Penny Illustrated Paper*, 14 March 1863, p. 180.

39   Henry Mayhew, 'The London Street Markets on a Saturday Night', in *London Labour and the London Poor*, vol. 1 (1851), p. 9; reprinted in *The Great World of London*, part 1 (March 1856), p. 61.

40   'London Sketches. No. 4 – Squalors' Market', *Illustrated Times*, 23 February 1861, p. 124. The article and accompanying illustration are reprinted as 'London Life. No. 8 – Squalors' Market', *Penny Illustrated Paper*, 2 December 1865, pp. 446–7.

41   Sala, *Gaslight*, p. 260. Cf. Schlesinger, *Saunterings*, p. 86. See also Thomas Hardy's descriptions of the butchers' stalls in this area in *A Pair of Blue Eyes* (first pub. 1872–3), discussed in Michael Slater, 'Hardy and the City', in Charles Pettit, ed. *New Perspectives on Thomas Hardy* (London: Macmillan, 1994), p. 50.

42   Mayhew, 'London Street Markets', p. 9.

43   Augustus Mayhew, *Paved with Gold: Or the Romance and Reality of the London Streets* (London: Chapman and Hall, 1858), p. 106. Cf. John Blackmore, *The London By Moonlight Mission: Being the Account of Midnight Cruises on the Streets of London* (London: Robson and Avery, 1860), p. 177: 'What a scene is any large city by gas-light! What a scene is London!'

44   On theatres and gas lighting see Frederick Penzel, *Theatre Lighting Before Electricity* (Middletown, Conn.: Wesleyan University Press, 1978), and Terence Rees, *Theatre Lighting in the Age of Gas* (London: Society for Theatre Research, 1978). On the representation of London in the Victorian drama see Michael R. Booth, 'The Metropolis on Stage', in H. J. Dyos and Michael Wolff, eds., *The Victorian City: Images and Realities*, vol. 1 (London, Henley and Boston: Routledge and Kegan Paul, 1973), pp. 211–22.

45   On Boucicault and his work see Peter Thomson, ed., *Plays by Dion Boucicault* (Cambridge: Cambridge University Press, 1984). On the sensation scene in *After Dark* see John McCormick, *Dion Boucicault* (Cambridge: Chadwyck-Healy Ltd, 1987), pp. 44–5.

46   'Scene from the New Play "The Streets of London" at the Princess's Theatre', *Illustrated Times*, 27 August 1864, p. 130. See also the review, 6 August 1864, p. 87.

47   On Astley's Amphitheatre in London see *ILN*, 28 October 1871, p. 407.

48   *Illustrated Times*, 6 August 1864, p. 87.

49   Sala, *Gaslight*, p. 156.

50   Charles Dickens, 'The Streets – Night', *Sketches by Boz: Illustrative of Every-Day Life and Every-Day People*, The New Oxford Illustrated Dickens (London: Oxford University Press, 1957), p. 53. The publication history of this piece is given in Michael Slater, ed., *Dickens' Journalism: Sketches by Boz and Other Early Papers, 1833–39* (London: J. M. Dent, 1994), p. 55, and Nicolas Bentley, Michael Slater and Nina Burgis, eds., *The Dickens Index* (Oxford and New York: Oxford University Press, 1988), pp. 236–7, 250–51.

51   Charles Dickens, 'Night Walks', *The Uncommercial Traveller* (London: Chapman and Hall, 1861), pp. 194–5.

52   Gaston Bachelard, *The Flame of a Candle*, trans. by Joni Caldwell (Dallas: Dallas Institute Publications, 1988).

53   John 9: 4. Also cited in Lieut. John Blackmore, *The London By Moonlight Mission: Being an Account of Midnight Cruises on the Streets of*

*London* (London: Robson and Avery, 1860), p. 47.

54  Ritchie, *Night Side Of London*, p. 56.

55  Sigmund Freud, 'The "Uncanny"', in *The Standard Edition of the Complete Psychological Works of Sigmund Freud*, trans. and edited by James Strachey, vol. XVII (London: Hogarth Press and the Institute of Psycho-Analysis, 1955), p. 220. Hereafter page references to this edition will be given in the text.

56  Freud describes the couple who move into a house with a wooden table carved with crocodiles and who, in the darkness of night, imagine ghostly crocodiles moving around the house, ibid., pp. 244–5.

57  Anthony Vidler, *The Architectural Uncanny: Essays in the Modern Unhomely* (Cambridge, Mass. and London: M.I.T. Press, 1992), p. 168. Foucault explores the ideal of the transparent society in a number of publications including 'The Eye of Power', in Colin Gordon, ed., *Power/Knowledge: Selected Interviews and Other Writing, 1972–1977* (Brighton: Harvester, 1980), pp. 146–65. The Freudian uncanny is worked into a compelling account of historical space in Michel de Certeau, 'Psychoanalysis and Its History', in *Heterologies: A Discourse on the Other*, trans. by Brian Massumi (Manchester: University of Manchester Press, 1986), pp. 3–16.

58  Between January and November 1864 the *Illustrated Times* ran a series of articles on 'The Hours A.M. and P.M. in London', comparing the same hour in the day and at night. A number of these pieces were illustrated by Florence and Adelaide Caxton. The format has been reworked in film in the twentieth century; see W. Ruttmann, *Berlin – Symphony of a Great City* (Germany, 1927). Biographical sources on Sala include his autobiography *The Life and Adventures of George Augustus Sala. Written by Himself*, 2 vols. (London, Paris, Melbourne: Cassell and Co. Ltd., 1895), Ralph Straus, *Sala: The Portrait of an Eminent Victorian* (London: Constable and Co. Ltd., 1942), and the excellent introductory essay in George Augustus Sala, *Twice Round the Clock: Or the Hours of the Day and Night in London*, with an introduction by Philip Collins (Leicester: Leicester University Press, 1971).

59  For a lancing attack on Sala see, 'Cheap Literature', *British Quarterly Review*, vol. 29 (1 April 1859), pp. 341–4: 'He is the head of a new school of writers, which may be called the Fast School. Consistency, common-sense,

fact, go for nothing; violence, excess, outrageous word-paintings, and unblushing effrontery are all in all' (p. 343).

60  George Augustus Sala, 'A Journey Due North', *Household Words*, 4 October 1856, p. 265.

61  Charles Dickens to W. H. Wills, 27 September 1851, in R. C. Lehmann, ed. *Charles Dickens as Editor. Being Letters Written by Him to Henry Wills his Sub-Editor* (London: Smith, Elder and Co., 1912), pp. 70–71.

62  Sala, *Life and Adventures*, vol. 1, p. 392. 'I never originated anything in my life, being totally destitute of the faculty of imagination.'

63  George Augustus Sala, *Twice Round the Clock; Or the Hours of the Day and Night in London* (London: Houlston and Wright, 1859), p. 318. On the cultural association of the Haymarket and midnight in this period see Lynda Nead, 'The Magdalene in Modern Times: Representations of the Prostitute in Victorian Art', unpublished B.A. dissertation, Department of Fine Art, University of Leeds, 1979.

64  'Mr Sala on Life in London', *Saturday Review*, 3 December 1859, p. 677.

65  Sala, *Gaslight*, p. 159.

66  James Joyce, *Ulysses: The Corrected Text*, ed. Hans Walter Gabler (Harmondsworth: Penguin, 1986), p. 416.

67  The best secondary source on E. T. Smith's period at Cremorne and on the general history of the Gardens is Warwick Wroth, *Cremorne and the Later London Gardens* (London: Elliot Stock, 1907).

68  Miles Ogborn, *Spaces of Modernity: London's Geographies, 1680–1780* (New York, London: Guilford Press, 1998), p. 122.

69  On some of the new forms of public entertainment in the first half of the nineteenth century see Richard D. Altick, *The Shows of London* (Cambridge, Mass., and London: Belknap Press of Harvard University Press, 1978).

70  Peter Bailey, *Leisure and Class in Victorian England: Rational Recreation and the Contest for Control, 1830–1885* (London: Routledge and Kegan Paul, 1978), p. 56. On the emergence of commercialised public leisure in the nineteenth century see also Hugh Cunningham, *Leisure in the Industrial Revolution, c.1780–c.1880* (London: Croom Helm, 1980).

71  'Shares Prospectus, 1860', in 'Papers Relating to the History of Cremorne Gardens, Chelsea. 1831–1878. Volume Two', pp. 58–9, CPL. There is no record of this company registered with Companies House.

72    'The Business of Pleasure', *All the Year Round*, 10 October 1863, pp. 149–52.

73    See Bailey, *Leisure and Class*, passim.

74    Edmund Yates, *The Business of Pleasure*, 2 vols. (London: Chapman and Hall, 1865).

75    'Papers Upon the History of Cremorne Gardens, Chelsea. 1840–1878', p. 29, CPL.

76    For ballooning reports see, for example, 'Ballooning at Cremorne', *ILN*, 17 September 1859, p. 275; 'M. Godard's Montgolfier Balloon at Cremorne Gardens', *ILN*, 30 July 1864, p. 113; 'The Second Ascent of the Godard Montgolfier Balloon from Cremorne Gardens', *Illustrated Times*, 6 August 1864, p. 81; 'Juvenile Balloon Fete at Cremorne Gardens', *Penny Illustrated Paper*, 14 July 1866, pp. 21–2.

77    *ILN*, 4 September 1852, p. 182.

78    'Parachute Descent from a Balloon', *ILN*, 11 September 1852, p. 199.

79    On the contemporary taste for dangerous spectacles: 'the public will rush to support and patronise any novelty which promises to stir the nerves', *ILN*, 25 July 1863, p. 82.

80    'Cremorne Gardens', *ILN*, 28 June 1851, p. 619.

81    'Cremorne Gardens', *ILN*, 14 August 1858, p. 149, illus. p. 150.

82    'The Tournament at Cremorne', *ILN*, 18 July 1863, p. 63. Dickens described the disappointment of a daylight visit to Vauxhall in 'Vauxhall Gardens by Day', in *Sketches by Boz*, pp. 126–31. See also 'Pleasure Gardens', *Penny Illustrated Paper*, 20 June 1868, p. 391.

83    On the 'Aristocratic Fête' see Wroth, *Cremorne*, p. 8. *Punch* ran an ongoing series of caricatures and articles on the taste for fashion and Cremorne amongst wealthy and aristocratic women. See 'Religion à la Mode', 26 June 1858, p. 257; 'Royal Gardens, Cremorne', 10 July 1858, p. 17; 'The Aristocratic Fête at Cremorne', 17 July 1858, p. 25; 'Aristocratic Amusements: "Confession, or Cremorne, My Lady?"', 24 July 1858, p. 35. My thanks to Michael Slater for bringing these to my attention.

84    See Oliver Impey, *Chinoiserie: The Impact of Oriental Styles on Western Art and Decoration* (London: Oxford University Press, 1977). On the use of orientalism in the architecture of leisure see Martin Zerlang, 'Orientalism and Modernity: Tivoli in Copenhagen', *Nineteenth-Century Contexts*, 20: 1 (1997), pp. 81–110.

85    On the alterations see 'Cremorne Gardens', *ILN*, 24 May 1851, p. 449, and the illustration of the site, 28 June 1851, p. 619.

86    Although this engraving was published in the *Illustrated Times* in July 1858, it is likely that it was drawn some time before 1857, when new and striking gas fittings were added to the platform (see below).

87    'The Lounger', 'Cremorne', *Illustrated Times*, 10 July 1858, p. 26. 'The Lounger' column in the *Illustrated Times* is referred to in Henry Vizetelly, *Glances Back Through Seventy Years: Autobiographical and Other Reminiscences*, vol. 2 (London: Kegan Paul, Trench, Trubner and Co. Ltd, 1893), p. 14.

88    For reports and illustrations of the 'Crystal Platform' see 'Royal Cremorne Gardens', *ILN*, 23 May 1857, p. 496, and 'Cremorne Gardens: "The Crystal Platform"', 30 May 1857, pp. 515–16.

89    On the gaslights and mirrors at the Argyll Rooms and the Holborn Assembly Rooms see William Acton, *Prostitution, Considered in Its Moral, Social and Sanitary Aspects in London and Other Large Cities and Garrison Towns with Proposals for the Control and Prevention of Its Attendant Evils*, second ed. (London: John Churchill and Sons, 1870), p. 19.

90    See 'Pleasure Gardens', *Penny Illustrated Paper*, 20 June 1868, p. 396. On the closure of Vauxhall see John Timbs, *Walks and Talks about London* (London: Lockwood and Co., 1865), pp. 29–30.

91    Sources on sheet music covers include Ronald Pearsall, *Victorian Street Music Covers* (Newton Abbot: David and Charles, 1972); Doreen and Stanley Spellman, *Victorian Music Covers* (London: Evelyn, Adams and Mackay Ltd, 1969); Catherine Haill, *Victorian Illustrated Music Sheets* (London: Her Majesty's Stationery Office, 1981).

92    On the growth in private ownership of pianos in the period see Haill, *Victorian Illustrated Music Sheets*, p. 5, and Bailey, *Leisure and Class*, p. 60.

93    On the galop, the polka and the quadrille see Mary Clarke and Clement Crisp, *The History of Dance* (London: Orbis Publishing, 1981), pp. 97–8, 101–2, 104; A. H. Franks, *Social Dance: A Short History* (London: Routledge and Kegan Paul, 1963), pp. 133–9, 140–47; and Philip J. S. Richardson, *The Social Dances of the Nineteenth Century in England* (London: Herbert Jenkins, 1960), pp. 69–70, 80–89, 72–6.

94    'Letters from Nigh Latitudes – No. 15. A Visit to Cremorne', *Fun*, 14 June 1862, p. 121.

95    On these genres see Martha Vicinus, 'Dark London', in *The Indiana University Bookman*, no. 12 (December 1977), pp. 67–79.

96  William Stephens Hayward, *London By Night* (London: William Oliver, 1870), pp. 122–6. On the emergence of 'yellow-back' fiction in the 1850s and its distinctive features see Michael Sadleir, 'Yellow-Backs', in John Carter, ed., *New Paths in Book Collecting: Essays by Various Hands* (London: Constable and Co. Ltd, 1934), pp. 127–61.

97  Hippolyte Taine, *Notes on England*, trans. by W. F. Rae (London: Strahan and Co., 1872), p. 44.

98  Acton, *Prostitution*, p. 17.

99  See Wroth, *Cremorne*, p. 11, and *ILN*, 3 October 1857, p. 335.

100  'The Battle of Cremorne', *Punch*, 24 October 1857, p. 175.

101  Ritchie, *Night Side*, p. 187.

102  For a detailed discussion of masculinity in Regency London see Jane Rendell, 'Ramblers and Cyprians: Gender and Architectural Space, London's St James's, 1821–8', unpublished PhD thesis, University of London, 1998. On male dress and manners in mid-nineteenth-century London see 'May in Town', *ILN*, 1 May 1852, pp. 345–6.

103  See Eric Partridge, *A Dictionary of Slang and Unconventional English* (London, Melbourne and Henley: Routledge and Kegan Paul, eighth ed. 1984), pp. 1185–6.

104  On fears about the influence of purposeless leisure on young men see Bailey, *Leisure and Class*, p. 93.

105  See Wroth, *Cremorne*, p. 19, and 'Echoes of the Week', *ILN*, 18 July 1863, p. 75.

106  'Papers Relating to the History of Cremorne Gardens . . . Volume Two', pp. 23–5. On masculinity in music-hall songs more generally see Peter Bailey, 'Champagne Charlie: Performance and Ideology in the Music-Hall Swell Song', in J. S. Bratton, ed., *Music Hall: Performance and Style* (Milton Keynes: Open University Press, 1986), pp. 54–5, 60.

107  Gareth Stedman Jones, 'The "Cockney" and the Nation, 1780–1988', in David Feldman and Gareth Stedman Jones, eds., *Metropolis: London Histories and Representations since 1800* (London and New York: Routledge, 1989), p. 290.

108  On entertainment licences see Cunningham, *Leisure*, p. 169.

109  'Petition received 26 September 1860 opposing renewal of licence from members of the Vestry of the Parish of Saint Luke Chelsea', *Middlesex Sessions Records* MR/LMD 11/9. See also MR/LMD 11/10. For Simpson's application for the renewal of Cremorne's Music and Dancing Licence see

110  'Minutes of Evidence Before the Select Committee on Theatrical Licences and Regulations', *Parliamentary Papers*, 1866, XVI, pp. 130–34.

111  Ibid., p. 134.

112  'Derby Night at Cremorne', *Days' Doings*, 27 May 1871, p. 274.

113  On Smith and Son's campaign against the *Days' Doings* see Lynda Nead, *Myths of Sexuality: Representations of Women in Victorian Britain* (Oxford: Basil Blackwell, 1988), pp. 65–6.

114  'In Favour of Cremorne', *Days' Doings*, 27 May 1871, p. 290.

115  'Puritanical Intolerance', *Days' Doings*, 14 October 1871, p. 186.

116  Ibid., p. 184. See also the double-page illustration 'Mayfair – How the Discreet, Delicate and Virtuous Diddlesex Dogberries and their Scholastic Friends Enjoy Themselves at Home', 'Chelsea – How the Discreet, Delicate and Virtuous Diddlesex Dogberries and their Scholastic Friends are Shocked by the Amusements of the People Out of Doors', 21 October 1871, pp. 200–1.

117  On the campaigns of the vice societies see M. J. D. Roberts, 'Making Victorian Morals? The Society for the Suppression of Vice and Its Critics, 1802–1886', *Historical Studies*, 21: 83 (October 1984), pp. 157–73, and Edward J. Bristow, *Vice and Vigilance: Purity Movements in Britain since 1700* (Dublin: Gill and Macmillan Ltd., 1977), esp. pp. 32–50.

118  'From the Ghost of the "Days' Doings"', *Here and There*, 9 March 1872, p. 35.

119  'The Chelsea Guys', *Days' Doings*, 4 November 1871, p. 226.

120  See *The Vestry of Chelsea. Supplemental Report of their Proceedings for the Years (March to March) 1872 to 1877, Inclusive* (London: Judd and Co., 1878), pp. 76–7.

121  *Twenty-Second Report of the Vestry of the Parish of Chelsea, Appointed Under the Metropolis Local Management Act, 1855. 1877–8* (London: G. Shield, 1879), p. 42. For Baum's application for 1877 see *Middlesex Sessions Records*, MR/LMD 20/3, and for a petition against it, see MR/LMD 20/5. London Metropolitan Archives.

122  'A. B. Chelsea', *The Trial of John Fox, or Fox John, or the Horrors of Cremorne*, 'Papers Upon the History of Cremorne Gardens 1840–1878', p. 121, CPL.

123  A number of these press reports are kept in

'Papers Upon the History of Cremorne Gardens 1840–1878', CPL.

124 On Whistler and his circle at Cremorne see *The Greaves Brothers and Victorian Chelsea: An Exhibition* (London: Royal Borough of Kensington and Chelsea, 1968).

125 On *Nocturne in Black and Gold* see Richard Dorment and Margaret F. MacDonald, *James McNeill Whistler* (London: Tate Gallery Publications, 1994), pp. 132–8. For a traditional treatment of the nocturnes more generally see Denys Sutton, *Nocturne: The Art of James McNeill Whistler* (London: Country Life Limited, 1963). For a meticulous account of the *Whistler v. Ruskin* trial see Linda Merrill, *A Pot of Paint: Aesthetics on Trial in 'Whistler v. Ruskin'* (Washington DC: Smithsonian Press, 1992), and also Costas Douzinas 'Whistler v. Ruskin: Law's Fear of Images', *Art History*, 19: 3 (September 1996), pp. 353–69.

126 As quoted in Merrill, *Pot of Paint*, p. 47.

127 Douzinas, '*Whistler v. Ruskin*', p. 357.

128 Merrill, *Pot of Paint*, p. 167.

129 Ibid., p. 36.

130 Ibid., p. 145.

131 See the announcement of the Cremorne auction 'Papers Relating to the History of Cremorne Gardens, Chelsea, 1831–1878, Volume Two,' p. 103, and auction catalogues in 'Papers Upon the History of Cremorne Gardens, Chelsea, 1840–1878', pp. 111–14, CPL.

132 See Paul Meritt [sic] and W. Howell Poole, *New Babylon or Daughters of Eve* (founded upon Paul Meritt's play 'New Babylon'), 3 vols. (London: Hurst and Blackett, 1882).

*Part 3*

1 *Hansard*, 3rd ser., vol. 145 (11 May 1857) c. 103.

2 On the use of the poison image in debates on obscenity in the 1920s see Beverley Brown, 'Troubled Vision: Legal Understandings of Obscenity', *New Formations – Perversity*, no. 19 (Spring 1993), p. 36.

3 *Hansard*, 3rd ser., vol. 145 (4 June 1857), c. 1093–4.

4 John Ruskin, 'The Stones of Venice, volume 3', in E. T. Cook and Alexander Wedderburn, *The Works of John Ruskin*, vol. 11 (London: George Allen, 1904), p. 201.

5 Ruskin, 'The Three Kinds of Engraving', in Cook and Wedderburn, *Works*, vol. 19 (1905), p. 150.

6 Ruskin 'Patience', in Cook and Wedderburn, *Works*, vol. 19 (1905), p. 89.

7 Ruskin, 'Lectures on Art. VI. Light', in Cook and Wedderburn, *Works*, vol. 20 (1905), p. 165.

8 *Daily Telegraph*, 6 April 1858, p. 5.

9 Ibid.

10 There is a substantial literature on the Victorian publishing industry and its readerships, see particularly Richard D. Altick, *The English Common Reader* (Chicago: Chicago University Press, 1957), and, in the context of censorship, Donald Thomas, *A Long Time Burning: The History of Literary Censorship in England* (London: Routledge and Kegan Paul, 1969).

11 Patricia Anderson, *The Printed Image and the Transformation of Popular Culture, 1790–1860* (Oxford: Clarendon Press, 1991), p. 11.

12 'Cheap Literature', *British Quarterly Review*, 29: 58 (1 April 1859), p. 316.

13 Ibid., p. 333.

14 'Mischievous Literature', *Bookseller*, 1 July 1868, p. 448.

15 On coloured illustrations, specifically in obscene publications, see ibid., p. 449.

16 The relationship between the Reform Act and mass consumption is examined in Gareth Stedman Jones, 'The "Cockney" and the Nation: 1780–1988', in David Feldman and Gareth Stedman Jones, eds., *Metropolis: London. Histories and Representations Since 1800* (London and New York: Routledge, 1989), pp. 272–324, on which the above argument on cultural debates post-1867 draws. For an excellent analysis of the emergence of these ideas concerning urban street culture pre-1867 see Edward Jacobs, 'Bloods in the Street: London Street Culture, "Industrial Literacy", and the Emergence of Mass Culture in Victorian England', *Nineteenth-Century Contexts*, 18 (1995), pp. 321–47.

17 'Nothing in the Papers', *ILN*, 6 June 1868, p. 570.

18 James Greenwood, *The Seven Curses of London* (first published London: Stanley Rivers and Co., 1869), reprinted with an introduction by Jeffrey Richards (Oxford: Basil Blackwell, 1981), p. 46.

19 Ibid., p. 45. The 'gaffs' were not licensed theatres and were not supposed to perform stage plays; performances tended to be physically broad and improvised.

20 Henry Mayhew, 'The London Street-Folk', *London Labour and the London Poor*, vol. 1 (London: Griffin, Bohn, and Company. 1861), p. 240. A similar topography of the trade in obscene images through street sellers

is described in 'Mischievous Literature', pp. 448–9. See also Thomas, *Long Time Burning*, p. 275.

21  'The Streets of London and Public Morals', *Saturday Review*, 25 (16 May 1868), p. 646.

22  A full analytical account of the Society for the Suppression of Vice is given in M. J. D. Roberts, 'Making Victorian Morals? The Society for the Suppression of Vice and Its Critics, 1802–1886', *Historical Studies*, 21: 83 (October 1984), pp. 157–73, on which the following brief discussion is based. For a detailed consideration of the role of the Society in the passing of Campbell's Act see M. J. D. Roberts, 'Morals, Art and the Law: The Passing of the Obscene Publications Act, 1857', *Victorian Studies* (Summer 1985), pp. 609–29. See also Edward J. Bristow, *Vice and Vigilance: Purity Movements in Britain since 1800* (Dublin: Gill and Macmillan, 1977).

23  Roberts, 'Making Victorian Morals?', p. 157.

24  Roberts, 'Morals, Art and the Law', p. 621, n. 31.

25  (1868) L. R. 3 Q.B. 360, at p. 371. As cited in Geoffrey Robertson, *Obscenity: An Account of Censorship Laws and their Enforcement in England and Wales* (London: Weidenfeld and Nicolson, 1979), p. 29.

26  See 'Indecent Photographs', *Photographic News* 17 (7 November 1873), p. 534. Many of the more explicit photographs were believed to be imported from France. For a detailed account of the production of photographic nudes in the very different context of mid-nineteenth-century France see Elizabeth Anne McCauley, *Industrial Madness: Commercial Photography in France, 1848–1871* (New Haven and London: Yale University Press, 1994), chap. 4.

27  See 'Indecent Photographs', *Photographic News*, 17 (31 October 1873), pp. 527–8; also McCauley, *Industrial Madness*, pp. 153–4.

28  Mr Sergeant Cox, as reported in 'More Alleged Indecent Photographs', *Photographic News*, 17 (21 November 1873), p. 555.

29  *Daily Telegraph* as cited in ibid., p. 556.

30  See Donald J. Olsen, 'Introduction: Victorian London', in David Owen, *The Government of Victorian London, 1855–1889: The Metropolitan Board of Works, the Vestries, and the City Corporation*, edited by Roy MacLeod, with contributions by David Reeder, Donald Olsen and Francis Sheppard (Cambridge, Mass., and London: Harvard University Press, Belknap, 1982), p. 7.

31  *Building News*, 16 (27 March 1868), p. 209.

32  This theme is fully explored in Richard Sennett, *Flesh and Stone: The Body and the City in Western Civilization* (London: Faber and Faber, 1994). See also Part 1, section 1 above.

33  George Augustus Sala, 'The Streets of the World. Paris: The Passage des Panoramas', *Temple Bar*, 10 (February 1864), p. 335.

34  For a reference to this legend see Edward Walford, *Old and New London: A Narrative of Its History, Its People, and Its Places*, vol. 3 (London: Cassell Petter and Galpin, ?1875), p. 32.

35  John Timbs, *London and Westminster: City and Suburb. Strange Events, Characteristics, and Changes, of Metropolitan Life*, vol. 1 (London: Richard Bentley, 1868), p. 173.

36  Peter Cunningham, *A Handbook for London, Past and Present*, vol. 1 (London: John Murray, 1849), pp. 388–9.

37  The derivation of Holywell Street's name is referred to in a number of sources including Walford, *Old and New London*, p. 33. See also cuttings in the Department of Maps and Prints, Guildhall Library, Corporation of London SW2 / HOL 3 Oct. 1889.

38  *Builder*, 31 May 1856, p. 293.

39  'London, As It Strikes a Stranger', *Temple Bar*, 5 (June 1862), p. 384.

40  Michel de Certeau, 'Practices of Space', in Marshall Blonsky, ed., *On Signs* (Oxford: Basil Blackwell, 1985), p. 140.

41  C. R. T., Letter to the Editor, *The Times*, 13 May 1857, p. 9.

42  *The Times*, 23 July 1857, p. 8.

43  This account of Holywell Street draws on a range of histories including: 'A Little Talk About Lyon's Inn', *ILN*, 27 December 1862, pp. 707–8; Walford, *Old and New London*, vol. 3, esp. chaps. 5 and 6; Henry B. Wheatley, *London: Past and Present. Its History, Associations, and Traditions. Based Upon the Handbook of London by the Late Peter Cunningham*, vol. 2 (London: John Murray, 1891), p. 228; Walter Besant, *London in the Time of the Tudors* (London: Adam and Charles Black, 1904), p. 44; Charles Gordon, *Old Time Aldwych, Kingsway and Neighbourhood* (London: Fisher Unwin, 1905), pp. 230–33; Walter Besant, *London: North of the Thames* (London: Adam and Charles Black, 1911), pp. 328–9; Charles G. Harper, *A Literary Man's London* (London: Cecil Palmer, 1926), pp. 11–21; Michael Sadleir, *Forlorn Sunset* (London: Constable, 1947).

44  On local government and parliamentary proposals for the demolition of Holywell Street

see Percy J. Edwards, *London County Council: History of London Street Improvements 1855–1897* (London: P. S. King and Son, 1898), and London County Council, *Opening of Kingsway and Aldwych by His Majesty the King, Accompanied by Her Majesty the Queen. On Wednesday, 18th October, 1905* (London: Southwood, Smith and Co. Ltd, 1905).

45  See, for example, *Builder*, 31 May 1856, p. 293, and *ILN*, 27 September 1856, p. 313.

46  See George Augustus Sala, 'Travels in the County of Middlesex', *Temple Bar*, 1 (December 1860), p. 80, for an early expression of this view.

47  'Elizabethan London', *Builder*, 6 April 1861, p. 229.

48  For biographical details of Frederick Crace (1779–1859) see Leslie Stephen, ed., *Dictionary of National Biography*, vol. 12 (London: Smith, Elder and Co., 1887), pp. 432–3, and obituaries in the *Gentleman's Magazine*, vol. 7, 3rd ser. (1861), p. 435, and the *Builder*, 1 October 1859, p. 647.

49  Harper, *A Literary Man's London*, p. 18.

50  There are a number of discrepancies relating to dates and captions between the information given on the mounts and the entries in the catalogue. The entries given here in the list of illustrations are taken from Crace's hand-written captions on the mounts.

51  'Wych-Street', *ILN*, 1 January 1870, p. 18.

52  See Jane Jacobs, *The Death and Life of Great American Cities* (London: Jonathan Cape, 1962), p. 29. James Winter has taken up this point in his excellent study *London's Teeming Streets, 1830–1914* (London and New York: Routledge, 1993), p. 11.

53  On the sign of the 'Half Moon' see 'The Houses and Shops of Old London', *Builder*, 18 December 1852, pp. 799–801.

54  G. W. M. Reynolds, *The Mysteries of London*, first published 1844–56 (London: George Vickers), edited and with an introduction by Trefor Thomas (Keele, Staffs.: Keele University Press, 1996), p. 157. My thanks to Michael Slater for drawing this reference to my attention. On topography in Reynolds's work and his involvement in Chartism see Anne Humpherys, 'The Geometry of the Modern City: G. W. M. Reynolds and *The Mysteries of London*', *Browning Institute Studies*, vol. 11 (1983), pp. 69–80.

55  The names George or Henry Vickers are entered as occupying 28 and 29 Holywell Street in *Kelly's Post Office London* (London: Kelly and Co.). See also Philip A. H. Brown, *London Publishers and Printers, c.1800–1870* (London: British Library, 1982). Vickers's shop is actually portrayed in a fascinating drawing in the Westminster City Archives (fig. 69). This shows the double-fronted 'Bookseller and Publisher' as an extremely restrained and reputable establishment. Little is known about the drawing; it is not clear why Vickers's shop should be the subject of an individual study. Perhaps it was made as a record of an older style of shop-front which was fast becoming replaced with plate-glass windows, or, perhaps Vickers's reputation as a publisher and seller of fast or indecent literature made his shop a worthy subject.

56  B. de Shrewsbury, Esq. [W. M. Thackeray], 'Codlingsby', *Punch* XII (1847), p. 166.

57  Robert Knox, *The Races of Man: A Philosophical Enquiry into the Influence of Race Over the Destinies of Nation* (London: Henry Renshaw, 1862), p. 194. See also J. Ewing Ritchie, *The Night Side of London* (London: William Tweedie, 1857), p. 67.

58  George Augustus Sala, *Gaslight and Daylight: With Some London Scenes They Shine Upon* (London Chapman and Hall, 1859), p. 93.

59  [Peter Cunningham], *A Handbook of London: As It Is* (London: John Murray, 1863), p. 272.

60  'Notes of the Week', *ILN*, 23 February 1856, p. 195.

61  The history of obscenity in the early nineteenth century and its links with popular politics is brilliantly described in Iain McCalman, *Radical Underworld: Prophets, Revolutionaries and Pornographers in London, 1795–1840* (Oxford: Clarendon Press, 1993). His account is superlative; my aim is to take the history of obscenity into the following decades.

62  See ibid., chaps. 9 and 10.

63  Ibid., p. 210.

64  On Dugdale see ibid., esp. chap. 10. On Dugdale's aliases and prison sentences see Thomas, *A Long Time Burning*, p. 280. Also on Dugdale and the law see the *Bookseller*, 1 July 1868, pp. 448–9. Dugdale's trials were well covered at the time in the daily national press.

65  See Michel de Certeau, 'Psychoanalysis and Its History', in *Heterologies: Discourse on the Other*, trans. by Brian Massumi (Manchester: Manchester University Press, 1986), p. 4.

66  *The Times*, 14 August 1857, p. 7. See also the *Bookseller*, 1 July 1868, p. 449.

67  It is possible that this watercolour belonged originally to the collection of John Edmund Gardner, who was, like Frederick Crace, a great mid-Victorian collector of London

images. Gardner's collection was dispersed, but is referred to, along with the work of C. J. Richardson, in Bernard Adams, 'London Illustrated, 1604–1851: A History', in *A Survey and Index of Topographical Books and their Plates* (London: The Library Association, 1983), pp. xviii–xix. For a description of the baulks and pavement displays of Holywell Street shops see Harper, *A Literary Man's London*, pp. 14–15, and Hanslip Fletcher, *London Passed and Passing: A Pictorial Record of Destroyed and Threatened Buildings* (London: Sir Isaac Pitman and Sons, 1908), p. 196.

68 'The London Shop-Fronts', *Chamber's Journal of Popular Literature, Science, and Art*, vol. 41, no. 42 (15 October 1864), p. 670. On the impact of display windows and commodity culture on the Victorian novel see Andrew H. Miller, *Novels Behind Glass: Commodity Culture and Victorian Narrative* (Cambridge: Cambridge University Press, 1995).

69 'London Shops, Old and New', *Chamber's Edinburgh Journal*, vol. 20, no. 511 (15 October 1853), p. 252.

70 Thomas Frost, *Reminiscences of a Country Journalist* (London: Ward and Downey, 1886), pp. 52–3. More recently, the interior of a Holywell Street bookshop and publisher is described in Sadleir, *Forlorn Sunset*, pp. 416–22. A visual representation of an interior is given in 'London's New Streets. 1. Sketches of Holywell-Street: To Be Pulled Down', *Pall Mall Budget*, 17 October 1889, p. 1329.

71 Frost, *Reminiscences*, pp. 53–4.

72 Ibid., pp. 54–5.

73 *Bookseller*, 1 July 1868, p. 448.

74 Adrian Rifkin, *Street Noises: Parisian Pleasure, 1900–1940* (Manchester and New York: Manchester University Press, 1993), p. 10.

75 See, for example, the leading article in *The Times*, 23 July 1857, p. 8: 'We would only ask any member of the House of Commons who may feel any doubt as to the propriety of applying some remedy to this evil, to step aside for five minutes in his walk from the West-end to the City, and to mark the age and dress of those who may be seen hanging about the windows [of Holywell Street] . . . and then, if he be a father, to ask himself how he would like to know that his own children were exposed to similar temptations.'

76 McCalman, *Radical Underworld*, p. 236. See also p. 216.

77 'Foul Literature', *Daily Telegraph*, 13 May 1857, p. 3.

78 *Hansard*, 3rd ser., vol. 146 (13 July 1857), c. 1363.

79 *Daily Telegraph*, 17 June 1857, p. 3.

80 On the attractions of the windows of the London printsellers in this period see Henry Vizetelly, *Glances Back Through Seventy Years: Autobiographical and Other Reminiscences*, vol. 1 (London: Kegan, Paul, Trench, Trubner and Co. Ltd, 1893), p. 88. On second-hand book and print shops as 'a great temptation when in a sauntering humour in the London streets', see 'Some Aspects of the London Shops', *Builder*, 25 December 1858, p. 874.

81 *Daily Telegraph*, 6 April 1858, p. 5.

82 John Ruskin, 'Fors Clavigera', Letter 29 (May 1873), in Cook and Wedderburn, *Works*, vol. 27 (1907), pp. 535–6.

83 *Yokel's Preceptor: Or, More Sprees in London. Where May be had a Catalogue of a Most Extensive Variety of Every Choice and Curious Facetious Work* (London: H. Smith, n.d.). H. Smith was one of the aliases used by Dugdale from his premises at 37 Holywell Street. The work was published *c*.1850–60.

84 E. L. L. [Eliza Lynn Linton], 'Out Walking' *Temple Bar*, 5 (April 1862), p. 135.

85 Henry Mayhew, *London Labour and the London Poor*, vol. 4 (London: Griffin, Bohn, and Company, 1862), p. 307.

86 Rafael Cardoso Denis, 'The Educated Eye and the Industrial Hand: Art and Design Instruction for the Working Classes in Mid-Victorian Britain', unpublished PhD thesis, University of London, vol. 1, 1995, pp. 108–71.

87 Ibid., p. 136.

88 Colin Campbell, *The Romantic Ethic and the Spirit of Modern Consumerism* (Oxford: Basil Blackwell, 1987). See also Colin Campbell, 'The Romantic Ethic and the Spirit of Modern Consumerism: Reflections on the Reception of a Thesis Concerning the Origin of the Continuing Desire for Goods', in Susan M. Pearce, ed., *Experiencing Material Culture in the Western World* (London and Washington: Leicester University Press, 1997), pp. 36–48. On the implications of Campbell's work on histories of the culture of consumption see Jean-Christophe Agnew, 'Coming Up For Air: Consumer Culture in Historical Perspective', in John Brewer and Roy Porter, eds, *Consumption and the World of Goods* (London and New York: Routledge, 1993), pp. 19–39.

89 Campbell, 'Reflections', p. 45.

90 Brief accounts of the passing of the 1857 Obscene Publications Act are given in Taylor

Croft, *The Cloven Hoof: A Study of Contemporary London Vices* (London: Denis Archer, 1932), chap. 10, and Thomas, *Long Time Burning*, pp. 260–63. An excellent, detailed account is provided by M. J. D. Roberts, 'Morals, Art, and the Law', pp. 609–29.

91  The cases against Dugdale and William Strange are reported in the *Daily Telegraph*, 11 May 1857, p. 3, and *The Times*, 11 May 1857, p. 11.

92  The second obscene libel, *The Women of London*, is most probably the sensation story written by Bracebridge Hemyng and published by George Vickers: [Bracebridge Hemyng], *The Women of London: Disclosing the Trials and Temptations of a Woman's Life in London, with Occasional Glimpses of a Fast Career* (London: George Vickers, *c*.1857).

93  For reports on Campbell's speech and the response see *The Times*, 12 May 1857, p. 5, and the *ILN*, 16 May 1857, p. 476.

94  'Notes of the Week', *ILN*, 16 May 1857, p. 465.

95  'An Act for the Punishment of Idle and Disorderly Persons, and Rogues and Vagabonds, in that Part of Great Britain called England', 1824, 5 Geo. 4, c. 83; the inclusion of indecent displays in shop windows is specifically reiterated in 'An Act to Amend an Act for Punishing Idle and Disorderly Persons and Rogues and Vagabonds', 1838, 1 & 2 Vict., c. 38; 'An Act for Further Improving the Police In and Near the Metropolis', 1839, 2 & 3 Vict., c. 47, and 'An Act for Consolidating in One Act Certain Provisions Usually Contained in Acts for Regulating the Police of Towns', 1847, 10 & 11 Vict., c. 89.

96  Beverley Brown, 'Troubled Vision', p. 33. See also Miles Ogborn, 'Ordering the City: Surveillance, Public Space and the Reform of Urban Policing in England 1835–56', *Political Geography*, vol. 12, no. 6 (November 1993), pp. 505–21.

97  *Hansard*, 3rd ser. vol. 146 (25 June 1857), c. 329.

98  For biographical notes on Lyndhurst (1772–1863) see Stephen, *Dictionary of National Biography*, vol. 12, pp. 182–9. On Campbell (1779–1861) see vol. 8, pp. 379–86.

99  *Hansard*, 3rd ser., vol. 146 (25 June 1857), c. 331. Lyndhurst's words took on a life of their own; they were quoted approvingly by the *Days' Doings* thirteen years later: 'Lord Lyndhurst on Art and Pictures', *Days' Doings*, 20 August 1870, p. 2.

100  *Hansard*, 3rd ser., vol. 146 (25 June 1857), c. 337, and 3 July 1857, c. 865.

101  *Daily Telegraph*, 27 June 1857, p. 3.

102  *The Times*, 29 June 1857, p. 8.

103  *Hansard*, 3rd ser. vol. 146 (3 July 1857), c. 864–5. For discussion of the legal ambiguities of the proposed legislation see the *Jurist*, 18 July 1857, p. 290.

104  Ibid., c. 866.

105  'An Act for more Effectually Preventing the Sale of Obscene Books, Pictures, Prints, and Other Articles', 1857, 20 & 21 Vict., c. 83. See Alec Craig, *The Banned Books of England and Other Countries: A Study of the Conception of Literary Obscenity* (London: George Allen and Unwin, 1962), pp. 42–4. For discussion of the 1868 definition of obscenity 'to deprave and corrupt', see Robertson, *Obscenity*, pp. 29–30.

106  Beverley Brown, 'Troubled Vision', p. 35.

107  On the law as a cartographic practice see Nicholas K. Blomley, *Law, Space and the Geographies of Power* (New York and London: Guilford Press, 1994), and Leslie J. Moran and Derek McGhee, 'Perverting London: The Cartographic Practices of Law', *Law and Critique*, vol. 9, no. 2 (1998), pp. 207–24.

108  On the derivation of the name Old Bailey see archive A446/4 T1970, Map and Print Room, Guildhall Library, Corporation of London.

109  On the organisation of the courtroom see 'The Old Bailey', *London Society*, 10 (1866), pp. 399–405. For analysis of the significance of courtroom space see Paul Rock, *The Social World of an English Crown Court: Witness and Professionals in the Crown Court Centre at Wood Green* (Oxford: Clarendon Press, 1993).

110  Reports of the arrests are given in *The Times*, 23 September 1857, p. 9, *Daily Telegraph*, 23 September 1857, pp. 2, 3, and *ILN*, 26 September 1857, p. 311. All of these papers closely followed the progress of the arrests and the following trials.

111  On Elliott's trial see *The Times*, 6 January 1858, p. 11; on her sentencing see *The Times*, 3 February 1858, p. 9.

112  'Notes of the Week', *ILN*, 26 September 1857, p. 311.

113  *Daily Telegraph*, 23 September 1857, p. 3.

114  For Campbell's call for a Return to show the effects of the Act see *Hansard*, 3rd ser., vol. 148 (7 December 1857), c. 226. See 'Return of the Informations laid under the Act, 20 & 21 Vict., c. 83 "for more effectually preventing the Sale of Obscene Books, Pictures, Prints and Other Articles" the Warrants issued thereupon, and the Result of the Proceedings in each case', House of Lords Record Office, Main Papers, Sess. 1857–8 (19 February 1858), 162.

115 The trial was held on 5 January 1858 in the Central Criminal Court and is reported in *The Times*, 6 January 1858, p. 11.

116 Public Record Office CRIM/4/592 (Indictments), 5 January 1858. On indictments see Rock, *Social World of an English Crown Court*, pp. 50, 62.

117 This was probably the title published by William Dugdale, *c.*1850–60, and listed in Pisanus Fraxi, *Index Librorum Prohibitorum: Being Notes Bio- Biblio- Icono-graphical and Critical on Curious and Uncommon Books* (London: Privately Printed, 1877), p. 118.

118 The seized titles are listed in the *Daily Telegraph*, 24 September 1857, p. 4, and in other press reports of the raids.

119 See *The Times*, 14 October 1857, p. 11, and the *Daily Telegraph*, 14 October 1857, p. 4.

120 'Notes of the Week', *ILN*, 14 November 1857, p. 483.

121 *The Times*, 11 February 1858, p. 11, and 18 February 1858, p. 11.

122 *The Times*, 11 February 1858, p. 11. My thanks to Alex Werner at the Museum of London and the Museum of London Archaeological Service for making the collection of smashed pipes available to me.

123 On the sentencing of Bleeketer see *The Times*, 3 February 1858, p. 9, and the *ILN*, 6 February 1858, p. 131.

124 *Hansard*, 3rd ser., vol. 148 (7 December 1857), c. 227.

125 *The Times*, 3 February 1858, p. 6.

126 On the renaming of Holywell Street see Walford, *Old and New London*, vol. 3, p. 34, and E. Beresford Chancellor, *Annals of the Strand: Topographical and Historical* (London: Chapman and Hall, 1912), p. 66.

127 'The Streets of London and Public Morals', *Saturday Review*, 25 (16 May 1868), p. 646.

128 Harper, *A Literary Man's London*, p. 12.

129 In these terms, Holywell Street can be described as a 'heterotopic' space, as defined by Michel Foucault, 'Of Other Spaces', *Diacritics*, vol. 16 (Spring 1986), pp. 22–7.

130 'London Improvements', *ILN*, 18 April 1868, p. 383.

131 Charles Dickens, *Bleak House*, first published in novel form 1853, Oxford Illustrated Dickens (Oxford: Oxford University Press, 1951), p. 2.

132 Some sources give later dates for the earliest references to Temple Bar. On the history of Temple Bar see 'A Member of the Inner Temple', *Temple Bar: The City Golgotha. A Narrative of the Historical Occurrences of a Criminal Character Associated with the Present Bar* (London: David Bogue, 1853); *Temple Bar; Its History, Memorials and Associations* (London: John Bursill, 1877); *The History of Temple Bar* (London: John Bursill, 1877); E. W. Godwin, *Temple Bar* (London: B. T. Batsford, 1877); L. Godfrey-Turner, *Old Temple Bar: Rambles, Reminiscences and Reflections* (London: King and Jarrett, 1921); Ben Weinreb and Christopher Hibbert, eds., *The London Encyclopaedia* (London: Macmillan, 1983), p. 881.

133 The ceremonial history of Temple Bar is described in Timbs, *London and Westminster*, pp. 97–112.

134 These events are reported in 'Temple-Bar, On the Night Before the Funeral of the Duke of Wellington', *ILN*, 11 December 1852, p. 525, and 'Illumination of Temple Bar in Honour of the Prince of Wales's Marriage', *ILN*, 21 March 1863, p. 358.

135 Godwin, *Temple Bar*, pp. 10, 11.

136 'London, As It Strikes a Stranger', *Temple Bar*, 5 (June 1862), p. 383. See also Sala's article 'Travels in the County of Middlesex: From Temple Bar to Kensington Turnpike', *Temple Bar*, 1 (December 1860), pp. 73–90, esp. p. 79.

137 *History of Temple Bar*, p. 3. The image is repeated in dreadful verse form in 'London Poems, 1. Temple Bar', *Temple Bar*, 1 (December 1860), pp. 99–102.

138 Henry Mayhew, 'The Great World of London', in Henry Mayhew and John Binny, *The Criminal Prisons of London and Scenes of Prison Life* (London: Griffin, Bohn and Co., 1862), p. 4.

139 See 'An Act for Widening and Improving the Entrance into the City of London near Temple Bar; for Making a More Commodious Street or Passage at Snow Hill; and for Raising, on the Credit of the Orphans' Fund, a Sum of Money for those Purposes', 35 Geo. 3, c. 126, and subsequent related legislation some of which is collected in 'Acts for Widening and Improving the Streets, etc. at Temple Bar and Snow Hill. From 1795 to 1804, both inclusive.' British Library, Rare Books and Manuscripts.

140 *ILN*, 22 October 1853, p. 354.

141 On the relationship between the City of London and other forms of London government, including the vestries and the Metropolitan Board of Works see Francis Sheppard, 'The Crisis of London's Government', in David Owen, *The Government of Victorian London*, pp. 23–30, and Ken Young and Patricia L. Garside, *Metropolitan London: Poli-*

142    Reported in *The Times*, 6 March 1858, p. 10.

143    The last years of Temple Bar in the 1870s are described in Sala, *Life and Adventures of George Augustus Sala. Written by Himself*, vol. 2 (London: Cassell and Co., 1895), pp. 312–16. In 1876 Sala campaigned for the demolition of Temple Bar, along with the architect, antiquarian and editor of the *Builder*, George Godwin.

144    The vote was taken on 27 September 1876 and reported in *The Times*, 28 September 1876, p. 4.

145    'Letter to the Editor', *The Times*, 22 September 1876, p. 7. For biographical details of Bowyer see Stephen, *The Dictionary of National Biography*, vol. 2 (Oxford: Oxford University Press, 1921–2), pp. 989–90.

146    *Daily Telegraph*, 23 September 1876, p. 5.

147    *The Times*, 4 January 1878, p. 6.

148    *The Times*, 7 January 1878, p. 9.

149    See also 'The Last of Temple Bar. – Sketched on Saturday, January 12, 1878' and the related article 'Temple Bar and Child's Bank', *ILN*, 19 January 1878, pp. 65, 68–70.

150    Gustave Doré and Blanchard Jerrold, *London: A Pilgrimage* (London: Grant and Co., 1872). The work was first issued in thirteen parts.

151    Ibid., p. 190.

152    Edward Gibbon, *The History of the Decline and Fall of the Roman Empire*, 6 vols. (London: Strahan and Cadell, 1776–88). Gibbon's use of the motif is referred to in James Belich, *Making Peoples: A History of the New Zealanders. From Polynesian Settlement to the End of the Eighteenth Century* (Auckland: Penguin Books, 1996), p. 297. The ideal was reworked in Constantin-François Volney, *Les ruines, ou, Meditation sur les revolutions des Empires*, which was first published in 1791 and translated into English as *Ruins of Empire* in the same year. Volney's work is discussed in Marilyn Butler, 'Romantic Manichaeism: Shelley's "On the Devil, and Devils" and Byron's Mythological Dramas', in J. B. Bullen, ed., *The Sun is God: Painting, Literature and Mythology in the Nineteenth Century* (Oxford: Clarendon Press, 1989), pp. 13–37. Shelley referred to a similar image in the Dedication to *Peter Bell the Third* (1819) in Thomas Hutchinson, ed., *The Complete Works of Percy Bysshe Shelley* (London, New York, Toronto: Oxford University Press, 1952), p. 347.

153    My thanks to Rod Edmond for generously sharing with me his references to Macaulay's New Zealander. T. B. Macaulay, 'Von Ranke', *Critical and Historical Essays Contributed to the Edinburgh Review* (London: Longman, Brown, Green and Longmans, 1851), pp. 535–6.

154    See Belich, *Making Peoples*, pp. 297–8.

155    Jno., *Archimago* (London: Ward and Lock, 1864). See also the hostile review in the *ILN*, 8 October 1864, p. 234.

# Works Cited

*Archival Sources*

British Library
  Rare Books and Manuscripts
Chelsea Public Library, The Royal Borough of
  Kensington and Chelsea Libraries and Arts
  Services
    'Papers Upon the History of Cremorne
      Gardens, Chelsea. 1840–1878'
    'Papers Relating to the History of
      Cremorne Gardens, Chelsea. 1831–
      1878. Volume Two'
Guildhall Library, Corporation of London
House of Lords Record Office
  Main Papers, Sess. 1857–8
London Metropolitan Archives
  *Middlesex Sessions Records*
  Minutes of Meetings of the Metropolitan
    Board of Works
Museum of London
  Letters from Amelia Roper to Martha
    Busher, 1849–58
Museum of London Archaeological Service
Public Record Office
  CRIM/4/592 (Indictments) 5 January
    1858
Westminster City Archives


*Statutes and Parliamentary Papers*

An Act for the Punishment of Idle and Disorderly Persons, and Rogues and Vagabonds, in
  that Part of Great Britain called England,
  1824, 5 Geo. 4, c. 83
An Act to Amend an Act for Punishing Idle
  and Disorderly Persons and Rogues and
  Vagabonds, 1838, 1 & 2 Vict., c. 38

An Act for Further Improving the Police In
  and Near the Metropolis, 1839, 2 & 3 Vict.,
  c. 47
An Act for Consolidating in One Act Certain
  Provisions Usually Contained in Acts for
  Regulating the Police of Towns, 1847, 10 &
  11 Vict., c. 89
An Act for more Effectually Preventing the
  Sale of Obscene Books, Pictures, Prints, and
  Other Articles, 1857, 20 & 21 Vict., c. 83
'Report from the Select Committee on Met-
  ropolitan Communications', *Parliamentary
  Papers, 1854–55*, X. 1.
'Minutes of Evidence Before the Select
  Committee on Theatrical Licenses and
  Regulations', *Parliamentary Papers, 1866*,
  XVI. 1.


*Newspapers and Periodicals*

*All the Year Round*
*British Quarterly Review*
*Builder*
*Building News*
*Chamber's Journal of Popular Literature, Science,
  and Art*
*Daily Telegraph*
*Days' Doings*
*Hansard's Parliamentary Debates*
*Household Words*
*Illustrated London News*
*Illustrated Times*
*Journal of British Studies*
*Journal of Gas Lighting, Water Supply, and
  Sanitary Improvement*
*Journal of Transport History*
*New Formations*

*New Left Review*
*Nineteenth-Century Contexts*
*Penny Illustrated Paper*
*Photographic News*
*Pictorial Times*
*Punch*
*Saturday Review*
*Temple Bar*
*Theory, Culture and Society*
*The Times*
*Victorian Studies*


## Unpublished Theses

Denis, Rafael Cardoso. 'The Educated Eye and the Industrial Hand: Art and Design Instruction for the Working Classes in Mid-Victorian Britain'. 2 vols. PhD thesis, University of London, 1995

Nead, Lynda. 'The Magdalene in Modern Times: The Representation of the Prostitute in Victorian Art'. BA dissertation, Department of Fine Art, University of Leeds, 1979

Pinkus, Rosa Lynn B. 'The Conceptual Development of Metropolitan London, 1800–1855'. PhD thesis, State University of New York at Buffalo, 1975

Rendell, Jane. 'Ramblers and Cyprians: Gender and Architectural Space, London's St James's, 1821–8'. PhD thesis, University of London, 1998


## Printed Sources

Acton, William. *Prostitution, Considered in Its Moral, Social and Sanitary Aspects in London and Other Large Cities and Garrison Towns with Proposals for the Control and Prevention of Its Attendant Evils*. 2nd edn, London: John Churchill and Sons, 1870

Adams, Annmarie. 'The Healthy Victorian City: The Old London Street at the International Health Exhibition of 1884'. In *Streets: Critical Perspectives on Public Space*, ed.

Zeynep Çelik, Diane Favro and Richard Ingersoll, 203–12. Berkeley, Los Angeles and London: University of California Press, 1994

Adams, Bernard. 'London Illustrated, 1604–1851: A History'. In *A Survey and Index of Topographical Books and their Plates*, xii–xxviii. London: The Library Association, 1983

Adburgham, Alison. *Shopping in Style: London from the Restoration to Edwardian Elegance*. London: Thames and Hudson, 1979

Agnew, Jean-Christophe. 'Coming Up For Air: Consumer Culture in Historical Perspective'. In *Consumption and the World of Goods*, ed. John Brewer and Roy Porter, 19–39. London and New York: Routledge, 1993

Altick, Richard D. *The English Common Reader*. Chicago: Chicago University Press, 1957

———. *The Shows of London*. Cambridge, Mass., and London: Belknap Press of Harvard University Press, 1978

Anderson, Nancy Fix. *Woman Against Women in Victorian England: A Life of Eliza Lynn Linton*. Bloomington, Ind.: Indiana University Press, 1987

Anderson, Patricia. *The Printed Image and the Transformation of Popular Culture, 1790–1860*. Oxford: Clarendon Press, 1991

Anderson, Perry. 'Modernity and Revolution', *New Left Review* 144 (1984): 96–113

Arscott, Caroline, with Griselda Pollock and Janet Wolff. 'The Partial View: The Visual Representation of the Early Nineteenth-Century City'. In *The Culture of Capital: Art, Power and the Nineteenth-Century Middle Class*, ed. Janet Wolff and John Seed, 191–233. Manchester: Manchester University Press, 1988

Bachelard, Gaston. *The Flame of a Candle*. Trans. Joni Caldwell. Dallas: Dallas Institute Publications, 1988

Bailey, Peter. *Leisure and Class in Victorian England: Rational Recreation and the Contest for Control, 1830–1885*. London: Routledge and Kegan Paul, 1978

———. 'Champagne Charlie: Performance and Ideology in the Music-Hall Swell Song'. In *Music Hall: Performance and Style*, ed. J. S.

Bratton, 49–69. Milton Keynes: Open University Press, 1986

Barlow, Thomas G. *On the Supply of Gas in the Metropolis.* London: W. B. King, 1859

Barton, Nicholas. *The Lost Rivers of London: A Study of their Effects Upon London and Londoners, and the Effects of London and Londoners Upon Them.* Rev. edn, London: Historical Publications, 1992

Belich, James. *Making Peoples: A History of the New Zealanders. From Polynesian Settlement to the End of the Eighteenth Century.* Auckland: Penguin Books, 1966

Benjamin, Walter. 'Paris – the Capital of the Nineteenth Century'. Trans. Quintin Hoare. In *Charles Baudelaire: A Lyric Poet in the Era of High Capitalism*, 155–76. London and New York: Verso, 1973

———. *Charles Baudelaire: A Lyric Poet in the Era of High Capitalism.* Trans. Harry Zohn. London and New York: Verso, 1973

———. *One-Way Street and Other Writings.* Trans. Edmund Jephcott and Kingsley Shorter. London and New York: Verso, 1979

Bentley, Nicolas, Michael Slater and Nina Burgis, eds. *The Dickens Index.* Oxford and New York: Oxford University Press, 1988

Berman, Marshall. *All That Is Solid Melts Into Air.* London: Verso, 1983

———. 'The Signs in the Street: A Response to Perry Anderson', *New Left Review* 144 (1984): 114–23

Besant, Walter. *London in the Time of the Tudors.* London: Adam and Charles Black, 1904

———. *London: North of the Thames.* London: Adam and Charles Black, 1911

Betts, Raymond F. 'The Allusion to Rome in British Imperialist Thought of the Late-Nineteenth and Early-Twentieth Centuries', *Victorian Studies* 15, no. 2 (December 1971): 149–59

Blackmore, John. *The London By Moonlight Mission: Being the Account of Midnight Cruises on the Streets of London.* London: Robson and Avery, 1860

Blomley, Nicholas K. *Law, Space and the Geographies of Power.* New York and London: Guilford Press, 1994

Booth, Mark Haworth. *The Golden Age of British Photography, 1839–1900.* London: Aperture, 1984

Booth, Michael R. 'The Metropolis on Stage'. In *The Victorian City: Images and Realities*, vol. 1, ed. H. J. Dyos and Michael Wolff, 211–22. London, Henley and Boston: Routledge and Kegan Paul, 1973

Bristow, Edward J. *Vice and Vigilance: Purity Movements in Britain Since 1700.* Dublin: Gill and Macmillan, 1977

Brown, Beverley. 'Troubled Vision: Legal Understandings of Obscenity', *New Formations – Perversity* 19 (Spring 1993): 29–44

Brown, Philip A. H. *London Publishers and Printers, c.1800–1870.* London: British Library, 1982

Buck-Morss, Susan. *The Dialectics of Seeing: Walter Benjamin and the Arcades Project.* Cambridge, Mass.: MIT Press, 1989

'Business of Pleasure (The)', *All the Year Round* x (10 October 1863): 149–52

Butler, Marilyn. 'Romantic Manichaeism: Shelley's "On the Devil, and Devils" and Byron's Mythological Dramas'. In *The Sun is God: Painting, Literature and Mythology in the Nineteenth Century*, ed. J. B. Bullen, 13–37. Oxford: Clarendon Press, 1989

Campbell, Colin. *The Romantic Ethic and the Spirit of Modern Consumerism.* Oxford: Basil Blackwell, 1987

———. 'The Romantic Ethic and the Spirit of Modern Consumerism*: Reflections on the Reception of a Thesis Concerning the Origin of the Continuing Desire for Goods'. In *Experiencing Material Culture in the Western World*, ed. Susan M. Pearce, 36–48. London and Washington: Leicester University Press, 1997

de Certeau, Michel. *The Practice of Everyday Life.* Trans. Steven Rendall. Berkeley, Los Angeles and London: University of California Press, 1984

———. 'Practices of Space'. Trans. Richard Miller and Edward Schneider. In *On Signs*, ed. Marshall Blonsky, 122–45. Oxford: Basil Blackwell, 1985

———. *Heterologies: Discourse on the Other.*

Trans. Brian Massumi. Manchester: University of Manchester Press, 1986

Chancellor, E. Beresford. *Annals of the Strand: Topographical and Historical*. London: Chapman and Hall, 1912

Chandler, Dean. *Outline of History of Lighting by Gas*. London: South Metropolitan Gas Company, 1936

Chandler, Dean, and A. Douglas Lacey. *The Rise of the Gas Industry in Britain*. London: British Gas Council, 1949

'Cheap Literature', *British Quarterly Review* 29 (1 April 1859): 313–45

Clark, T. J. *The Painting of Modern Life: Paris in the Art of Manet and His Followers*. London: Thames and Hudson, 1985

Clarke, Mary, and Clement Crisp. *The History of Dance*. London: Orbis Publishing, 1981

Cleminshaw, C. G. *A Few Remarks on the Pamphlet Entitled 'Metropolitan Gas Legislation Past and Prospective'*. London: Longmans, Green and Co., 1867

——. *The Gas Supply of the Metropolis: A Word to the Public, the Companies, and the Shareholders*. London: Longman, Green and Co., 1868

Collins, Philip. Introduction to George Augustus Sala, *Twice Round the Clock: Or the Hours of the Day and Night in London*, 7–22. Leicester: Leicester University Press, 1971

Conrad, Peter. *The Victorian Treasure-House*. London: Collins, 1973

Cook, E. T., and Alexander Wedderburn, eds. *The Works of John Ruskin*. 39 vols. London: George Allen, 1903–12

Cosgrove, Denis, ed. *Mappings*. London: Reaktion, 1999

Craig, Alec. *The Banned Books of England and Other Countries: A Study of the Conception of Literary Obscenity*. London: George Allen and Unwin, 1962

Croft, Taylor. *The Cloven Hoof: A Study of Contemporary London Vices*. London: Denis Archer, 1932

Croll, A. Angus. *The Great Central Gas Company: Its Origin and History*. London: Samuel Harris and Co., 1875

Cullen, M. J. *The Statistical Movement in Early Victorian Britain: The Foundations of Empirical Social Research*. Hassocks, Sussex: Harvester Press, 1975

Cunningham, Hugh. *Leisure in the Industrial Revolution, c.1780–c.1880*. London: Croom Helm, 1980

Cunningham, Peter. *A Handbook for London, Past and Present*. 2 vols. London: John Murray, 1849

[Cunningham, Peter]. *Handbook of London As It Is*. London: John Murray, 1863

Curtin, Michael. *Propriety and Position: A Study of Victorian Manners*. New York and London: Garland, 1987

Darlington, Ida, and James Howgego. *Printed Maps of London, c.1553–1850*. London: George Philip and Sons, 1964

Davidoff, Leonore. *The Best Circles: Society, Etiquette and the Season*. London: Croom Helm, 1973

[Day, C. W.]. *Hints on Etiquette and the Usages of Society: With a Glance at Bad Habits*. London: Longman, Brown, Green, and Longmans, 1849

Derrida, Jacques. *Memoirs of the Blind: The Self-Portrait and Other Ruins*. Trans. Pascale-Anne Brault and Michael Naas. Chicago and London: University of Chicago Press, 1993

Dickens, Charles. *Sketches by Boz: Illustrative of Every-Day Life and Every-Day People*. Oxford: Oxford University Press, 1957

——. *The Uncommercial Traveller*. London: Chapman and Hall, 1861

——. *Dombey and Son*. Harmondsworth: Penguin, 1970

——. *Barnaby Rudge*. Harmondsworth: Penguin, 1997

——. *Bleak House*. Oxford: Oxford University Press, 1951

Doré, Gustave, and Blanchard Jerrold. *London: A Pilgrimage*. London: Grant and Co., 1872

Dorment, Richard, and Margaret F. MacDonald. *James McNeill Whistler*. London: Tate Gallery Publications, 1994

Douzinas, Costas. '*Whistler v. Ruskin*: Law's Fear of Images', *Art History* 19:3 (September 1996): 353–69

Dyos, H. J. 'Railways and Housing in Victorian London', *Journal of Transport History* II (1955–6): 11–21, 90–100

————. 'Some Social Costs of Railway Building in London', *Journal of Transport History* III (1957–8): 23–9

Edwards, Percy J. *London County Council: History of London Street Improvements, 1855–1897*. London: P. S. King and Son, 1898

*Etiquette for Ladies*. London: Frederick Warne and Co., 1866

Fletcher, Hanslip. *London Passed and Passing: A Pictorial Record of Destroyed and Threatened Buildings*. London: Sir Isaac Pitman and Sons, 1908

Flukinger, Roy. *The Formative Decades: Photography in Great Britain, 1839–1920*. Austin: University of Texas Press, 1985

Foucault, Michel. *Discipline and Punish: The Birth of the Prison*. Trans. Alan Sheridan. London: Allen Lane, 1977

————. 'The Eye of Power'. Trans. Colin Gordon. In *Power/Knowledge: Selected Interviews and Other Writings, 1972–1977*, ed. Colin Gordon, 146–65. Brighton: Harvester, 1980

————. 'Of Other Spaces'. Trans. Jay Miskowiec. *Diacritics* 16 (Spring 1986): 22–7

Franks, A. H. *Social Dance: A Short History*. London: Routledge and Kegan Paul, 1963

Fraser, Nancy. 'Rethinking the Public Sphere: A Contribution to the Critique of Actually Existing Democracy'. In *Habermas and the Public Sphere*, 109–42, ed. Craig Calhoun. Cambridge, Mass.: MIT Press, 1992

Fraxi, Pisanus. *Index Librorum Prohibitorum: Being Notes Bio- Biblio- Icono- graphical and Critical on Curious and Uncommon Books*. London: privately printed, 1877

Freedgood, Elaine. 'Groundless Optimism: Regression in the Service of Egos, England and Empire in Victorian Ballooning Memoirs', *Nineteenth-Century Contexts* 20:1 (1997): 61–80

Freud, Sigmund. 'The Uncanny'. In *The Standard Edition of the Complete Psychological Works of Sigmund Freud*, vol. XVII, trans. and ed. James Strachey, 219–52. London: Hogarth Press and the Institute of Psycho-Analysis, 1955

Frisby, David. *Fragments of Modernity: Theories of Modernity in the Work of Simmel, Kracauer and Benjamin*. Cambridge: Polity Press, 1985

Frost, Thomas. *Reminiscences of a Country Journalist*. London: Ward and Downey, 1886

F. W. R. and Lord Charles X. *The Laws and Bye-Laws of Good Society: A Code of Modern Etiquette*. London: Simpkin, Marshall and Co., 1867

*Getting London in Perspective*. London: Barbican Art Gallery, 1984

Gibbon, Edward. *The History of the Decline and Fall of the Roman Empire*. 6 vols. London: Strahan and Cadell, 1776–88

Gilroy, Paul. *The Black Atlantic: Modernity and Double Consciousness*. London and New York: Verso, 1993

Gledhill, David. *Gas Lighting*. Aylesbury: Shire Publications Ltd, 1981

Godfrey-Turner, L. *Old Temple Bar: Rambles, Reminiscences and Reflections*. London: King and Jarrett, 1921

Godwin, E. W. *Temple Bar*. London: B. T. Batsford, 1877

Gordon, Charles. *Old Time Aldwych, Kingsway and Neighbourhood*. London: Fisher Unwin, 1905

*Greaves Brothers (The) and Victorian Chelsea: An Exhibition*. London: Royal Borough of Kensington and Chelsea, 1968

Greenwood, James. *The Seven Curses of London*. London: Stanley Rivers and Co., 1869

*Habits of Good Society, The: A Handbook of Etiquette for Ladies and Gentlemen. With Thoughts, Hints, and Anecdotes Concerning Social Observances; Nice Points of Taste and Good Manners; and the Art of Making One's-Self Agreeable. The Whole Interspersed with Humorous Illustrations of Social Predicaments; Remarks on the History and Changes of Fashion; and the Differences of English and Continental Etiquette*. London: James Hogg and Sons, 1859

Haill, Catherine. *Victorian Illustrated Music Sheets*. London: Her Majesty's Stationery Office, 1981

Hardy, Anne. 'Parish Pump to Private Pipes: London's Water Supply in the Nineteenth Century'. In *Living and Dying in London* (Medical History, Supplement no. 11), ed. W. F. Bynum and Roy Porter, 76–93.

London: Wellcome Institute for the History of Medicine, 1991

Hardy, Thomas. *A Pair of Blue Eyes*. Oxford: Oxford University Press, 1985

Harley, J. B. 'Maps, Knowledge and Power'. In *The Iconography of Landscape: Essays on the Symbolic Representation, Design and Use of Past Environments*, ed. Denis Cosgrove and Stephen Daniels, 277–312. Cambridge: Cambridge University Press, 1988

————. 'Deconstructing the Map'. In *Writing Worlds: Discourse, Text and Metaphor in the Representation of Landscape*, ed. Trevor J. Barnes and James S. Duncan, 231–47. London and New York: Routledge, 1992

Harper, Charles G. *A Literary Man's London*. London: Cecil Palmer, 1926

Harvey, David. *Consciousness and the Urban Experience*. Oxford: Basil Blackwell, 1985

Hayward, William Stephens. *London By Night*. London: William Oliver, 1870

[Hemyng, Bracebridge]. *The Women of London: Disclosing the Trials and Temptations of a Woman's Life in London, with Occasional Glimpses of a Fast Career*. London: George Vickers, c.1857

Hill, Nancy K. *A Reformer's Art: Dickens' Picturesque and Grotesque Imagery*. Athens, Oh., and London: Ohio University Press, 1981

Hindley, Diana, and Geoffrey Hindley. *Advertising in Victorian England, 1837–1901*. London: Wayland, 1972

*History of Temple Bar, The*. London: John Bursill, 1877

Hogarth, Paul. *Arthur Boyd Houghton*. London: Victoria and Albert Museum, 1975

————. *Arthur Boyd Houghton*. London: Gordon Fraser, 1981

Hollingshead, John. *Underground London*. London: Groombridge and Sons, 1862

'How a Blind Man Saw the International Exhibition', *Temple Bar* 7 (January 1863): 227–37

Humpherys, Anne. 'The Geometry of the Modern City: G. W. M. Reynolds and *The Mysteries of London*', *Browning Institute Studies* 11 (1983): 69–80

Hunt, Charles. *Gas Lighting*. Vol. III of *Groves and Thorp's Chemical Technology or Chemistry Applied to Arts and Manufactures*. London: J. and A. Churchill, 1900

————. *A History of the Introduction of Gas Lighting*. London: Walter King, 1907

Hussey, Christopher. *The Picturesque*. London: G. P. Putnam, 1927

Hutchinson, Thomas, ed. *The Complete Works of Percy Bysshe Shelley*. London, New York and Toronto: Oxford University Press, 1952

Hyde, Ralph. *Printed Maps of Victorian London, 1851–1900*. Folkestone, Kent: William Dawson and Sons, 1975

————. *Panoramania! The Art and Entertainment of the 'All-Embracing' View*. London: Trefoil Publications and Barbican Art Gallery, 1989

Impey, Oliver. *Chinoiserie: The Impact of Oriental Styles on Western Art and Decoration*. London: Oxford University Press, 1977

Jacobs, Edward. 'Bloods in the Street: London Street Culture, "Industrial Literacy", and the Emergence of Mass Culture in Victorian England', *Nineteenth-Century Contexts* 18 (1995): 321–47

Jacobs, Jane. *The Death and Life of Great American Cities*. London: Jonathan Cape, 1962

Jno. *Archimago*. London: Ward and Lock, 1864

Jones, Gareth Stedman. 'The "Cockney" and the Nation, 1780–1988'. In *Metropolis: London Histories and Representations since 1800*, ed. David Feldman and Gareth Stedman Jones, 272–324. London and New York: Routledge, 1989

Joyce, James. *Ulysses: The Corrected Text*, ed. Hans Walter Gabler. Harmondsworth: Penguin, 1986

*Kelly's Post Office London*. London: Kelly and Co.

Knox, Robert. *The Races of Man: A Philosophical Enquiry into the Influence of Race Over the Destinies of Nation*. London: Henry Renshaw, 1862

Larking, Albert. *History of the Early Closing Association and How the Saturday Half-Holiday Was Won*. London and Woking: Unwin Brothers Ltd, 1912

Layard, G. S. *Mrs Lynn Linton: Her Life, Letters,*

*and Opinions*. London: Methuen and Co., 1901

Lehmann, R. C., ed. *Charles Dickens as Editor. Being Letters Written by Him to Henry Wills his Sub-Editor*. London: Smith, Elder and Co., 1912

'Letters from Nigh Latitudes – No. 15: A Visit to Cremorne', *Fun*, 14 June 1862: 121

Lewis, R. A. *Edwin Chadwick and the Public Health Movement, 1832–1854*. London: Longmans, Green, 1952

E. L. L. [Linton, Eliza Lynn]. 'Out Walking', *Temple Bar* 5 (April 1862): 132–9

[Linton, Eliza Lynn]. 'Passing Faces', *Household Words* 263 (7 April 1855): 261–4

Linton, Eliza Lynn. *Ourselves: A Series of Essays on Women*. London and New York: G. Routledge and Sons, 1870

———. *The Girl of the Period and Other Social Essays*. 2 vols. London: Richard Bentley and Son, 1883

———. *The Autobiography of Christopher Kirkland*. 3 vols. London: Bentley, 1885

———. 'Town or Country?', *New Review* IX (October 1893): 373–83

———. *My Literary Life*. London: Hodder and Stoughton, 1899

'London, As It Strikes a Stranger', *Temple Bar* 5 (June 1862): 379–88

London County Council. *Opening of Kingsway and Aldwych by His Majesty the King, Accompanied by Her Majesty the Queen. On Wednesday 18th October, 1905*. London: Southwood, Smith and Co. Ltd, 1905

'London Gas', *British Quarterly Review* LXIX (1879): 1–39

'London Shop-Fronts, The', *Chamber's Journal of Popular Literature, Science, and Art* 41:42 (15 October 1864): 670–72

'London Shops, Old and New', *Chamber's Edinburgh Journal* 20:511 (15 October 1853): 250–53

'London's New Streets, 1: Sketches of Holywell-Street: To Be Pulled Down', *Pall Mall Budget*, 17 October 1889: 1328–9

Macaulay, T. B. 'Von Ranke'. In *Critical and Historical Essays Contributed to the Edinburgh Review*. 535–56. London: Longman, Brown, Green and Longmans, 1851

Marin, Louis. *Utopics: Spatial Play*. Trans. Robert A.Vollrath. London: Macmillan, 1984

———. *Portrait of the King*. Trans. Martha M. Houle. London: Macmillan, 1988

Mayhew, Augustus. *Paved with Gold: Or the Romance and Reality of the London Streets*. London: Chapman and Hall, 1858

Mayhew, Henry. *The Great World of London*. London: David Bogue, 1856

———. *London Labour and the London Poor*. 4 vols. London: Griffin, Bohn and Co., 1861–2

Mayhew, Henry, and John Binny. *The Criminal Prisons of London and Scenes of Prison Life*. London: Griffin, Bohn and Co., 1862

Mayne, Jonathan, ed. and trans. *Charles Baudelaire: The Painter of Modern Life and Other Essays*. London: Phaidon, 1964

McCalman, Iain. *Radical Underworld: Prophets, Revolutionaries and Pornographers in London, 1795–1840*. Oxford: Clarendon Press, 1993

McCauley, Elizabeth Anne. *Industrial Madness: Commercial Photography in France, 1848–1871*. New Haven and London: Yale University Press, 1994

McCormick, John. *Dion Boucicault*. Cambridge: Chadwyck-Healy Ltd, 1987

McKendrick, Neil, John Brewer and J. H. Plumb. *The Birth of Consumer Society: The Commercialization of Eighteenth-Century England*. London: Europa, 1982

Member of the Inner Temple, A. *Temple Bar: The City Golgotha. A Narrative of the Historical Occurrences of a Criminal Character Associated with the Present Bar*. London: David Bogue, 1853

Meritt, Paul, and W. Howell Poole. *New Babylon or Daughters of Eve*. 3 vols. London: Hurst and Blackett, 1882

Merrill, Linda. *A Pot of Paint: Aesthetics on Trial in 'Whistler v. Ruskin'*. Washington DC: Smithsonian Press, 1992

Metz, Nancy Aycock. '*Little Dorrit's* London: Babylon Revisited', *Victorian Studies* 33, no. 3 (Spring 1990): 465–86

Miller, Andrew H. *Novels Behind Glass: Commodity Culture and Victorian Narrative*. Cambridge: Cambridge University Press, 1995

Minto, W., ed. *Autobiographical Notes of the Life*

*of William Bell Scott and Notices of His Artistic and Poetic Circle of Friends, 1830 to 1882.* 2 vols. London: Osgood, McIlvaine, 1892

'Mischievous Literature', *Bookseller*, 1 July 1868: 445–9

Moran, Leslie J., and Derek McGhee. 'Perverting London: The Cartographic Practices of Law', *Law and Critique* IX:2 (1998): 207–24

Nead, Lynda. *Myths of Sexuality: Representations of Women in Victorian Britain.* Oxford: Basil Blackwell, 1988

O'Dea, William T. *The Social History of Lighting.* London: Routledge and Kegan Paul, 1958

Ogborn, Miles. 'Ordering the City: Surveillance, Public Space and the Reform of Urban Policing in England, 1835–56', *Political Geography* 12:6 (November 1993): 505–21

———. *Spaces of Modernity: London's Geographies, 1680–1780.* New York: Guilford Press, 1998

'Old Bailey, The', *London Society* 10 (1866): 399–405

*Old Paris: Twenty Etchings by Charles Méryon.* With an Essay by Philip Gilbert Hamerton. Liverpool: Henry Young and Sons Ltd, 1914

Olsen, Donald J. 'Introduction: Victorian London'. In David Owen, *The Government of Victorian London, 1855–1889: The Metropolitan Board of Works, the Vestries, and the City Corporation,* ed. Roy MacLeod, with contributions by David Reeder, Donald Olsen and Francis Sheppard, 1–19. Cambridge, Mass., and London: Harvard University Press, Belknap, 1982

'On Being Cut', *All the year Round* 19 (1868): 208–10

Osborne, Peter. 'Modernity is a Qualitative, Not a Chronological Category', *New Left Review* 192 (1992): 65–84

Owen, David. *The Government of Victorian London, 1855–1889: The Metropolitan Board of Works, the Vestries and the City Corporation,* ed. Roy MacLeod, with contributions by David Reeder, Donald Olsen and Francis Sheppard. Cambridge, Mass., and London: Harvard University Press, Belknap, 1982

Partridge, Eric. *A Dictionary of Slang and Unconventional English.* 8th edn. London, Melbourne and Henley: Routledge and Kegan Paul, 1984

Pearsall, Ronald. *Victorian Sheet Music Covers.* Newton Abbot: David and Charles, 1972

Penzel, Frederick. *Theatre Lighting Before Electricity.* Middletown, Conn.: Wesleyan University Press, 1978

Pick, Daniel. 'Stories of the Eye'. In *Rewriting the Self: Histories from the Renaissance to the Present,* ed. Roy Porter, 186–99. London and New York: Routledge, 1997

Pinkney, David H. *Napoleon III and the Rebuilding of Paris.* Princeton, NJ: Princeton University Press, 1958

Pointon, Marcia. *William Dyce, 1806–1864: A Critical Biography.* Oxford: Clarendon Press, 1979

Pollock, Griselda. 'Vicarious Excitements: *London: A Pilgrimage* by Gustave Doré and Blanchard Jerrold, 1872', *New Formations* 2:1 (1988): 25–50

———. *Vision and Difference: Femininity, Feminism and Histories of Art.* London and New York: Routledge, 1988

Potts, Alex. 'Picturing the Metropolis: Images of London in the Nineteenth Century', *History Workshop* 26 (Autumn 1988): 28–56

'Rape of the Glances, The', *Saturday Review* XIII (February 1862): 124–5

Rappaport, Erika D. '"The Halls of Temptation": Gender, Politics and the Construction of the Department Store in Late Victorian London', *Journal of British Studies* 35 (January 1996): 58–83

Rees, Terence. *Theatre Lighting in the Age of Gas.* London: Society for Theatre Research, 1978

Reynolds, G. W. M. *The Mysteries of London,* ed. and with an introduction by Trefor Thomas. Keele, Staffs: Keele University Press, 1996

Richards, Thomas. *The Commodity Culture of Victorian England: Advertising and Spectacle, 1851–1914.* London: Verso, 1991

Richardson, Philip J. S. *The Social Dances of the Nineteenth Century in England.* London: Herbert Jenkins, 1960

Rifkin, Adrian. *Street Noises: Parisian Pleasure, 1900–1940.* Manchester and New York: Manchester University Press, 1993

Ritchie, J. Ewing. *The Night Side of London*. London: William Tweedie, 1857

Roberts, M. J. D. 'Making Victorian Morals? The Society for the Suppression of Vice and Its Critics, 1802–1886', *Historical Studies* 21:83 (October 1984): 157–73

———. 'Morals, Art and the Law: The Passing of the Obscene Publications Act, 1857', *Victorian Studies* (Summer 1985): 609–29

Robertson, Geoffrey. *Obscenity: An Account of Censorship Laws and Their Enforcement in England and Wales*. London: Weidenfeld and Nicolson, 1979

Rock, Paul. *The Social World of an English Crown Court: Witness and Professionals in the Crown Court Centre at Wood Green*. Oxford: Clarendon Press, 1993

Ross, Kristin. 'Streetwise: The French Invention of Everyday Life', *parallax* 2 (February 1996): 67–76

Rostron, Laurence W. S. *The 'Powers of Charge' of the Metropolitan Gas Companies. A History of the Question of Price in London, from the Introduction of Gas Lighting to the Year 1899*. London: Ernest Benn for the South Metropolitan Gas Company, 1927

Ryan, Jenny. 'Women, Modernity and the City', *Theory, Culture and Society* 11:4 (1994): 35–64

Ryan, Mary P. *Women in Public: Between Banners and Ballots, 1825–1880*. Baltimore and London: Johns Hopkins University Press, 1990

Sadleir, Michael. 'Yellow-Backs'. In *New Paths in Book Collecting: Essays by Various Hands*, ed. John Carter, 127–61. London: Constable and Co. Ltd, 1934

———. *Forlorn Sunset*. London: Constable, 1947

Sala, George Augustus. *Gaslight and Daylight: With Some London Scenes They Shine Upon*. London: Chapman and Hall, 1859

———. *Twice Round the Clock; Or the Hours of the Day and Night in London*. London: Houlston and Wright, 1859

———. 'Travels in the County of Middlesex', *Temple Bar* 1 (December 1860): 73–90

———. 'The Streets of the World: The Passage des Panoramas', *Temple Bar* 10 (February 1864): 335–41

———. *The Life and Adventures of George Augustus Sala. Written by Himself*. 2 vols. London, Paris and Melbourne: Cassell and Co. Ltd, 1895

Schivelbusch, Wolfgang. *Disenchanted Night: The Industrialisation of Light in the Nineteenth Century*. Trans. Angela Davies. Oxford, New York and Hamburg: Berg, 1988

Schlesinger, Max. *Saunterings In and About London*. English edn. by Otto Wenckstern. London: Nathaniel Cooke, 1853

Schlör, Joachim. *Nights in the Big City*. Trans. Pierre Gottfried Imhof and Dafydd Rees Roberts. London: Reaktion, 1998

Sennett, Richard. *The Fall of Public Man*. Cambridge: Cambridge University Press, 1977

———. *The Conscience of the Eye: The Design and Social Life of Cities*. London: Faber and Faber, 1991

———. *Flesh and Stone: The Body and the City in Western Civilization*. London: Faber and Faber, 1994

Serres, Michel, with Bruno Latour. *Conversations on Science, Culture and Time*. Trans. Roxanne Lapidus. Ann Arbor: University of Michigan Press, 1995

Sheppard, Francis. *London, 1808–1870: The Infernal Wen*. London: Secker and Warburg, 1971

Slater, Michael, ed. *Dickens' Journalism: Sketches by Boz and Other Early Papers, 1833–39*. London: J. M. Dent, 1994

———. 'Hardy and the City'. In *New Perspectives on Thomas Hardy*, ed. Charles Pettit, 41–57. London: Macmillan, 1994

Soja, Edward J. *Postmodern Geographies: The Reassertion of Space in Critical Social Theory*. London and New York: Verso, 1989

Spellman, Doreen, and Stanley Spellman. *Victorian Music Covers*. London: Evelyn, Adams and Mackay Ltd, 1969

*Stanford's Library Map of London and Its Suburbs*. Introduced by Ralph Hyde. Lympne Castle, Kent: Harry Margaray in association with Guildhall Library, London, 1980

Stansell, Christine. *City of Women: Sex and Class in New York, 1789–1860*. New York: Alfred Knopf, 1986

Straus, Ralph. *Sala: The Portrait of an Eminent Victorian*. London: Constable and Co. Ltd, 1942

Sutcliffe, Anthony. *The Autumn of Central Paris: The Defeat of Town Planning, 1850–1970*. London: Edward Arnold, 1970

Sutton, Denys. *Nocturne: The Art of James McNeill Whistler*. London: Country Life Ltd, 1963

Tagg, John. 'The Discontinuous City: Picturing and the Discursive Field'. In *Visual Culture: Images and Interpretations*, ed. Norman Bryson, Michael Ann Holly and Keith Moxey, 83–103. Hanover, NH, and London: Wesleyan University Press, 1994

Taine, Hippolyte. *Notes on England*. Trans. W. F. Rae. London: Strahan and Co, 1872

*Temple Bar; Its History, Memorials and Associations*. London: John Bursill, 1877

Tester, Keith, ed. *The Flâneur*. London and New York: Routledge, 1994

von Thal, Herbert. *Eliza Lynn Linton: The Girl of the Period: A Biography*. London: George Allen and Unwin, 1979

Thomas, Donald. *A Long Time Burning: The History of Literary Censorship in England*. London: Routledge and Kegan Paul, 1969

Thomson, Peter, ed. *Plays by Dion Boucicault*. Cambridge: Cambridge University Press, 1984

Tickner, Lisa. *The Spectacle of Women: Imagery of the Suffrage Campaign, 1907–14*. London: Chatto and Windus, 1987

Timbs, John. *Walks and Talks About London*. London: Lockwood and Co., 1865

———. *London and Westminster: City and Suburb. Strange Events, Characteristics, and Changes, of Metropolitan Life*. 2 vols. London: Richard Bentley, 1868

Trench, Richard, and Ellis Hillman. *London Under London: A Subterranean Guide*. London: John Murray, 1984

Tristan, Flora. *The London Journal: or, the Aristocracy and the Working Class of England*. Trans. Jean Hawkes. London: Virago, 1982

Trotter, David. *Circulation: Defoe, Dickens and the Economies of the Novel*. London: Macmillan, 1988

*Twenty-Second Report of the Vestry of the Parish of Chelsea, Appointed Under the Metropolis Local Management Act, 1855. 1877–8*. London: G. Shield, 1879

Urry, John. *The Tourist Gaze: Leisure and Travel in Contemporary Societies*. London: Sage, 1990

———. *Consuming Places*. London and New York: Routledge, 1995

*Vestry of Chelsea (The). Supplemental Report of their Proceedings for the Years (March to March) 1872 to 1877, Inclusive*. London: Judd and Co., 1878

Vicinus, Martha. 'Dark London', *The Indiana University Bookman* 12 (December 1977): 67–79

Vickery, Amanda. 'Golden Age to Separate Spheres? A Review of the Categories and Chronology of English Women's History', *Historical Journal* 36:2 (1993): 383–414

Vidler, Anthony. *The Architectural Uncanny: Essays in the Modern Unhomely*. Cambridge, Mass., and London: MIT Press, 1992

Vizetelly, Henry. *Glances Back Through Seventy Years: Autobiographical and Other Reminiscences*. 2 vols. London: Kegan Paul, Trench, Trubner and Co. Ltd, 1893

Walford, Edward. *Old and New London: A Narrative of Its History, Its People, and Its Places*. 6 vols: vols I, II by Walter Thornbury; vols III–VI by Edward Walford. London: Cassell Petter and Galpin, 1873–8

Walker, Lynne. 'Vistas of Pleasure: Women Consumers of Urban Space in the West End of London, 1850–1900'. In *Women in the Victorian Art World*, ed. Clarissa Campbell Orr, 70–85. Manchester and New York: Manchester University Press, 1995

Weinreb, Ben, and Christopher Hibbert, eds. *The London Encyclopaedia*. London: Macmillan, 1983

Wheatley, Henry B. *London: Past and Present. Its History, Associations, and Traditions. Based Upon the Handbook of London by the Late Peter Cunningham*. 2 vols. London: John Murray, 1891

Wilson, Elizabeth. *The Sphinx in the City: Urban Life, the Control of Disorder, and Women.* London: Virago, 1991

———. 'The Invisible *Flâneur*', *New Left Review* 191 (1992): 90–110

———. 'The Rhetoric of Urban Space', *New Left Review* 209 (1995): 146–60

Winter, James. *London's Teeming Streets, 1830–1914.* London and New York: Routledge, 1993

Wohl, Anthony S. *Endangered Lives: Public Health in Victorian Britain.* London: Dent, 1983

Wolff, Janet. 'The Invisible *Flâneuse*: Women and the Literature of Modernity', *Theory, Culture and Society* 2:3 (1985): 37–48

———. 'The Artist and the *Flâneur*: Rodin, Rilke and Gwen John in Paris'. In *The Flâneur*, ed. Keith Tester, 111–37. London and New York: Routledge, 1994

*World's Guide to London in 1862 (The), by Day and by Night.* London: Darton and Hodge, 1862

Wroth, Warwick. *Cremorne and the Later London Gardens.* London: Elliot Stock, 1907

Yates, Edmund. *The Business of Pleasure.* 2 vols. London: Chapman and Hall, 1865

*Yokel's Preceptor: Or, More Sprees in London. Where May be had a Catalogue of a Most Extensive Variety of Every Choice and Curious Facetious Work.* London: H. Smith, n.d.

Young, Ken, and Patricia L. Garside. *Metropolitan London: Politics and Urban Change, 1837–1901.* London: Edward Arnold, 1982

Zerlang, Martin. 'Orientalism and Modernity: Tivoli in Copenhagen', *Nineteenth-Century Contexts* 20:1 (1997): 81–110

# Index

*Page numbers in italics represent illustrations*